Volume 34, Number 3

differences

Social Bonds and Catastrophic Acts

Guest Editor: Elizabeth Stewart

ELIZABETH STEWART

Dropping the Bond or Dropping the Act?

*W*hen COVID-19 unleashed itself in the United States in early 2020, large numbers of Trump followers—many of them working-class white Americans with bad or no health insurance, with an unsurprising distrust in government and the various institutions that have catastrophically failed most if not all of them in the last several decades, and who were easily persuaded by theories of hostile governmental takeover of their lives—refused to get vaccinated, to wear masks, or to keep a minimal distance from others, and then became very ill, infected many others due to their behaviors, and died. They had been primed by QAnon conspiracy theories about Joe Biden, Hillary Clinton, and Democrats in general as ringleaders of a widespread sexual-abuse-of-children network, itself preceded by Trump's prepresidential Obama "birther" conspiracy and others along those lines. Now they became entangled in the chaotic whirlwinds of an endless supply of increasingly bizarre conspiracy theories about the disease, which many believed did not really exist but was in fact a twisted way for the "power elites" to reinforce their total power over them.

Volume 34, Number 3 DOI 10.1215/10407391-10898171

© 2023 by Brown University and d i f f e r e n c e s : A Journal of Feminist Cultural Studies

Bizarre beliefs were matched by bizarre behaviors, and incredible stories circulated; we all know them and there is no need to go into great detail. A handful of moments among them, however, can teach us something about our moment in time: Nurse Kathryn Ivey's account of behaviors sticks in the mind, talking about veritable breaks in reality are hard to forget. COVID deniers, she observed, "won't see COVID for the monster it is even when it stands shrieking in front of them." She describes patients at the very moment of death in "the intensive care unit, all gasping and dying and begging for a miracle" (Ivey). Dramatic stories proliferated, which produced strange martyrdoms in a context in which other regular, enraged people were tearing down mask racks in stores, coughing on babies, and "sneezing" on produce in grocery stores, acts recorded by bystanders on their phones and then viewable online for all to watch. These same antivaxxers and their families died in droves. On October 5, 2020, Trump followers were further spurred on to try to enact strange COVID-19 suicides when Trump, leaving the hospital where he had been seriously ill with COVID, tweeted, "Don't be afraid of COVID. Don't let it dominate your life!"[1] and back at the White House tore off his mask on national television, even though he was still contagious. The idea of suffering, struggling to the death with COVID, increasingly transformed into an enacted political oath of loyalty to Trump, to a certain view of "America," to "freedom," and to the free market, an expression of belief and, more importantly, of *being* (or dying) American. Dan Patrick, the lieutenant governor of Texas, infamously declared that "there are more important things than living" (Stieb) (namely, the free market) in a bid to reopen Texas in late March of 2020 without any testing equipment or disease-mitigating regulations in place.

Politics began sporadically to degrade to simple violence: in May of 2017, running for governor of Montana, Greg Gianforte "body-slammed" *Guardian* reporter Ted Jacobs for asking a question that annoyed him (an audio recording of the incident circulated online) (LaFrance; Guardian). The act was publicly praised and encouraged by Trump who, during his campaign and after he became president, repeatedly encouraged police brutality (Porter) and openly wished the Secret Service would just "beat the crap out of" protesters and critics (Parker). Also in May of 2020, the country witnessed the murder of George Floyd by police officers, a horrific murder recorded by bystanders on their phones, passed on to the public, and watched online by an entire country in various stages of lockdown due to the pandemic. Trump's incitements to violence continued unabated. What had begun with direct, encouraging remarks was first raised into a more symbolic and institutionalizing display of violence when on June 1, 2020, Trump had troops use tear gas, pepper, and rubber pellets against citizens peacefully protesting police brutality in Lafayette Square in DC in order to clear a path for him (Rogers), accompanied by Ivanka and Jared Kushner, Attorney General William Barr, and Chairman of the Joint Chiefs of Staff General Milley, for a photo-op in front of St. John's Church while holding up a Bible. Throughout that summer, he thundered about "dominating" protesters in the streets. By January 6, 2021, having lost the presidential election, Trump turned to a second form of violence: badly organized, furious MAGA followers who camouflaged, for the perennially watching national viewership, the truly serious and disciplined violent paramilitary organizations who also heeded Trump's call and helped storm the Capitol.

On the one hand, Trumpism has inspired his devoted followers to martyr their own bodies by putting them through the COVID wringer; on the other, Trumpism has proudly displayed to the world the body of the Trumpian alpha male, first in the police officer not afraid to assault "criminals" and then, increasingly, in the paramilitary soldier. This latter trend is traditionally fascist, of course, and it is not surprising that Trump did eventually turn to it in a disturbing revival, though a weirdly perverted and distorted one, of the fascist adulation of the body in struggle, the body that marches, fights, and dies. The more specifically Trumpian body, however, seems to be not only a body that struggles but also a body that *throws itself away* and that lashes out in a sort of unpredictable short-circuiting of violent rage. This is a mundane rage that crashes mask stands at CVS, hisses at mask-wearers, and so on. Both are characteristic of the Trump era, and both can be seen as instances of what Jacques Lacan called the *passage à l'acte,* "passing to the act": sudden, impulsive, rash acts, violent and often ending in death, individual or collective; moments that dissolve the social bond and tear holes into the structures of the social order itself.

Lacan discussed the *passage à l'acte* in his seminar on anxiety, Seminar X (*Anxiety* 109). The notion emerges for us, he contends, in Freud's "Psychogenesis of a Case of Homosexuality in a Woman." The event animating that case is a culminating moment when the woman impulsively, in a split-second act, throws herself suicidally over a parapet and onto the railway tracks when she encounters the disapproving gaze of her father, who sees her walking with her female companion. By suddenly jumping in this suicidal sort of way, she radically "let[s] herself drop" (110), says Lacan:

> *The scene unfolds very rapidly. The loved one, for whom this adventure is doubtless but a somewhat lowly entertainment, who*

clearly starts to get a bit fed up with all this and doesn't want to expose herself to any great difficulties, says to the young woman that this has gone on long enough, that they are going to leave it at that, and for her to stop lavishly sending her flowers every day and following her around on her heels. With that, the young woman flings herself straight off a bridge. (110)

The impulse takes off in such a radical way at a moment (and Lacan claims this is always the case in a *passage à l'acte*) of "supreme embarrassment": "All of this, this entire scene, is what meets the father's eye in the simple encounter on the bridge. And this scene [aspiring to show the father what love should look like], which had gained the subject's full approval, nevertheless loses all its value with the disapproval felt in this look. It is to this extent that there next occurs what we might call [. . .] supreme embarrassment" (111). Honing in on this key gesture of the *passage à l'acte*, "letting oneself drop," Lacan says: "It is not for nothing that the melancholic subject has such a propensity to fling himself out of the window, which he always does at such disconcerting speed, in a shot. Indeed, inasmuch as it calls to mind the limit between the stage and the world, the window indicates for us what is meant by this act—in some way, the subject comes back to the state of the fundamental exclusion he feels himself to be in" (110).

Dropping Out of the Social Bond

Dropping out, murder-suicide, exclusion, violence, embarrassment, mortification: they stake out the emotional and phenomenological frameworks within which pro-Trumpian "politics" move. The subject swept up in a *passage à l'acte* falls catastrophically through the cracks and out of both symbolic structures and the social bond—even out of the frame of subjectivity itself. People critically ill with COVID, and sometimes their families (who often were not allowed into ICUs to be with their dying family members) provided example after example (Larkin) of the *passage à l'acte*: a last act of totally impotent violence in an attempt to obliterate the crude fact of the virus's existence, arguably in various ways representative of the predatory "power elites." A likely source also of the "supreme embarrassment" experienced by people in such positions is an unacknowledged, enraged sense of betrayal and a mortifying final confirmation of absolute impotence. Trump in office tossed the nation, and certainly his followers, back and forth in everyday tempests of outrage, hate, and increasingly irrational and jouissance-filled conspiratorial inventiveness. In other words, dying also came with enjoyment: jouissance. The Trumpian subject, in a mix of mortification, embarrassment, rage, and masochistic enjoyment, breaks out of symbolic structures and jumps into modes of simply elemental living and dying. The *passage à l'acte* provides an instantaneous, catastrophic, and ostentatious smashing open of the structures of the social bond; it opens up and then compels the subject, a subject no longer, to throw itself away. In the Trumpian scenario, this dropping out seems to be laced with enjoyment.

What is it that is being thrown away? Staying with Lacan, it is the object *a*, that little piece of the real, remnant of our most primitive yet also most sublime substance, that thing of enjoyment that, psychically, gets us attached to, seduced toward, the world, society, others, to be a social, and eventually also political, creature, even as simultaneously we must also sacrifice it, that impossible jouissance, let it go—in other words, drop it—as we attach ourselves to law and society. This very moment and spot (simultaneous attachment and evacuation) is the kernel of the Oedipus complex, the pivot into the symbolic order. Object *a* is our most prized possession, our "essence," and our relinquishing of it is our sacrifice to the social; without object *a*, no civilization. Attachment and evacuation must occur simultaneously, however, leaving us with the impasse that the object *a* is never present in itself, never tangible and definable, and yet it is our everything that promises redemption and fulfillment. The Trumpian *passage à l'acte* is of this sort: enjoyment while simultaneously dying for it, relinquished for the sake of the Other. Something is seriously off in the Trumpian scenario, however: the object *a* is supposed to be an object, something "*in* you" and "*more than you*" (Lacan, *Four* 263), but not your actual, entire body. When dropping the object *a* transforms into throwing away one's entire body in an act of suicide, something else is going on.

The various ways in which we "deal with" object *a*, according to Lacan, determines "who" we are, what we do to ourselves, and how we live our social bond. This knot, this process, lies at the heart of Lacan's discourse theory, presented in Seminar XX, which gives us entry into thinking about politics in the Lacanian mode. By *discourse* Lacan means a specific way of configuring power; object *a* is psychically and unconsciously inscribed in a certain way by every subject (conducive to sublimation, to sacrifice, to disavowal, and so on), thus *configuring power in a certain way*. The advantage of bringing Lacan into political theory is that it allows us, by definition, to include the dimension of the unconscious in politics: political theories, fantasies, processes, and acts are in part unconsciously determined; in Lacanian theory, the subject who thinks, feels, and operates politically is psychically determined by the play of discursive inclinations unconsciously dominating it from within and is usually dominated by one preponderant modality. That is, the range of available subjective discursive positionings for Lacan—their *modus operandi,* their aims, their needs—usually tilt toward one of the four possibilities that constitute the discursive landscape:

1) In the *master's discourse* the dominant value is the subject's certainty, and the Other is configured (for the subject) in such a way that it supports such certainty. The master masks their castration while drawing out the castration of the (supporting) "slaves"; the master catches the others' surplus labor and, from that, sublime profit and enjoyment. It is not difficult to see Trump in this position.

2) The *university's discourse* is dominated by the value of (supposedly neutral) knowledge (the sciences, the arts, and so on) and is always already unconsciously infected with the drive toward mastery. In our contemporary context, this discourse is partially but crucially in crisis when we think of the vilifications of scientific knowledge (and its representatives in Dr. Fauci, the CDC, "progressives" on the side of mitigation, and so on), as well as the widespread attacks on academics and the academy in general, in particular the Humanities, that came to such a head during the pandemic.

3) At the heart of the *hysteric's discourse* is the subject aware of its own division that asks the Other the key question animating all power-laden relationships: "Who am I to you and who are you to me?" It is a discourse of questioning and struggle that defines the relationship between parent and child, master and slave, master and disciple, in short, the subject qua divided subject, symptomatically challenging its masters. A key image for the hysteric's discourse is the gesture of "tearing itself open" for the master to see, witness, and justify. It is in these ways the quintessential discourse of politics; in its questioning and doubt, it is the discourse of the neophyte and reflects most essentially the structure of the social bond.

4) In the *analyst's discourse* the highest value is the object *a,* with which the analyst wants the analysand to identify. We saw earlier that the Trumpian subject leaves its position within the sym-

bolic order and identifies totally with its own object *a* in order to throw itself away. In contrast, the analyst wants to provoke identification with *a*, with the difference that, in the successful analysis, the analysand will not throw themself away, but will experience object *a* via the analyst and be held (by the analyst) in suspension, as opposed to landing on the trash heap, in order to reconnect with their drive—to then finally reenter symbolic networks in a different way, namely by passing through and beyond identification, which is where, in a lethal way, the Trumpian subject is located.

The Trumpian subject desires a master, rejects knowledge and university, and, I would say, is in part hysterical in that, as a hysteric, they tear themself open for the Other—in this case, the master. As hysterics, Trumpian subjects demand to know of the Other: What is truth? Who am I to you? but then almost immediately enter an epistemological whirlwind that presents truth as failed, worthless, irrelevant; truth is and should be destroyed, as should logos, the word, on the whole. As failed hysterics, they begin to drop out of the social bond very quickly. The Trumpian subject engages with the Other but almost simultaneously prepares itself as a delicious sacrifice, as, refusing doubt, it refuses its own hystericization. With this refusal, both politics and the social bond dissolve. While the analyst's discourse is that of the object *a* presenting itself for the analysand in order to restart the analysand's desire and get them to question their own division, the Trumpian subject identifies completely, lock, stock, and barrel, with object *a* and throws itself away—for Trump and for the free market that kicks working people in the shins day in and day out—fused together with the object that drops, object *a*: pure enjoyment and pure waste, pure burning trash heap, little piece of the real, sublime and abject simultaneously, pure jouissance and pure abjection.

Slavoj Žižek provides a felicitous example of the object *a* that also works within our context. He offers an image that flashes up for an instant, revealing our time, the age of hypercapitalism, its heavens now almost fully coinciding with its hells, wonderful and horrible at once, with the hells gaining in volume and sheer force every day. It also features a dropping corpse:

> *Here is this scene that Hitchcock wanted to insert in* North by Northwest, *as reported in Truffaut's conversations with the Master:* "I wanted to have a long dialogue between Cary Grant and one of the factory workers /at a Ford automobile plant/ as they walk along the assembly line. Behind them a car is being

assembled, piece by piece. Finally, the car they've seen being put together from a simple nut and bolt is complete, with gas and oil, and all ready to drive off the line. The two men look at each other and say, 'Isn't it wonderful!' Then they open the door of the car and out drops a corpse." (Žižek)

In my mind this corpse can be seen to represent our social bond, which is now fully identified with the sacrificed object that takes the whole body and mind with it out onto the trash heap. Žižek's zeroing in on this image helps us anchor the Trumpian body thrown in the garbage within an extreme capitalism that has grown deadlier for more and more people every day.

In his discussion of the *passage à l'acte* scenario in Seminar X Lacan shows us when and why it takes place: namely, when the fantasy of a functioning social order no longer works and collapses. Why and how does it collapse? It is the function of object *a* to underwrite the particular fantasy that enables any social order to constitute itself (and float and work, so to speak), to promise subjects the substance they "deserve," which will enable them to attach to and "buy into" any particular master signifier and its corresponding social "scene." With the failure and dissolution of the fantasy—and that means the social bond itself—the object *a* must exit the crumbling scenario, and language and subjectivity themselves, and to flush itself down the toilet. The corollary of this state of affairs is that, as symbolization itself decreases, excess jouissance becomes increasingly less disguised. Object *a* as surplus value, that extra enjoyment (in the form of profit), becomes increasingly obscene on the part of the rich and powerful, while working conditions, where the surplus is extracted, are more and more openly brutal, coercive, often lethal, as seen, for example, in the sweatshop fires in Bangladesh and other such events (see CBC). This is what we might see in Hitchcock/Žižek's image of the corpse that rolls out of the resplendent new car and thuds down onto the factory floor. A downtrodden American white working class surely sees itself there as well. Roberto Harari writes, "The object that provokes anxiety in the neurotic is the a-Thing [the *objet a* prepared as a sacrifice for the Other], that is, the desire of the Other, as the Other requires that the subject erase its borders, handing itself over to it in an unconditional manner. Lacan points out that in this place is to be found, supposedly, a kind of jouissance that is reached through abdication" (75). We see Harari referring to the jouissance I am alleging seduces subjects into self-sacrifice. An alternative to this hellish sacrificial furnace (for the white American worker) is to insert into this plan a rewriting of the scene in such a way as to quickly and defensively transform the workers' own potential passive inclusion in capitalism's world of suffering into a scene of active, semidelusional exclusion of those "others" (like the rows of young female Bangladeshi corpses burned alive or crushed to death lined up in the video footage) that Western workers consider to be on the outside, beyond the pale—who, they believe, are not-they but who nevertheless, the fantasy goes, are threatening to engulf them. In any case, the fantasy in which what steps out of the shiny new car would be a new, white, and living working-class car owner has collapsed, and the worker has thrown himself onto the imagined garbage heap of history. To say it more psychoanalytically: when the worker performs self-immolation, or is already quietly dead without anyone noticing, he or she had already at the start of the fantasy thrown him- or herself at the feet of the master, ready to perform self-sacrifice. Castration, the inauguration of the split subject as negotiator into the social order, has been transformed into a perverted assembly line of self-sacrifice—for example, in the ragged diseased flesh efficiently produced in pandemic hospitals. The Trumpian subject has committed to exiting the symbolic order and simply does so, quickly and traumatically, in a suicidal plunge. Thus, this subject's psychic itinerary goes from specular identification (with the leader), sought after for its stabilizing effects (the heavy-handed far-right, racist, anti-Semitic, anti-immigrant, and so on identifications) that divide the world into "friend" and "foe," to a short-circuiting drop into nothingness, all while knowledge and politics, like the social bond itself, devolve into utter nonsense.

But of course, it is not to Trump that this violent sacrifice—murderous and suicidal—is really made, but rather to the obscure gods of corporate capitalism. In his later work Lacan alludes to a fifth discourse that, however, lies outside of the social bond: the discourse of the capitalist ("Milan"). Its obscurity is its essence: a relentless drive of a blotted out, opaque, and sadistic order of corporate totalitarianism.

"Sadopopulism"

It seems clear that Trump supporters operate from a place—or nonplace—of exclusion and neglect by the entire political class, including most Republican lawmakers. Bizarrely, when Republicans are in power, they work diligently to undo all social and economic safety nets—including health insurance, food stamps—for these very segments of the American population, their most fervent supporters; such legislative undoings directly victimize those very groups, and their effects create untold suffering and distress for the population that will enthusiastically and enragedly continue voting for them. (Legislative cruelties of this sort victimize other parts of the population as well, of course, but it is stunning to see economically struggling Trump supporters vow revenge for Trump and his supporters, the very people who do everything they can to render those supporters more destitute.)

Timothy Snyder uses the felicitous term "sadopopulism" to name the socioeconomic and political scenario defined by this constantly emergent and clamoring Trumpism, with its grievances and readiness to "fight" ("Sadopopulism"). Trump in power as president was not even remotely about thinking, legislating, and making policy; his activity was simply about ceaseless distraction from actual governing by keeping his supporters suspended in a constant oscillation between outrage and gleeful enjoyment (of Trump "sticking it to the libs"), and about the disavowed production of suffering (in the form of minimal or entirely lacking health insurance, economic misery, drug addiction, crumbling and quickly disappearing government support, devastation of American cities and towns, zero new infrastructure and infrastructure maintenance) precisely for the blue-collar white working class that blindly and unshakably supports him. Of course, this works for populist agitators: the suffering and rage that is thereby generated can be manipulated and turned against immigrants, people of color, "wokeism," academics, and so on.

Snyder has defined the socioeconomic order of our moment in the United States as "wannabe oligarchy" (American oligarchy, though emergent, being less developed than Russian oligarchy, for example [see "America"]), and our politics (with Trump in power) as "not even fascism" (see "On Language"), because an American Trumpist state has shown itself to be capable of *doing* only three things: tax cuts for the wealthy, political and personal corruption, and *being* white. The latter means: looking back at a fictional America of the past, "real" and "great," which supposedly cherished and respected a resplendently white working class living in harmony within a resplendently white American society that pulled itself up by its bootstraps and thereby became "great," where women were obedient and stayed at home while children knew that they were either boys or girls, and so on. In reality, of course, such an America never existed in the past, certainly does not exist in the present, and will not exist in the future. Neoliberalism and American oligarchy have created untold suffering by way of economic misery, fear, and distress in a sea of violence that mounts exponentially day by day, where people of color, women, immigrants, LGBTQ+ folks, children, and other "minority" groups have become open prey. Ridiculous projections of an America of the past go hand in hand with historical amnesia and, increasingly, attempts to revise history entirely, as print-based culture is increasingly censored, abridged, and taken off the shelves altogether in schools and libraries. Snyder calls the form of politics defining the neoliberal era, which maintains the volatility and sheer misery of what others have called "technofeudalism,"[2] the "politics of eternity." This is a politics in which change (and with it time past, present, and future), seems (and possibly is) doomed; all political "doing" has either transformed into a politics of eternal "being" (race, gender, nationality) and "feeling" (hate, mockery, sacrificial enjoyment) or has degenerated to a dimension of "doing" that is pure violent acting: hourly mass shootings, assaults and attempted murder on politicians and their families, constant death threats against judges, jurors, election workers, Democratic members of Congress, and so on. While planned and coherently executed murder and mass murder attempts and executions are often not instances of a *passage à l'acte* insofar as they are not impulsive, but are, rather, meticulously planned, and because they may lack any element of supreme embarrassment and subjective mortification, nonetheless, cars or vans ramming into protesters (especially if they are of color) and horrific (and often unnecessary) bouts with and deaths by COVID-19 *are* impulsive, as there we see a breakdown of the social bond and a sort of explosion of the subject as it falls out of and leaves the scene entirely.

Chris Hedges, via Karl Polanyi and Sheldon Wolin, refers to this structure of oligarchical contemporary American society and sadopopulist governance as "corporate totalitarianism" ("Conversation"). Polanyi's lesson in his *The Great Transformation*, regarding the rise of fascism, was how the economic and social elites, including big business and financial institutions, consistently turn to fascist movements when the free market has powerful antisocial side effects, the likes of which we are clearly experiencing now. The self-destructiveness that buoys and favors Trump politically has been a long time coming and is, I am arguing, a result of dissolving social bonds. With technological, social, and political change comes the weakening of shared assumptions, values, and beliefs, of consistent and meaningful ways of working in the world, of a shared sense of the very fabric of reality, and of a sense of participation in a political system. Hedges contends that with the formal establishment of the corporate state, its power clinched by the *Citizens United* case[3] and maintained by the constant flow of dark money into politics that increasingly bolsters corporate power, and with the ever-increasing concentration of wealth within the tiniest fraction of the population, with all of its ramifications, it is not hard to see how median-to-low wage earners can quickly become hopeless. As of the end of 2022, 68.2 percent of the nation's wealth is in the hands of the top 10 percent of the population, while the lower 50 percent of the population have only 3 percent of the nation's wealth (Statista). One of the most striking symptoms of this obscene disparity was, before Trump even arrived on the scene, the opioid crisis. Social mobility is dead. Émile Durkheim's notion of *anomie* (normlessness, rule-lessness) and the connection he draws between anomie and suicide have again become highly relevant as the strangulating power of the corporate elite and, more importantly, absolute corporatism in the United States have sentenced huge swaths of the population to a state of constant economic fear and distress and attending emotional and social consequences. By now, one of Hannah Arendt's definitions of totalitarianism, namely that the totalitarian regime's targets and victims come to cooperate in their own destruction, has come true, as the Trumpist, largely white, struggling working classes often call for the destruction of "Obamacare," which supports them, and the dismantling of the welfare state that in many cases aids them. Arendt also clearly lays out the closely linked phenomena of dissolving social bonds, radical loneliness, totalitarian affinities, and (self-)destructive tendencies (317, 474). Not only are the possibilities for public and political action destroyed but people's emotional lives, their capacity to communicate with others and themselves—to think, to have feelings of happiness and serenity—are being shattered: "Totalitarian government, like all tyrannies, certainly could not exist without destroying the public realm of life, that is, without destroying, by isolating men, their political capacities. But totalitarian domination as a form of government is new in that it is not content with this isolation and destroys private life as well" (475).

It is precisely in this space, there where the Trumpian subject turns against itself in order to throw itself away, that our attention must be directed. Psychoanalysis can help us understand the dimension of this singularity, this impasse that takes place by way of an absolute mirroring, there where the subject not only pronounces a loyalty oath with its hand on its own life, or where it realizes that its only space for being is in not-being, but where it is also persuaded to throw itself away. What takes place at this impasse, this glitch where it feels that the master demands nonexistence of it, is a sort of magical transposition away from itself and its suffering—but toward what?

Some of the new savagely authoritarian segments of U.S. society—vulnerable to sadopopulist rapture and self-ejection from the scene of politics (and life) through violence against themselves and others, driven to despair by a growing inability to survive economically within a technofeudal corporate totalitarianism (Brown), falling prey to the fantasy of a past America that endures only in fictional and fantasized accounts of "America," mortified by their own weakness, their apparent inability to be seen, cherished, respected, and loved back by the beloved father—turn to an often shocking form of *passage à l'acte*, most of the time enacted against racialized others, the fantasized "caravans" or "incursions" of migrants at the southern border, women, trans kids, and other "minorities," and themselves.

Passage à l'acte *and Statelessness*

How can we understand this self-relegation to the trash heap—in addition, that is, to Lacan's description of this dropping and tossing of the body when it occurs as a consequence of the subject's abject identification with object *a* in the *passage à l'acte*? I have said that this reckless, uncontrolled tossing of the body occurs when the social bond is lacerated and dissolving and the subject, crazed without a social bond, falls apart. Such bodies—and the psyches that inhabit them—are like errant flies searching for a container or stabilizer without being able to find it. Here, Lacan's later addition to his classical discourse theory takes us a bit farther with a fifth discourse, that of the capitalist ("Milan").

The capitalist discourse lies outside of the bounds of the social bond. It is associated with a new kind of symptom, one that is about immediate jouissance unencumbered by fantasy. These symptoms do not signify, they are not addressed to the Other: they include anorexia, bulimia, cutting, addiction and are all associated with the capitalist command to enjoy immediately, via consumption. All consumption is immediately followed by disappointment (the commodity was not "it") and then by more consumption. Capitalist discourse is "pestilent" (11) in the sense of infectious obscene consumption driven by suicidal object *a*, its version of desire, namely unending greed, a mouth that never closes, an object *a* not just materially but literally ever present, pure sublime substance: alcohol, opioids, porn, and so on. The subject lets go of the word, the address to the Other. The Trumpian who throws themselves away for Trump enjoys their own dissolving physical, often fatal positioning within the world. It is an actual literal dissolution that produces *plus-de-jouir*. And crucially, others' bodies, dissolving *them*, can do the trick as well.

This notion of a dissolving body and taking pleasure in it might also evoke a different psychoanalyst: Sándor Ferenczi and his understanding of the psychic shattering that occurs when a child is being traumatized. Ferenczi is also the theorizer of the victim's identification with the aggressor, later developed and translated into political theory by Arendt. Both Ferenczi and Arendt develop an understanding of a subject without social bond. In his famous paper "Confusion of Tongues between Adults and the Child" (1933) and in various parts of his *Clinical Diaries* (1932), Ferenczi describes what occurs to a psyche and body traumatized by sexual assault as well as physical and emotional neglect and abuse—which he calls, specifically, "authoritarian abuse."

The most fundamental effect of this abuse is a catastrophic psychic *Erschütterung* (fragmentation): "If a trauma strikes the soul [. . .] [t]he power that would hold the individual fragments and elements together is absent. Fragments and elements of organs, psychic fragments and elements become dissociated" (*Clinical* 69). This "power" that is "absent" is precisely the familial and social bond. In severe trauma, which for Ferenczi means essentially psychic murder and death, the psyche whirls in a state of dissolution; it then attempts to cure itself by way of a deeply unconscious act of reassembly, even in the face of almost inexorable dissociations. The combination of dissociation—dissociation between intellect and emotion, mind and body, agent and patient, predator and prey—and the unconscious reassembly (the idea is in part deeply Kleinian) that can sometimes come to "rewire" such subjects, sever and reconnect them in symptomatic ways (though such "last-resort" self-salvations are not the typical outcome), should be of enormous interest in contemporary psychoanalytic and political theory.

Can Ferenczi help us read this perplexing moment in American society and politics and its sadomasochistic pleasures and horrors? I want to suggest that his extraordinarily clear and visual depictions of traumatic psychic shattering in what he calls authoritarian abuse and various possible instances of "rewiring" by a psyche that is attempting to cure and save itself can help us if we briefly, maybe even just as a sort of theoretical exercise, transplant it into the wider social arena that is normally governed not only by the familial but also the social bond. I do not think that it is entirely coincidental that Ferenczi was working, thinking, and writing in this vein during the rise of fascism in Europe (1932–1933).

Let us single out three potentially relevant ideas in Ferenczi. The first is that for Ferenczi victims of authoritarian abuse are characterized by "extreme impressionability" (*Clinical* 148): in response to the lethal attack coming from without, they turn to mimicry as a mode of defense and make themselves conform to the agent attacking them, while "they," or, rather, their previous selves, have a "tendency to fade away," lacking any support in effective "self-protection." Instead, what takes place is an "immediate resignation and adaptation of the self to the environment" (148).

The second idea, more image than idea, is Ferenczi's paraphrase of a patient's verbal description of the status of her body that emerged from a fantasy she had involving a "gigantic" rape: "She sees her body unnaturally laid out, like that of a dead person; powerful heart palpitations accompany this fantasy. After about twenty or twenty-five violent jolts [*Erschütterungen*] which overwhelm her like waves of pain, she feels nothing more but regards herself, her body, as a stranger, from the outside" (*Clinical* 66–67). In our context, the image works isomorphically for the pervasive alienation of enormous groups of people and for what Hedges, with Durkheim, calls *anomie*: the alienated body lying outside the bounds of social bond.

The third idea is Ferenczi's identification of a key dissociative—and consequently murderous and simultaneously suicidal—mechanism: identification with the aggressor. Recognizing that it is in mortal danger as the victim of a life-threatening assault of whatever nature, the psyche suicidally leaves its own body and identity behind in order not to be the victim and thus to survive what it recognizes as a murderous attack. Better to be the aggressor, the murderer, through identification, than the victim—for the sake of survival.

All three ideas depict a form of profound displacement and "statelessness"; that is, all three scenarios are about a devastating disappearance. All three are also images of a dissolving social bond. It seems clear to me that they are related to another similar state, namely the state of the subject in a "state of exception" as formulated by Carl Schmitt (*Concept*) and picked up by Giorgio Agamben, who depicted "bare life" in a literal, physical sphere in which life and death themselves roam about unpredictably, lacking any sort of civil protections or a place in the social bond.[4] These theories are well known and need not be rehearsed here.

No less urgent is yet another isomorphism in this series of dissociations: a scenario we have all heard about that seems, on the surface, clearly distant, but not only because the actual context is geographically detached, which makes displacement that much easier. On May 20, 2023, the *New York Times* ran a front-page video-article titled "Greece Says It Doesn't Ditch Migrants at Sea: It Was Caught in the Act" (Stevis-Gridneff). The video, taken surreptitiously from quite a distance but with a zoom lens that leaves no doubt about the nature of the events taking place, records the following: "On April 11 on the Greek island of Lesbos, 12 migrants—men, women, children and an infant—were locked inside this unmarked van, forced onto a speedboat, transferred to a Greek Coast Guard vessel, and then abandoned in the middle of the Aegean Sea, in violation of Greek, European Union and international law. They were left adrift in an inflatable emergency raft." One sees clearly police and coast guard helping adults and children onto the boat before abandoning them on a raft. We see, particularly clearly, the baby handed off by one of the officials. It is no secret that this particular form of atrocity has occurred repeatedly and is occurring in the Aegean and Mediterranean Seas as well as the Atlantic Ocean this very instant and will continue to occur as migration from the South grows only more desperate given the ramifications of climate change and endless wars. Migrants as "merely living" and desperate stateless creatures would seem to offer an ample supply of targets for the sadism of our age. Migrants, through their literal statelessness, are and will increasingly become open prey, perfectly suited for sacrifice, the object *a*'s act of "falling away," and are in this way identified with object *a*: identified, targeted, and eliminated, thrown out, evacuated. Certainly, in sentiment and action, such abandonments and killings in no-places (the middle of the ocean) of nameless, stateless men, women, and children that occur without record are linked to, and are symptoms of, the growing anomie and sadomasochism produced by a global capitalism that increasingly suspends basic human rights and protections. The destruction of basic human rights and protections has become a pastime offered up not only to xenophobic mobs but to governments as well.[5]

Arendt warned repeatedly that statelessness played a crucial role in the generation of atrocity and crimes against humanity. In *Origins of Totalitarianism* she declared statelessness the problem of our age, as events like the one that took place in Greece were becoming the norm. Statelessness, she wrote, is

> *the newest mass phenomenon in contemporary history, and [indicates] the existence of an ever-growing new people comprised of stateless persons, the most symptomatic group in contemporary politics. Their existence can hardly be blamed on one factor*

> *alone, but if we consider the different groups among the stateless it appears that every political event since the end of the first World War inevitably added a new category to those who lived outside the pale of the law, while none of the categories, no matter how the original constellation changed, could ever be renormalized. (277)*

Loss always takes place when formulating the existence of fundamental human rights (namely, to have the right to exist and to be alive in a particular place in the world, the right to "mere life"), in fact, the right to have rights, for when a right is formulated it inexorably brings along with it its negation. Again, in *Origins of Totalitarianism* she writes, "[T]his calamity arose not from any lack of civilization, backwardness, or mere tyranny, but, on the contrary [. . .] could not be repaired, because there was no longer any 'uncivilized' spot on earth, because whether we like it or not we have really started to live in One World. Only with a completely organized humanity could the loss of home and political status become identical with expulsion from humanity altogether" (296–97). Statelessness, literal and figurative, is the reality but also the symptom of our time. We are left with the question of what sorts of acts can mitigate, or even overturn, the relegation—forced or chosen—of certain bodies and lives to such zones of lethal anomie. How do we navigate the sadomasochism of our age, which has a flavor all its own? The essays that follow give us some indications.

ELIZABETH STEWART is an associate professor of English at Yeshiva University, the author of *Catastrophe and Survival: Walter Benjamin and Psychoanalysis* (Continuum, 2010), and translator and editor of *Lacan in the German-Speaking World* (State University of New York Press, 2004). She is currently working on a book on intergenerational relations from a psychoanalytic and philosophical perspective in German society and culture during the twentieth century, with a focus on the postwar period. She is a contributor to *Understanding Lacan, Understanding Modernism*, edited by Thomas Waller, which will appear in 2024 (Bloomsbury) and has contributed chapters to several edited volumes.

Notes

1   Trump's full tweet read, "I will be leaving the great Walter Reed Medical Center today at 6:30 P.M. Feeling really good! Don't be afraid of COVID. Don't let it dominate your life. We have developed, under the Trump Administration, some really great drugs & knowledge. I feel better than I did 20 years ago!"

2   See Morozov, who engages critically with the use of the term and writes:

On the right, the most vocal proponent of the "return to feudalism" thesis has been the conservative urban theorist Joel Kotkin, who targeted the power of "woke" techno-oligarchs in The Coming of Neo-Feudalism *(2020). [. . .] On the left, the list of people who have flirted with "feudalist" concepts is*

*long and growing: Yanis Varou-
fakis, Mariana Mazzucato, Jodi
Dean, Robert Kuttner, Wolfgang
Streeck, Michael Hudson and,
ironically, even Robert Brenner, of
the eponymous Brenner Debate on
the transition from feudalism to
capitalism.*

We might add Ellen Brown to the
list.

3   The Brennan Center for Justice
explains, "A conservative nonprofit
group called Citizens United challenged campaign finance rules
after the FEC stopped it from promoting and airing a film criticiz-
ing presidential candidate Hillary
Clinton too close to the presidential primaries. A 5–4 majority of
the Supreme Court sided with
Citizens United, ruling that corporations and other outside groups
can spend unlimited money on
elections" (Lau).

4   Carl Schmitt, the legal theorist
for the National Socialist takeover
in Germany, defines "mere life"
(*bloßes Leben*) in *The Concept of
the Political* as mere existence
devoid of any social, political, or
cultural meaning that lies outside
of what Lacan calls the Symbolic
and is deprived of the most fundamental human rights; one could
say, in fact, that its dimension is
the damned space inhabited by
Polyneices's body in *Antigone*.
This space of statelessness and
everything in it therefore ceases to
be recognized as human.

5   Famously, for example, Governor
of Florida Ron DeSantis organized
what was essentially the kidnap-
ping of a group of migrants by
flying them to Martha's Vineyard
to drop them, literally, on the door-
steps of vacationing Democratic
politicians (see Sandoval et al.).

Works Cited

Agamben, Giorgio. *Homo Sacer: Sovereign Power and Bare Life*. Trans. Daniel Heller-Roazen. Stanford: Stanford UP, 1998.

Arendt, Hannah. *The Origins of Totalitarianism*. Cleveland: Meridian, 1958.

Brown, Ellen. "How America Went from Mom-and-Pop Capitalism to Techno-Feudalism." *AMASS* 25.4 (2021): 30–34.

CBC News: The National. "Bangladesh Factory Collapse." *YouTube*. https://www.youtube.com /watch?v=ISj8BECf40Q (accessed 29 June 2023).

Durkheim, Émile. *Suicide: A Study in Sociology*. London: Routledge, 1952.

Ferenczi, Sándor. *The Clinical Diary of Sándor Ferenczi*. Cambridge MA: Harvard UP, 1988.

——————. "Confusion of Tongues between Adults and the Child: The Language of Ten- derness and of Passion." *Contemporary Psychoanalysis* 24.2 (1988): 196–206.

Freud, Sigmund. "The Psychogenesis of a Case of Homosexuality in a Woman." 1920. *The Standard Edition of the Complete Psychological Works of Sigmund Freud*. Trans. and ed. James Strachey. Vol. 18. London: Hogarth, 1955. 145–72. 24 vols. 1953–74.

Guardian News. "Republican Greg Gianforte 'Body Slams' Guardian Reporter in Montana— Audio." *YouTube*. https://www.youtube.com/watch?v=KQwu4wff7lI (accessed 29 June 2023).

Harari, Roberto. *Lacan's Seminar on Anxiety: An Introduction*. Trans. Jane C. Lamb-Ruiz. New York: Other Press, 2001.

Hedges, Chris. *America: The Farewell Tour*. New York: Simon and Schuster, 2019.

———————. "A Conversation with Chris Hedges: Corporate Totalitarianism." New York City Bar Association. *YouTube*. https://www.youtube.com/watch?v=EiAXKiTS6HA&t=377s (accessed 10 July 2023).

Ivey, Kathryn. "Nurses Struggle through a New COVID Wave with Rage and Compassion: A Critical Care Nurse Confronts the Omicron Surge Filling Her Hospital." *Scientific American* 11 Jan. 2022. https://www.scientificamerican.com/article/nurses-struggle-through-a-new -covid-wave-with-rage-and-compassion/.

Lacan, Jacques. *Anxiety: The Seminar of Jacques Lacan Book X*. Ed. Jacques-Alain Miller. Trans. A. R. Price. Malden: Polity, 2014.

———————. *Encore: Feminine Sexuality, the Limits of Love and Knowledge: The Seminar of Jacques Lacan Book XX*. Ed. Jacques-Alain Miller. Trans. Bruce Fink. New York: Norton, 1998.

———————. *The Four Fundamental Concepts of Psychoanalysis: The Seminar of Jacques Lacan Book IX*. Ed. Jacques-Alain Miller. Trans. Alan Sheridan. New York: Norton, 1998.

———————. "Milan Discourse—Lacan [On Psychoanalytic Discourse]." *Lacan in Italia. En Italie Lacan*. Milan: La Salmandra, 1978, 32–55. Trans. Jack W. Stone, 1–15.

LaFrance, Adrienne. "A Transcript of the Greg Gianforte 'Body-Slam' Audio." *Atlantic* 25 May 2017. https://www.theatlantic.com/technology/archive/2017/05/a-transcript-of-the-greg -gianforte-body-slam-audio/528102/.

Larkin, Howard. "Navigating Attacks against Health Care Workers in the COVID-19 Era." *JAMA* 325.18 (2021):1822–24. doi:10.1001/jama.2021.2701.

Lau, Tim. "Citizens United Explained." *Brennan Center for Justice*. 12 Dec. 2019. https://www .brennancenter.org/our-work/research-reports/citizens-united-explained.

Morozov, Evgeny. "Critique of Techno-Feudal Reason." *New Left Review* 133/34 (2022). https:// newleftreview.org/issues/ii133/articles/evgeny-morozov-critique-of-techno-feudal-reason.

Parker, Ashley. "In 'Good Old Days,' Donald Trump Says, 'Campaign Protesters Got More Than Just an Escort Out.'" *New York Times* 27 Feb. 2016. https://archive.nytimes.com/www .nytimes.com/politics/first-draft/2016/02/27/in-good-old-days-donald-trump-says-campaign -protesters-got-more-than-just-an-escort-out/.

Polanyi, Karl. *The Great Transformation: The Political and Economic Origins of Our Time*. New York: Beacon, 2001.

Porter, Tom. "Police Condemn Trump for Speech 'Condoning Law Enforcement Brutal- ity.'" *Newsweek* 29 July 2017. https://www.newsweek.com/police-condemn-trump-speech -condoning-law-enforcement-brutality-643816.

Rogers, Katie. "Protesters Dispersed with Tear Gas So Trump Could Pose at Church." *New York Times* 1 June 2020. https://www.nytimes.com/2020/06/01/us/politics/trump-st-johns -church-bible.htm.

Sandoval, E., M. Jordan, P. Mazzei, and J. D. Goodman. "The Story behind DeSantis's Migrant Flights to Martha's Vineyard." *New York Times* 2 Oct. 2022. https://www.nytimes.com/2022 /10/02/us/migrants-marthas-vineyard-desantis-texas.html.

Schmitt, Carl. *The Concept of the Political*. 1932. Chicago: U of Chicago P, 2008.

—————————. *Political Theology 2: The Myth of the Closure of Any Political Theology.* Hoboken: John Wiley, 2014.

Snyder, Timothy. "America and the Politics of Pain." *New Statesman* 28 Oct. 2020. https://www.newstatesman.com/long-reads/2020/10/america-donald-trump-healthcare-politics-pain-covid-illness-hospital.

—————————. "On Language and 'Not Even Fascism.'" *American Academy in Berlin.* 14 Jan. 2019. https://www.americanacademy.de/timothy-snyder-on-language-and-not-even-fascism/.

—————————. "Sadopopulism: Timothy Snyder Speaks, ep. 4." *YouTube* 2 Dec. 2017. https://www.youtube.com/watch?v=oOjJtEkKMX4.

Statista Research Department. "Wealth Distribution in the United States in the Fourth quarter of 2022." 5 April 2023. https://www.statista.com/statistics/203961/wealth-distribution-for-the- us/#:~:text=In%20the%20fourth%20quarter%20of,percent%20of%20the%20total%20wealth.

Stevis-Gridneff, Matina, et al. "Greece Says It Doesn't Ditch Migrants at Sea: It Was Caught in the Act." *New York Times* 19 May 2023. https://www.nytimes.com/2023/05/19/world/europe/greece-migrants-abandoned.html.

Stieb, Matt. "Dan Patrick of Texas on State Reopening: 'There Are More Important Things Than Living.'" *New York Magazine* 21 Apr. 2020. https://nymag.com/intelligencer/2020/04/dan-patrick-there-are-more-important-than-living.html.

Trump, Donald J. (@realDonaldTrump). "I will be leaving the great Walter Reed Medical Center today at 6:30 P.M. Feeling really good! Don't be afraid of COVID. Don't let it dominate your life. We have developed, under the Trump Administration, some really great drugs & knowledge. I feel better than I did 20 years ago!" 5 Oct. 2020, 2:37 p.m. Tweet.

Wolin, Sheldon S. *Democracy Incorporated: Managed Democracy and the Specter of Inverted Totalitarianism.* Princeton: Princeton UP, 2008.

Žižek, Slavoj. "Is there a Proper Way to Remake a Hitchcock Film?" *Lacan.com.* https://www.lacan.com/hitch.html (accessed 29 June 2023).

The Social Bond Adrift

*W*hile the paradigm shift inaugurating our contemporary era tends to hinge on the fall of the Berlin Wall or the attacks of September 11, 2001, little attention has been paid to an event that, in an approach to what Sigmund Freud characterized as the clinic of civilization in *Civilization and Its Discontents*, could be considered a symptom of a changing subjectivity. On February 12, 1993, Robert Thompson and Jon Venables, two children from Liverpool barely ten years old, kidnapped, tortured, and murdered two-year-old James Bulger. The social commotion and repercussions that followed the unprecedented case were massive, taking not only public opinion but also the British judicial system by surprise. Due to the underage nature of the assassins, they were judged under the denominations of "Child A" and "Child B" and sentenced to prison following special security measures, all under strict secrecy, to prevent the release of their names.

The impossibility of finding a motive to explain the commission of such a monstrosity, combined with the failure of psychological evaluations to provide any clear and evident clinical diagnoses, cannot but evoke Hannah Arendt's considerations regarding the banality of evil in her famous

Volume 34, Number 3   DOI 10.1215/10407391-10898185

essay about Adolf Eichmann (*Eichmann*). The tragedy of the crime laid bare something new. If Auschwitz had definitively shattered the false hope placed on the superiority of human reason, revealing the dark side of enlightened modernity, the assassination of James Bulger destroyed the last remaining myth of the West: childhood innocence. Not only did we have to renounce all ideas of redemption of the human condition, but to make matters worse, we had to accept that children are also capable of monstrous and gratuitous actions whose disproportionality exceeds any possibility of attributing meaning to them, even the most perverse imaginable. It was the overwhelmingly incomprehensible nature of this event, along with the impotence of sociologists, psychologists, and experts of all kinds to offer a convincing explanation based on the socioeconomic, cultural, and familial contexts of the children, as well as their respective biographies, that authorizes me to interpret the crime as the breaching of a new limit, the rupture of a moral barrier once believed to be inviolable. Of course, I am not suggesting that we have reached a point in civilization in which children have become potential assassins. Nor do I propose to employ the tools of psychoanalysis to establish a clinical hypothesis about what happened, given that this isn't my interest in the case. I find it important to highlight its symptomatic status in that it reveals the momentum reached in our time by the "disentanglement" of the drive, a term used by Freud to refer to the rupture of inhibition that Eros can exert on the devastating action of the death drive (*Beyond*). "Liquid society," postulated by Zygmunt Bauman as a consequence of the historical process of globalization, has its correlate in the decomposition and decline of the paternal function, a phenomenon through which psychoanalysis condenses the collapse of narrativity structured by great normative, moral, religious, and ideological values, as well as their effects on the plane of the subject (Bauman and Dessal).

One could argue that the exceptional nature of the event in Liverpool detracts from its illustrative value. However, I reaffirm my hypothesis precisely because of the near total absence of studies on the case. This apparent lack of interest itself incites suspicion. It would appear as though the notable effort to invisibilize the actors, to erase them from public existence, had extended to all disciplines involved in an event with these characteristics (judicial, sociological, philosophical, forensic), thereby increasing through silence the overwhelming dimension of what is at play: the terrible disproportionality between an act and any possibility of classifying it within the order of rational discourse. If until the Bulger murder we knew that childhood has always been—and still is—the object of the same abominations that human beings can exert on their fellow human beings, regardless of age, gender, or condition; and if we were fully and sadly aware that a child (as the embodiment of a sacred space in which we attempt to safeguard a damaged and degraded humanity) is a historical-cultural figure that is annihilated and reestablished based on the ups and downs of that same history and culture, then the Liverpool crime blows to pieces the last vestiges of an order in which we believed that the ethical dimension of the impossible still retained a minimum guarantee of survival. If we had to summarize in a single characterization the principle that rules the capitalist regime's current modality (a system whose chameleonic variability allows it to adopt an astonishing array of forms, from a liberal spirit to a pending totalitarianism), we should highlight its tendency to promote a perversion of the ideal of liberty as an unrestricted acceptance of the prerogatives of the market. To benefit the supreme objectives of capital, it has been considered necessary to progressively and consistently eliminate those limits on which the social state relied, which for decades was responsible for mitigating the hardships and precarities of the weakest strata of the system and for serving the reconstruction of an economy devastated by World War II. The dismantling of this structure (once the economic fabric was recomposed in the postwar period and the terrain secured for plundering with renewed energy) and its replacement by social engineering based on the calculated and extreme exploitation of man's helplessness has required the cooperation of various forces necessary to configure the transformation of the Zeitgeist that could accompany, consent to, and even become a docile ally of the new doctrine. The dissolution of local societies in the globalized cloud has birthed an era that at times seems to augur an unprecedented threat against the human condition, as if the action of the destructive forces of the death drive were approaching its definitive and final realization.

This portrait of society in no way supposes a naïve model of a self-conscious power capable of intentionally redesigning a new socioeconomic architecture. Although power is not an abstract entity, given that it is represented by real people, structures, and organizations, we nonetheless recognize the autonomous action of dynamics that exceed the will of its supposed actors, whose freedom of movement, despite its indisputable magnitude, is neither full nor exempt from the backlashes of the Real.

The search for safety constitutes an aspiration as ancient as humankind itself. It takes its impulse from the original uncertainty and helplessness of man, whose existential sense lacks a predetermined foundation. This ontological weakness makes the speaking being a creature tormented by indeterminacy, vulnerable to the cosmic feeling of the incommensurable and unpredictable. Here, we find the roots that have given rise to the greed for identificatory references and to the emergence of religious and ideological representations capable of injecting meaning into the Real of a world that, to the subject, presents itself inhabited by all sorts of perils. Those threats were clearly formulated by Freud in *Civilization and Its Discontents,* in which he classifies the three great sources of human fear: those coming from the forces of nature, those generated by the social bond, and those that originate from the feeling of corporal fragility. In this sense, the fear of God has entailed an extraordinary sublimating conquest and an enormous advantage, condensing in a single source the countless fears that prey upon human beings (Lacan, *Psychoses* 266–68). For centuries, the existential vulnerability of man has been partially alleviated by the different narrative orders constructed by political and religious powers, which have simultaneously played with "terror and hope" (Borges 102). Until the Age of Reason, the Sovereign (earthly or divine) and the slave sealed a pact by virtue of which the former embodied terror, whose source was now localizable and created bonds of obedience and fidelity, while the latter alienated its existence in exchange for the hope of protection, fundamentally derived from faith in the omnipotence and omniscience of the former.[1] At the whim of God or Master, subjects could concentrate the senseless randomness of existence and convert it into a coherent argument, a relatively regulated order capable of exorcising the terrifying feeling of abandonment in the face of life's uncertainty and precarity. Despite its terrible disproportion, bartering freedom for supposed security constituted one of the most solid social contracts in history, more or less intact until the Enlightenment, which introduced the ideal of a brotherhood of human reason struggling against manipulation by primitive ghosts. But if the Enlightenment promised to bring us out of the cave and the captivity of false representations, humanity would soon witness the Restoration of darkness promoted by capitalism, which, hand in hand with the Industrial Revolution, opened the path to the empire of the technological society under whose regime we currently live, and which again stirs up the fallacy of security as an instrument of political domination.

Communism represented the new promise of happiness elaborated by a society artificially designed according to the criteria of rationality "clean" of all ideological impurities. As with all social hygienics—and consonant with the National Socialist project—the purification process could only be ensured through the removal of all obstacles that interfered with the achievement of the final objective. The communist creed, like Nazi millenarianism, constituted the embodiment of the bloodthirsty superego that promised the myth of the motherland in exchange for the definitive death of desire. If, in its successive phases, the capitalist order has demonstrated until now immunity to all social experiments of emancipation, it is due to its acute perception of the unconscious mechanisms ruling human subjectivity and its ability to put them at its service. Capitalism largely owes its long life and capacity for constant regeneration to its grasp of human nature as not merely sustained by the needs that ensure its survival but closely linked with a regime of satisfaction that doesn't respond to the logic of *primum vivere*. To put it ironically, though in response to a reality which is impossible to ignore, man does not live on bread alone but also on those objects in which we see the extraordinary clinical understanding of the subject that Marx displayed in his analysis of commodity fetishism. As Bauman aptly points out, "[I]n the liquid stage of modernity capitalism opted out from that competition: its wager was put instead on the potential *infinity* of human desires, and its efforts have focused since on catering for their infinite growth: on desires desiring more desire, not their satisfaction; on the multiplying instead of the streamlining of opportunities and choices; on letting loose, not 'structuring,' the play of probabilities" (36). It is perhaps at this point that sociology runs up against the limits of its understanding. Indeed, the "unlimited growth" that makes up part of today's market creed is completely tributary to the impossibility of desire's satisfaction, as only unconscious experience can attest to it. That desire is, in its most intimate essence, "desire for desire" is not something we should attribute to capitalist discourse. On the contrary, such discourse would be incapable of sustaining its hegemony if it did not employ the properties of unconscious desire as a fundamental base for its imperatives. Given that the root of desire originates in an inaugural loss conceptualized by Freud under the term "experience of satisfaction" (*Interpretation*, esp. 550–72), desire as such is engaged in an incessant search whose destination is the impossible reunion with the severed part of the self, a forced consequence of alienation to the order of word and language.

Security becomes the bargaining chip of an era in which the inconsistency of the symbolic Other is experienced with extreme rawness and brutality. Under the rule of current modernity, the fateful combination of psychic and social helplessness has found unprecedented expression, as the subject is stripped of the narratives that once provided a reason for his existence, no matter how painful it may be. Today, millions of people lack the slightest moral compass that would grant them a place in the world. To make matters worse, their marginality, their belonging to an extraterritoriality that is part of neither real nor virtual social space, turns them into carriers of a strangeness conducive to embodying that alterity that every human group requires to simultaneously house evil and acquire a false consistency. The growth of populist and nationalist movements in the United States and Europe, waving the immemorial flags of economic and existential insecurity, is the direct consequence of the dispossession produced by globalization and the uncontrollable flow of capital (and its correlate of unprecedented levels of inequality). The same powers that have condemned millions of the planet's inhabitants to chronically experience uncertainty assert themselves as the preachers and heralds of the supreme value of guaranteed security. Political speeches have turned into contests where candidates exhibit their zero-tolerance policies toward all those factors that put the security of citizens at risk, taking great care to keep hidden the true causes of the insecurity they suffer and heightening the focus on extrinsic factors. The primordial function of contemporary politics is the calculated manipulation of various figures of the Other, which fulfill the expiatory function of the evils caused by agents administering the Discourse of the Master. Anyone who aspires to consolidate their leadership in the obscenity of a political career must know how to connect with the primal fears of the masses and then convince them to sacrifice their liberty to the calf of security. In order to do so, the anguish and resentment of the people must be redirected toward imaginary enemies, thus distancing them from the real causes of their misfortune. The lie, the political weapon par excellence, is as old as humankind, but it finds renewed potency thanks to technologies that allow disinformation and mystification to spread at the speed of light. The very notion of truth loses all consistency, since there are no longer any instances or institutions capable of opposing the capacity to create false and accommodating narratives or of exercising at least minimal control. On social media, real subjects are not even required to sow hatred. Bots can also take on this task.

But haven't uncertainty and ontological unprotectedness always existed? Haven't we said they are intrinsic to the human condition? Why, then, make them a key to deciphering the direction of contemporary discourse?

One fundamental difference is that uncertainty is no longer a hardship to defeat, or at least to conceal. On the contrary, it has acquired a new phenomenal form, accompanied by a procession of signifiers that grant it justification and legitimacy: flexibility, autonomy, outsourcing, discontinuity. Precarity becomes the new virtue of modernity, insofar as it is supposed to be healthy stimulus for personal reinvention, for the autobiographical overcoming of the system's "challenges," a source of energy to stimulate personal growth and the fitness necessary in the race for the survival of the fittest. In light of this current spirit, the welfare state (or what little is left of it) is viewed as a narcotic, a formula that has only served to create generations of subjects unfit for battle, morally weak in the conquest of socioeconomic ideals, inclined to self-pity, and addicted to begging from the state.

Although it is undoubtedly not our intention to establish a causal link, it is worth noting the extent to which social media has contributed to forging this model of adaptive identity, in which all the traits and values of high-performance individualism are reinforced. The paradox of social media is in its creation of a simulacrum of society, a false community, a preaching of "sharing" that is actually a purely mechanical action devoid of any authentic content. The modern winner is the one who refuses all expectations based on solidarity, the common good, or empathy, instead emphasizing the spirit of combat in the pursuit of an imagined personal and autonomous security. Social media provides the platform for the exhibitionism needed to success-fully and competitively promote the self. From this perspective, it is worth asking whether this decade's trend toward autistic protagonists in various novels, films, and television shows does not constitute a metaphor for a func-tional subjectivity characterized by isolation, affective disconnection, and the capacity for multiple as well as mechanical performances.

The exponential growth in the ideology of security's followers is directly proportional to the increase in social and economic uncertainty that is deliberately hidden behind the lucrative business of making visible the external threats (terrorism, immigration) from which our government must protect us. Such ideology has not only failed to diminish our feelings of defenselessness but has instilled suspicion, distrust, and the principle of "every man for himself" as a defense mechanism.

In short, the polarity between security and ethics brings us back to a contemporary and dramatic form manifesting the incessant struggle between Eros—the principle of conservation and communion—and Thanatos, which seeks separation, segregation, and destruction. Surrendered to the imperative of reason, we run the risk of forgetting that it carries within it the counterpoint to barbarism.

Why do totalitarian systems triumph? Why do human beings submit to political systems that subjugate them? What is the cause of this passivity that can reach the limits of collective humiliation and the suffer-ing of nearly all? It is not only a problem of political philosophy but also an enigma of subjectivity. Already in the sixteenth century, a young French jurist named Étienne de La Boétie wrote a treatise titled *Discourse on Voluntary Servitude*, where he posed this same question: how is the existence of a tyrant explained? Undoubtedly, any response based on the idea of physical coercion is insufficient. Nietzsche took this question to an extreme, concluding that servitude is always voluntary.

History is a constant and truthful witness that, under certain circumstances, humans can overcome the fear that keeps them in subjugation. Peoples revolt, they confront domination, sometimes without weapons or resources, animated solely by the desire for freedom from the same yoke that they tolerated for years, even decades. Those who presumably submitted out of physical fear will not hesitate to leave themselves exposed to face the bullets. How is it possible that we have arrived at this situation, the destruction of dignified forms of work, the submission to modes of exploitation that are introduced into all aspects of human life? The classic concept of exploitation denounced by Marx in the nineteenth century has evolved into much more sophisticated versions. We are exploited on a daily basis and in subtle ways, scammed by advertisements, the media, and corporations, by the larceny of banks and the lies of politicians, institutions, and agents of power. We are exploited by the mediocrity of television and the obscenity of characters who assume the new spiritual direction of the collective consciousness. We live, as the French philosopher Gilles Lipovetsky argues in *L'Ère du vide*, in an era where ideologies no longer represent the subject's lived experience of reality. There is nothing more auspicious than the void to facilitate the rise of innumerable servitudes, as many as there are masters willing to satisfy them. Salvation and rescue are no longer expected from political actions, but are promoted as individual will: everyone founds their own narrative, assumes themself the architect of their destiny, becomes the promoter of themself, seeks a way out in their personal opportunities, and abandons all confidence in social and collective answers.

The flip side of this "era of the void" is plenitude, the neoliberal belief in the infinite multiplication of products. It is a plenitude provided by the superabundance of things, an excess that is even compatible with poverty: in places where everything is lacking, there may be an excess of weapons, drugs, and cell phones. The subject moves between emptiness and plenitude without realizing that they are equivalents. Plenitude is, ultimately, the revelation of emptiness in the contemporary era.

It is not that we now live in greater uncertainty than that which has always lain beneath existence, but that the pandemic has intervened as a reagent that has unleashed an undisguised rawness. At the same time, this feeling becomes hostage to a new form of exploitation, an ideology that has, after the dissolution of traditional political representations, come to fill the void as a sovereign and universal rule: security. Paradox of our time, generalized uncertainty is manipulated through the supreme concept of security, a security that COVID demolished despite all the voices that foretold what was to come but were ignored by those who should have taken notice.

Capitalism, as opposed to former and coexisting political experiments, has been pointed out by different authors as a system characterized by the creation of weak identities, poorly defined identifications (see Nancy and Lacoue-Labarthe). Totalitarian, nationalist, and tribal regimes all foster strong, monolithic identifications, which, on the one hand, ensure social cohesion and, on the other, facilitate the domination of the masses. In the uncertainty and lack of ontological foundation that characterize the human being, tyranny finds fertile ground in which to germinate. The tyrant and the dictator captivate through the solidity with which they deliver an epic, raise a promise, and trace a path to salvation. They don't conceal their perversions; they mock laws; they establish themselves as their own masters and as masters of everyone else—and this thanks to their extraordinary ability to fabricate stories and tales that people like, stirring the collective archetypes with which societies weave their dreams. Faced with a world where everything blurs together, where the edges of reality become foggy, the New Prince represents the virtue of clarity, precision, and the unambiguous. He defends the most reactionary values, which have the advantage of providing tangible references at a time when life decomposes to infinity in the infinite slippage of social media. The masters, the tyrants, the kinglets return. A revolution is no longer necessary to install them.

The movement is twofold: on the one hand, the globalized and predatory economy generates a flow of ungovernable power that crushes any ideology and threatens to irreversibly discredit the weak trust that citizens have in political action. Ontological precariousness aims to conceal itself with the superabundance of consumer goods, and the subject experiences a solitude and disorientation that withdraws him deep into his small island, less and less capable of a collective response to the pillaging to which he is subjected. On the other hand, like carrion birds waiting for the sign of death to descend on their prey, "personalities" sense a popular appetite for meaning and enter public discourse. There's nothing simpler than taking advantage of the structural condition of a human being, who needs the nourishment of dreams and who is always ready to attribute to his peer a misfortune whose true explanation requires a longer, more committed look. The disturbing rise of the populist far right in Europe and the United States feeds on contemporary mental fragility caused, in turn, by the devitalization of the political, which languishes under the mortifying effects of capital.

A few nuances.

The progressive decline of a narrative that forms the backbone of the course of life of contemporary modern societies simultaneously produces a series of paradoxical and symptomatic phenomena that deserve to be positively taken into account. First of all, there is no denying that the increasing empowerment of individualism, with its consequent disaffection and insensitivity to social reality, is notably offset by the fact that never before in history have we experienced such a heightened consciousness of the hardships that torment human beings and of the need to take action that transcends local worries, a sort of globalized moral solidarity that has reached unprecedented efficacy thanks to new technologies. The Internet not only executes infamous financial operations that condemn millions to misery but also allows for fabulous public opinion campaigns to be launched, often capable of stopping, or at least delaying, infamies. Ecology, although in some instances threatening to become an alternative to religious discourse, is also an important social force, not just because of its direct objective but also because it is a discourse that legitimizes itself in defense of an ethic that derives from philosophical thought in an era in which market laws work mechanically, as amoral forces of nature. These laws produce a new form of alienation, one that deprives subjects of any possibility of articulating the causal relationship between the degradation of their living conditions and the behaviors they adopt to improve them.

Faced with the discrediting of politics and the progressive withdrawal of governmental mechanisms for social rescue, citizenship is organized in a fragmentary manner around traits that permit the formation of self-management collectives, reciprocal protection, and the search for recognition. The decomposition of traditional ideologies has opened up the possibility for new forms of existence, in many cases multiplying identity formulas that allow human beings to group themselves not only around normative ideals as in the past but also around their symptoms, that is, particularities that deviate from the universal model. Whether organized around sexual preferences or physical or mental health, group mechanisms meant to alleviate solitude and exclusion are currently undergoing an exponential growth in the world.

Those like Hannah Arendt who have deeply reflected on power and violence have comprehended that these terms oppose one another. Power is maintained not through violence but rather through the legitimacy granted it, even if it is despotic. Power resorts to violence only when threatened, which is to say, when it falters. Therefore, if power can assert dominance, it is because it takes advantage of a circumstance in which the masses find themselves driven and willingly swept along by the allure of an idea. This idea can be political or religious, but currently, wherever these kinds of references have lost their prestige, they can be replaced by other kinds of attachments. The value of a brand, object, or television program can be manipulated. Anything can become a hook that the subject, lost in a world without desire, bites in order to fill their emptiness and conceal from themselves their own disorientation. If there is enjoyment in the exercise of power, there is also pleasure in letting oneself be dominated, in submitting to the dictates of a doctrine, a trend, an object of worship, or any other representation on which we confer power to lead us. There would be no master without a willing slave, who is thus spared the confrontation with their desire.

We are hostages of a state that is, in turn, prisoner of a globalized and supranational dictatorship. To the extent that it has lost its traditional role, the state can only continue to justify its existence with the specter of security and its threats. Hence, the writing of a new gospel, preached from all forms of media, consisting of the calculated fabrication of the myth of security. Politics has become, on the one hand, an instrument for the execution of private interests, while on the other, a sworn watchdog for a population intoxicated by the supreme value of security and the multiplicity of risks that call it into question.

The world of infinite things, created by technical and industrial rationality, is paradoxically a new take on the belief in magic. The height of technological sophistication has brought with it a regression to a naïve and prescientific mentality, where objects are inhabited by spirits, are animate beings that speak or have a soul, although their lives are more ephemeral than that of butterflies: they are only fabricated to replace one another at a speed that must constantly increase to sustain the dream of continuous growth and to satisfy the ever more voracious appetite of the contemporary superego, convinced that progress is the confluence of plenitude and immortality. The consequence of this imperative is a life without desire. Given that desire is a timer of satisfaction, it introduces a distance from the object, traces the perimeter of its absence, and translates in us the feeling of lack. But in the world of infinite things, the impossible is inconceivable and satisfaction is demanded and required immediately, discarding all that implies a detour, a slight delay, or an effort to know.

In *The Protestant Ethic and the Spirit of Capitalism*, Max Weber noted that modern science had produced a disenchantment of the world in the sense that man had ceased believing in the magical forces of nature. And yet, the magical has returned in the modern subject's belief in the things of technology. The new form of alienation is the knowledge assumed by objects. Things "know," "think," are "smart," are gifted with a knowledge that we do not possess, and we give in to their power, entrust ourselves to them and hope that their knowledge will exempt us from our own.

Perhaps the question about the submission and indifference of citizens to the abuses of globalization deserves an answer that goes beyond easy explanation. Servitude is pleasurable, and the only reaction so far has been to assume victimhood in a perverted form of rebellion. In this regard, I recommend Pascal Bruckner's book *The Temptation of Innocence* on mechanisms for nurturing the culture of subjects convinced that the world is indebted to them. The victim is the counterpart of the subject drugged by the joy of ignorance, infantilized in a reality filled with music, images, and colors that accompany and surround him everywhere: at work and at leisure, in public life and in intimacy.

An honest reflection, stripped of the victimhood that pollutes social thought, cannot fail to contemplate this "happiness of passivity" and recognize it as a disastrous yet effective ingredient in service of exploitation and the maintenance of the great chain of production and unlimited enrichment. Each must take charge of his own perverted happiness, his own ignorance, his own moral cowardice. It is not enough to take on a position of denunciation. Evil is not depleted by the external agents that torment us. It also exists within us, and it becomes the best ally of a system perpetuated by unanimous complicity. Of course, it's not a matter of promoting a discourse of asceticism, the renunciation of goods, or a bucolic return to nature, which constitute diversions that capitalism assumes as perfectly compatible with its goals. An industry can also be made of such abstention. It is, rather, about awakening from the vain narcissism of happiness, employing technology in service of life and not the other way around, overcoming the temptation of perpetual hedonism and the imposture of plenitude. This is the ethical sense of the cure, understood not from a medical perspective that seeks to return us to normality, but on the contrary as a reencounter with our absolute difference, with what departs from the norm, with what does not make mass or totality, with what is subtracted from the inertia of current discourse, which runs in the direction of banality, stupidity, and moral weakness: a reencounter with what makes us exceptional, from which no exception or privilege is derived nor any justification to reject all debt. Only then, freed from the mirage fabricated by the collusion of our childish dreams and the prophets that announce their realization, will we be in a position to open our eyes to the world that surrounds us, to read between the lines of the messages that traverse us, to resist succumbing to the temptation of looking to a new and obscure authority for redemption from the evils that rush in when the news announces that life has ceased to be a party.

One of the most notable consequences of the COVID-19 pandemic was the unveiling of a complex of political, social, and economic forces that in less critical times remain hidden. On this occasion, I would like to emphasize psychosis and the important role it plays in the current drift of capitalism.

The category of ordinary psychosis proposed by Jacques-Alain Miller has demonstrated a fecundity that is not only clinical but also useful for analyzing the current state of civilization. Social media is no doubt everybody's heritage, but it constitutes a space that is particularly fit for hosting the discourse of the ordinary psychotic. As we know, ordinary psychosis is a clinical variant that, thanks to a supplementary knotting, achieves a functionality well adapted to the current discourse. Ordinary psychosis does not lack the delusional nucleus—usually within reach of analytic listening—which remains latent and without noticeable amplifications. In many cases, the absence of a structured ideational development allows psychotics to establish a social bond between one another that is organized around a shared delusion. The flat-earther example is eloquent. The delusional belief does not function individually; rather, it acts as an amalgam that unites subjects in a community where they mutually recognize each other, achieve a sort of insignia that distinguishes them, and manage to find a way to collectivize the symptom of suppletion. The clinic does not collect individual flat-earth cases of delusion. Although a psychotic might constitute himself as the "case zero"—the "inventor" of the delusion—it is more interesting to formulate a logical sequence in which the delusion precedes its followers. It is a narrative construction made according to the laws of paranoia, which allow the jouissance that returns through the hole of foreclosure to be forwarded to the field of the Other. Such a construction has a status similar to myth, which manages to give meaning to the primary Real, possesses an explanatory virtue that makes it possible to locate evil, and seeks to awaken consciences that are asleep or hypnotized by manipulative forces. From the social circulation of delusion, currently exacerbated by the multiplying effect of social media, psychotic subjects—particularly those who clinically respond to the ordinary form—link the singularity of their subjective position to the universality of the delusional belief that is already "edited" in the discourse that runs through the *alethosphere* (see Lacan, *Other*).[2] Such a link has the advantage of granting more credibility to the nuclear idea, reinforced by the feeling of belonging to a *religio*, in the original sense of the Latin term *religare*, to strongly unite. These delusional links have always existed, but the contemporary paradigm characterized by the decline of the Name of the Father has no doubt notoriously pluralized them. To be sure, delusional theories also find an incalculable number of adherents who could not be considered clinically psychotic, given that a delusional condition is not an intrinsically morbid trait, or in any case, that it responds to the essential madness of language and its effects on the body.

Conspiracy theories are longstanding and have, at times, played an interesting historical role, as is the case with the belief that King George III had orchestrated a secret plan to enslave all the inhabitants of the North American colonies. This theory set the stage for the revolt against the British Crown and the war of emancipation. But despite their age, such theories are currently more powerful and influential than ever before in the history of civilization. Never before has the survival of factual truth been threatened to such an extent, which—as Hannah Arendt notes—can only be established through the testimony of witnesses who are generally unreliable and by reports, documents, and monuments that can be easily fabricated. Arendt is even more radical when she states that nothing can impede most witnesses from veering from the truth and that, under certain circumstances, the feeling of belonging to a majority can stimulate false testimony ("Truth"). We might add, from a psychoanalytic perspective, that this stimulus can also stem from a minority joined by a delusional theory. The thin and blurred line separating factual truth from opinion, along with the lack of self-evident facts, which could always have occurred differently, is manifested in the possibility that history can be rewritten before the eyes of those who have been its direct witnesses. There's no fact that cannot be denied or overlooked, which represents on the political level an expression of the force with which delusional belief imposes itself on the psychotic subject. Truth as fictional construct is at the root of all political action, which by definition relies on lies as a fundamental instrument of mobilization. The current novelty is that the lie no longer possesses a verso: its unmasking changes absolutely nothing, nor does it bring about any consequence insofar as belief is able to survive any denial.

There is no intrinsic relationship between delusional ideas and political ones. Psychosis is a modality of being that traverses the entire ideological spectrum, and yet the delusional ideas that gain strength in social discourse and win over a significant number of adherents and disseminators end up finding an enthusiastic welcome in right-wing and far-right ideologies. An interesting knot between psychosis, delusional theory, and political ideology arises here.

The COVID-19 pandemic is the first to occur on a global scale since the appearance of the World Wide Web. This circumstance cannot be put aside in the analysis of what occurred and of the medium- and long-term consequences, given that the Internet is the network in which we are all unfailingly confined, unable to conceive a space outside of it. The virus, and those to come, constitutes the best example of the devastating return of jouissance that the *parlêtre* has spread over the earth. If man is inseparable from the waste he produces, and if waste is finally the most real thing about man, that with which he identifies to the point of producing on an industrial scale, as was seen in the Holocaust, then this identification has been reinforced and multiplied infinitely by the action of manufacturing technical objects on an inhuman scale. That they are the prolongation of the voice and the gaze is their immediate and manifest aspect. Their obverse, realized in the unstoppable flow of trash that coats the planet's surface, is undoubtedly excrement. It is what will drown us. COVID-19 is proof not only that jouissance has released an evil that has no remedy but also of the impotence of science to deal with the Real of life. Science is ruled by immutable laws, while jouissance cannot be calculated. The letters of science are useless. That is precisely the linchpin, the grain of truth that, as Freud demonstrated in "Constructions in Analysis," underlies all delusional constructions. Distrust or disbelief in science, the most notorious expression of which is a denial of the very existence of the virus by right-wing and far-right collectives, has accompanied the development of the pandemic. Trump is perhaps the best example for appreciating the interconnection between psychosis and politics: a psychotic subject who completely disbelieves scientific truth in the name of his own intuition and who manages to captivate millions of ordinary and extraordinary psychotics (and many others who are not, in a clinical sense) through the assertion that science constitutes a threat to freedom. We know the libertarian argument is a favorite of far-right movements, which violently reject the legitimacy of the master signifier and obey the knowledge of the leader. Trump holds a knowledge that comes from delusional enlightenment. The paranoid treatment of the Real finds perfect conditions in far-right ideologies, which base themselves on the mechanisms of reintroducing evil into the field of the Other. We know the fascist declinations of the Other. The "Chinese virus," as Trump's knowledge has named it, is today a perfect metaphor for the fundamental service that the alliance between psychosis and the far right provides to present-day capitalism, which is engrossed in the vertiginous acceleration of its own destruction without so much as glimpsing (despite the enthusiastic millenarian positions that augur it) the emancipatory step that would save us.

Although psychoanalysts are not accustomed to anticipating the effects of the Real in subjectivity and therefore on social bonds, certain phenomena already observed as a result of the pandemic's planetary expansion allow us to venture a few ideas, undoubtedly provisional given that, following Freud, we recognize that trauma is realized in two events: the moment of seeing and the moment of concluding. What's missing in between is time to comprehend. In other words: trauma is the impact of a true nonsense, which precipitates a variable symptomatic effect. What characterizes trauma between the first event and the resulting effect is the freezing of the process of comprehension, the reopening of which often requires clinical intervention. We must therefore await the residual effects of the coronavirus on the subject and the social bond and content ourselves with venturing a few possibilities that will have to be reaffirmed or retracted in view of developments in the coming years.

Social relationships are complex and conflictual even in the best of conditions. Given our current circumstances, the complexity and conflict will increase. We can already note at least two types of conduct in apparent opposition that really belong to all human ties: on one hand, the emergence of a sort of hypomanic "epidemic" of universal love, solidarity, and fraternity; on the other, aggression. We have seen that the neighbor, with whom I identify myself and whom I turn into an object of love through a transfer of narcissistic libido, can become my enemy, my threat, a strange, hostile, and invasive body that endangers my life. The spontaneous community concerts and balcony choirs of March 2020 gave way to vigilantes who insulted those walking down the street, or to neighborhood associations that left anonymous notes at the doors of health workers "inviting" them to find other housing. The absence of God has become too noticeable. In antiquity, plagues were punishments from Heaven. These are not the times for such beliefs, but culprits are needed just the same. Social media offers all kinds of scapegoats and paranoid theories that delight millions of people.

We have all become suspects. The lamentable expression "social distance" begins to make itself felt. It happened before as a consequence of the attacks on the Twin Towers and Madrid's Atocha train station. Airport lounges became spaces where everyone mistrusted those around them. A bomb could be inside any suitcase or backpack. Similar scenes happened everywhere, in atmospheres charged with suspicion. Now, with the pandemic, we will all be a little suspicious for a while. Perhaps this fear will fade, but on the streets, many do not respond to greetings or they react fearfully to the possibility of their peers getting too close. The contrary also happens: the denial that leads to negligence, the narcissistic arrogance of those who consider themselves immune, who privilege their misunderstood right to freedom over the care of others. This doesn't come as a shock to psychoanalysis, which discovered early on that the search for good does not govern human conduct. Under certain circumstances, the suicidal tendency that lives deep within every subject can awaken and spring into action. The pandemic is a propitious circumstance to stir up turbulent passions and bring to the surface the destructive and latent power in everyone. Without a doubt, these collective morbid forms alternate and often coexist with manifestations that weigh the value of love and devotion.

Remote communication devices, which have shown their advantages and risks in recent decades, have become an ever-increasing complement to everyday life. Huge masses of work energy have been transferred to virtual space. So-called telework, so desired and requested by workers, was imposed by the unprecedented circumstances of the pandemic. Shortly afterward, employers discovered its benefits, which they exploited and extended once the health crisis had passed. People work harder at home. They are permanently connected, reachable, and available twenty-four hours a day. They don't incur the costs of workspace leases, catering vouchers, or the various expenses derived from the maintenance of classic offices. Workers, who imagined working from home as a path to greater scheduling freedom and reduced commutes, will stop smiling when they see the degree of alienation to which this modality pushes them and the claustrophobia that the nonexistent border between public or work life and private life entails. Moreover, the social isolation of teleworking poses significant obstacles to unionizing, which benefits companies that are keen to obstruct such associations.

In the educational sphere, pandemic responses were improvised given the surprising nature of the crisis (which might not have been so disruptive had global authorities heeded warnings). Classroom attendance has been supplemented in various ways, and virtual teaching will likely be incorporated into training methods. Online learning, however, cannot replace the indisputable benefits of the real-life encounter between teacher and student. The transmission of knowledge does not function through a simple transfer of information; it implies a particular relation between those who teach and those who learn, a relation that includes intimate aspects and in which important transferential forces converge. Learning does not occur only through the absorption of knowledge. Love and ideals, the unconscious satisfaction garnered from the sublimating act, cannot be so simply replaced by robotic functions, just as telemedicine makes sense only for initial contact between a doctor and patient. Nevertheless, online learning may bring advantages for socially and geographically remote communities that, given the necessary means, are able to access continuous education.

The virtual environment, as can be verified by the progressive extension of the metaverse and its multiple applications, is increasingly confiscating the terrain of face-to-face life. It is difficult to predict the extent to which speaking beings will be able to progressively dispense with sensible presence and real contact. Advances in artificial intelligence and virtual reality anticipate a future where sensory experiences induced and created by telematic means will enable us to visit cities, bathe in the sea, and tour museums with an absolutely convincing sense of reality. In fact, a whole variety of sexual encounters via videocalls already exists, although these methods will surely be made obsolete in the not-so-distant future. The Zoom platform, which overnight saw its use multiply by millions of people, is working frantically to prevent telematic orgies, apparently a trend that took off as a result of confinement (see López). Will the virtual body, even in its most accomplished realism, replace the physical one? Will this be the dream of a disinfected humanity, free of contagion?

In light of the first quarter of the twenty-first century, what can be said of psychoanalysis, of its form of existence, of what it has led to, and of the crossroads it faces? First and foremost, it can be said that psychoanalysis has managed to survive, which is no small feat. If a few decades ago a survey had asked which discourse was more likely to survive into the twenty-first century, psychoanalysis or Marxism, there is no doubt as to which would have been the nearly unanimous answer. Psychoanalysis was seen as an intellectual fad, especially among Marxists, many of whom do not seem to have noticed the slap in the face that history has dealt them. But psychoanalysis is not an intellectual fad, possibly because it wasn't conceived as a matter of the intellect—which does not mean, of course, that intellect is alien to it. Psychoanalysis is an experience and a praxis—surely not the only one, although probably the only one in our Western culture—that deals with being. Of course, there have been plenty of discourses about being, but none accompanied by a praxis and an experience, or rather, none resulting from a praxis and an experience of the Real. If psychoanalysis has managed to survive fads, the twists and turns of history, and even the vicissitudes of the psychoanalytic movement itself, it is due to three main reasons: first, the structural impossibility of establishing any kind of alliance with the mechanisms of power, whatever they may be; second, its unavoidable will to protect the truth as a singular event, never extrapolated, in no case extensible to the universal, and above all separate from any moral pretension; and third, its determined orientation toward the Real, the Real of the speaking being's suffering.

No doubt, these three reasons would not have been enough had they not unfolded on the firm ground of an extraordinarily particular therapy beholden to the tradition of logos but at the same time forever detached from the discourse of medicine, which is both captive to the ancient ideals of health and homeostasis and overtaken by the rise of bioengineering. Because a therapy that makes disease the prodromal sign of the human condition, a therapy that seeks not to cure the human being of his essence but rather to confront him with his incurability, a therapy that neither promises nor consoles, is at the very least a particular therapy. What is curious, marvelous, truly thrilling is that many people, even in the twenty-first century, prefer to entrust themselves to the uncertainties of this therapy instead of betting on others that are consumed like any product in the current market—like objects acquired to remedy castration in vain.

Castration. No one wants to know anything about it. Through the most varied forms, contemporary discourse extols the virtues of an era in which the subject is ever closer to the promised land, to paradise within reach, to the democratization of enjoyment, to the prolongation of life, to the definitive avoidance of pain, to the right to immediate satisfaction and perpetual novelty. Psychoanalysis does not oppose any of this. To oppose or question the direction of history, to try to rescue values that are constantly changing, is not the business of psychoanalysis. That is what religions are for. And when some people casually judge psychoanalysis to be a form of religion, they only prove that they haven't understood a word, either about psychoanalysis or religion. Religion has nothing to worry about. It has won its battle, won it forever, because there never has been nor will be a period in history free from obscurantism, not even the present one, so modern and endorsed by scientific rationality. And religion represents this, the human need to remain partially submerged in the dark.

For this reason, because psychoanalysis is not a religion despite sharing with it that undecided domain called spirituality, neither is it in its power nor is it its purpose to promote a moral discourse about all that in modernity serves as an alibi to hide castration from the subject. Psychoanalysis is not a method of denunciation or a moral judgment, nor is it a form of philosophy or psychology. It limits itself to receiving those who say they have a symptom, and if they say so, it's because they have it, and if they have it, its measure, its objectivity, or its importance will not be judged. No method can claim an objectification of suffering except the one that lets the sufferer speak and accompanies him on the path to his truth.

After more than a century of existence, psychoanalysis has known all sorts of opposition, and renewed figures and hostile discourses are continually added to the long list of its adversaries. If we see something unprecedented in the twenty-first century, it is that for the first time in the history of psychoanalysis, modern states are putting a spotlight on this strange praxis that has always flowed through extraterritorial circuits to political and university spaces, that has been at work in mental health facilities in a way that has remained relatively hidden from public powers. These powers are now taking measures to subject psychoanalysis to examination, verification, scientific testing, balance sheets, and quality measurements. In the initial phase of this process, democratic states, through their officials and bureaucrats, seemed to grant psychoanalysis a specificity that relatively exempted it from the supervision and control that the state sought to exercise over every aspect of the various therapeutic instruments of health. Initially, it was accepted that psychoanalysis is not exactly psychotherapy, that its method, its procedure, and its conceptions of health, illness, cure, and well-being couldn't be evaluated with statistical or performance criteria. But after this initial phase, a program to expel psychoanalysis from the public sphere and relegate it to the private sphere was undertaken in Europe, although there are now signs that the state will also take action in the private sphere. What policy, strategy, and tactics will psychoanalysis need to adopt to try to cross this new century and reach the other shore? A frontal battle against the powers of the state, one that employs the media, public debate, and alliances with other groups of psychotherapists? A strategic retreat into private spaces, which have undoubtedly provided psychoanalysis with shelter and respectability for decades? A reconversion or recycling of our doctrine and our clinic to adapt them to the paradigms of scientificity and efficacy that dominate the discourse of calculation and evaluation? Some currents of psychoanalysis are already contemplating the latter option, and their representatives will not hesitate, if need be, to sacrifice any concept or principle that might be inconvenient in order to receive the ministerial seal of approval. "One must adapt to the times," some might say. Others, more resigned, will say that "it is better to exist halfway than to disappear completely." We Lacanian analysts do not want to adapt, or recycle, or renounce the principles that govern our treatment because those principles are nonnegotiable; they are part of the fundamental fabric of psychoanalysis, without which analytic practice loses not only its form but also its essence, its sense, its specificity, or even worse, its ethics.

In the twenty-first century, no one is shocked to hear about the unconscious, childhood sexuality, the Oedipus complex, the decline of the paternal imago, or the death drive. This is surely the century in which all knowledge will be admitted, for the simple reason that no one will care in the least. Only figures, accounts, and formulas that show us the cost of eradicating a phobia, dissolving an obsession, or silencing a delusion will matter. Surely, we are defeated in advance, because when it comes to cutting costs, psychoanalysis always ends up losing. Psychoanalysis does not give rebates or discounts. It bets on desire at all costs and does not reimburse the subject for the satisfaction he dreams of.

Freud employed the term *future* in the title of two of his articles: "The Future Prospects of Psychoanalytic Therapy," written in 1910, and *The Future of an Illusion* from 1927. Despite the difficulties he faced throughout his life, Freud was personally convinced that psychoanalysis would endure and occupy an undisputed and permanent place in the history of ideas. It has been pointed out almost unanimously that Freud's wish has been fulfilled and that psychoanalysis, even with the usual attacks of criticism, has gained recognition, appending itself to Western culture as one of its fundamental components.

Where is the subject? How to conceive it in the present? For Hegel, the subject of history was the slave. For Marx, the proletarian. For Freud, the neurotic. Each one had their particular vision as to how to conceive "emancipation." For Hegel, a direct product of the Enlightenment, emancipation would be obtained through knowledge. For Marx, it would be through revolution, and for Freud, through the experience of the unconscious. Having exhausted illusions of knowledge and faced the failure of revolutions, how to situate the historical role of the subject in this new epoch? Can psychoanalysis contribute something to this reflection, which undoubtedly requires the simultaneous participation of diverse contributions of thought?

What are the difficulties psychoanalysis faces in the present? It is instructive to compare them with those that stood in the way of Freud and other pioneers of psychoanalysis. Psychoanalysis is no longer a scandal. Sexuality, the Oedipus complex, and other concepts that once infuriated a great part of society no longer astonish anyone. Nearly everyone has heard of the Oedipus complex, and there's no need to expound on cultural changes regarding sexuality. Compared to what is seen and heard on television, the discourse that takes place in the analyst's office is modest and discreet. No one particularly questions the ideological stratum of psychoanalysis, if I may say so. Today's fundamental adversities stem from other sources, which question our discourse inasmuch as they propagate a new paradigm of being.

In recent years, Europe has taken a spectacular turn in its conception of the role of the state as guarantor of the welfare of its citizens, which beyond its indisputable progress has resulted in the promotion of the subject as a real or potential creditor with the right to demand the share of enjoyment owed to him. This way of conceiving social policy created an ethical position, demanding from the state aid or the solution to life's setbacks or misfortunes, even those in which the state has neither responsibility nor influence. But the situation has dramatically changed and with unusual speed for historical time. The discourse of crisis has served as an alibi to introduce a new paradigm, which makes the subject responsible for taking charge, as an individual, of the problems that exceed the scope of his action, since they belong to the sphere of those who administer political decisions. In other words, we are obliged to assume exclusive responsibility for our social destiny. We can no longer expect anything at the level of work, health, or education. Everyone must provide for their own survival in all these spheres and relearn a way to subsist on their own. States, reduced to operating as gendarmes of the transnational interests of financial power, justify their existence through imposture, keeping citizens safe from the threats that capitalism has manufactured, as is the case with terrorist organizations that represent a return to the Real.

A quick review of the contemporary era allows us to immediately appreciate a growing discordance between the political devices of nation-states and the extraterritoriality of economic, commercial, and financial flow. The impossibility of the former to maintain control over the latter generates a first form of violence: not only the violence implied by the impunity of economic powers but also the violence implied by the erasure of different ways of understanding existence and life. Since the global arena is itself beyond the reach of the institutions that watch over, or should watch over, existing forms of decency and ethical responsibility, responsibility for what occurs in the world has become a practically extinct abstraction. People notice the impotence of states and prevailing radical impunity, which generates a second form of violence: the feeling of moral helplessness that reigns everywhere. This feeling goes hand in hand with the evidence that society, as an artifice that is both coercive and protective, is ceasing to exist, forcing the individual to take charge of what was until now the responsibility of society as a whole. The contemporary world forces subjects to seek biographical solutions to systemic problems, as Ulrich Beck notes in *Risk Society: Towards a New Modernity.* Here, we can find an unequivocal form of violence: it is perfectly clear that this demand is unrealizable since the politics of life cannot resolve the contradictions of the system. This is one of the many manifestations of the cruelty exerted by the contemporary super-ego, whose root we must situate in Lacan's observation regarding capitalist discourse, a modality of discourse in which the limit of impotence between the production of surplus-enjoyment and the truth of the subject as castration has been surpassed.

The historical perspective shows the signs of a subjectivity that progressively withdraws from its relation to the unconscious for the benefit of a scientism that encourages diverse modalities of foreclosure. It would be a mistake to believe that our battle consists in opposing the advances of science and technology that will definitively change the very concept of humanity. We shouldn't feel authorized to point out what in our time could be considered symptomatic forms. The voice of analyzing discourse is needed to point them out, so that psychoanalysis can offer itself as an alternative way of addressing the malaise in society, beyond generalized biologization and medicalization. And it is vital that we assume our role stripped of all hope, given that even Lacan didn't deny that ours is a lost cause, that humanity will be cured of psychoanalysis, and that religion—in its strictest sense of belief—will triumph. This, however, does not exempt us from fulfilling our ethical duty to militate for the cause of the unconscious.

Psychoanalysis is neither an adaptive nor adaptable discourse. The flexibility of its technique must not be confused with a position that accommodates the winds of fashion, political movements, or trending social values. If speed has become a sacred virtue, we will not be faster. If suffering in the West has become a completely unacceptable experience, even in minimal doses, we will not renounce truth to spare the subject the discomfort that knowing it may cause. Lacan believed that in the United States, psychoanalysis had condemned itself by trying to conform to the American way of life. What we must not forget is that the American way of life is now the global way of life. Therefore, the future of psychoanalysis will depend on the capacity of analysts to resist the temptation to resign ourselves to the conditions of the time, which does not mean entrenching ourselves in a dogmatic and outdated orthodoxy. The conditions of the time promote ideologies that suppress the subject, ideologies that erase psychic causality and install in its place organic, genetic, or bacteriological causality. The unprecedented flirtation of some psychoanalysts with neuroscience reveals that there will always be those who seek salvation at any price.

Psychoanalysts must remain sensitive to the horizon of their time. They must not camouflage themselves with the prevailing discourse or bend to their circumstances. Rather, they must embody the symptom, which is an obstacle to the master's discourse, which incompletes the illusions of contemporary consciousness, which reintroduces the impotence between the object of jouissance and the subject. We must keep in mind that we are not completely alone in this task, despite the rejection we endure from academics and omniscient intellectuals. Many trust the analytical method because they do not blindly believe in happiness, the philosophy of social triumph, suggestive formulas, spiritual directors, or self-help books. Many reject the morality of victimhood and are willing to assume their share of responsibility for the disorder of which they complain, according to the famous expression that Lacan took from Hegel.[3] Many seek not normality but *varité*, the variety of truth (see Lacan, *L'insu*), and prefer to find it in their own discourse rather than in the chatter of media prophets. These people are part of the future of psychoanalysis.

And, of course, there are still psychoanalysts willing to commit to action and who, like Freud's first disciples, have long understood that a fundamental part of their daily work consists in protecting the existence of psychoanalysis. I personally continue to believe that such existence requires a singular space in which to secure its roots, a space that is neither fully inside nor outside the institutional, social, and political order. Psychoanalysis requires independence from public powers, and to a certain extent even from analytic institutions, to safeguard its specificity. The logic of any institutional structure tends to impose a norm that interprets the spirit that the institution supposedly serves, and proclaims as heresy all that does not correspond to the established canon. But at the same time, institutions preserve a tradition of knowledge, laws, and rites, mitigating the emergence and propagation of individual delusions. The analytic act takes place simultaneously on the plane of the encounter, alone with the analysand, and the plane of the institutional conversation, where knowledge is laid bare to construct new paradigms. Both planes converge and reclaim one another. A solitary analyst runs the risk of hiding his castration, and an institution that does not rely on clinical experience only serves to reproduce an empty word.

The future of psychoanalysis lies fundamentally in the training of future analysts, and for that, it is necessary to support and shepherd postulants through the unavoidable passage through a structure that includes a personal analysis, supervision, and the study of the texts. In particular, we must insist that personal analysis is a prolonged experience and that its profundity will depend on the solvency and efficacy with which a cure is pursued. Freud was adamant on this point, and Lacan dedicated his entire work to investigating the different ways this depth could be theorized.

Analytical training must tune its instruments to aim at the current configurations of the symptom and the demand for a cure rather than at media debates and efforts to be heard in the fora where power decides the coming misfortunes of citizens. This does not mean that our discourse will not be present in certain debates where the rules of the game provide for respect. But let us not forget that our main strength lies in the intimacy of the act of speaking and listening, in the art of becoming the object for the transference of the subject, in the suspension of critical, moral, or pedagogical judgment, in the disidentification with the signifiers of the master, the director of conscience, or the healer of souls. In short, our strength must continue to concentrate on what has allowed us to offer to the suffering subject a place where their life's work encounters an ethical form of interrogation.

Psychoanalysis has managed to live and develop within democratic states as a praxis that, due to its singular mechanisms of production and reproduction, has remained outside bureaucratic, academic, and professional regulations. Until now, states have admitted that only analytic institutions were legitimately authorized to take charge of the training and oversight of analysts. But the consciousness of the state has changed and is heading toward a totalitarianism exercised not through the tyrant's brutality, but rather, through a hypertrophied control over private life based on the inflationary value of security. This new consciousness begins to take an interest in psychoanalysis: it wants to know who, how many, and what we are like. Do we converge with the interests of the state? Do we want to? It seems to me that reflecting on these two questions can provide some clarity for betting on the future of psychoanalysis.

GUSTAVO DESSAL is a member or the World Association of Psychoanalysis, a professor at the Freudian Field Institute, and a practicing psychoanalyst. In addition to writing essays on psychoanalysis, he writes novels and short stories. He has lived in Madrid since 1982.

ESTEBAN BUJANDA and JACINTA BUJANDA SUÁREZ are based in New York City and Barcelona, Spain, respectively.

Notes

1 Dessal's reading of the Hegelian master-slave dialectic follows Lacan, who, like many French theorists, draws on Alexander Kojève's reading of Hegel. In Lacan's theory of the four discourses in Seminar XX, he notes that "the concept of discourse should be taken as a social link (*lien social*), founded on language" (*Encore* 17). In the "master's discourse," the master is the master signifier (S1, agent) that makes the slave (S2, knowledge, the other) produce a surplus (*objet a*) that the master signifier aims to appropriate—an attempt at totalization, present in all classical Western philosophy and ontology, but one that cannot not fail. For Lacan, this is the dominant discourse in which the subject ("subject" understood as the effect of language) is caught up in the impossible split between knowledge and being. For David S. Marriott's consideration of the ways Lacanian readings are challenged and expanded when the structural "slave" coincides with the *historically* enslaved subject, see *Lacan Noir: Lacan and Afro-Pessimism*, and *Whither Fanon? Studies in the*

Blackness of Being. Much more has, of course, been written on the relation between Hegel's master-slave dialectic (*Herr und Knecht* in the German, which until relatively recently was often translated as "lord and bondsman") and his writing on slavery in history. See, for example, Chu; Fanon, esp. ch. 7, which has generated an enormous body of work; and Terada, esp. sect. 3. [*Eds.*]

2 The term *alethosphere* is from Lacan's Seminar XVII. See also Copjec, who explains, "In Lacan's new ultra-modern myth, there is no heavenly sphere, naturally; it has been demolished. All that remains of the world beyond the subject is the 'alethosphere,' which is a kind of high-tech heaven, a laicized or 'disenchanted' space filled none the less with every technoscientific marvel imaginable: space probes and orbiters, telecommunications and telebanking systems, and so on" (96).

3 The famous expression is "One is always responsible for one's position as subject," which Lacan develops in Seminar VII (*Ethics*).

Works Cited

Arendt, Hannah. *Eichmann in Jerusalem: A Report on the Banality of Evil.* New York: Penguin, 2006.

—————. "Truth and Politics." *New Yorker* 25 Feb. 1967: 49–88.

Bauman, Zygmunt. *Collateral Damage: Social Inequalities in a Global Age.* Malden: Polity, 2011.

—————, and Gustavo Dessal. *El retorno del péndulo: Sobre psicoanálisis y el futuro del mundo líquido.* Trans. Lilia Mosconi. Buenos Aires: Fondo de Cultura Económica de España, 2014.

Beck, Ulrich. *Risk Society: Towards a New Modernity.* Trans. Mark Ritter. London: Sage, 1992.

Borges, Jorge Luis. "The Lottery in Babylon." *Collected Fictions.* Trans. Andrew Hurley. London: Penguin, 1998. 101–6.

Bruckner, Pascal. *The Temptation of Innocence: Living in the Age of Entitlement.* New York: Algora, 2000.

Chu, Andrea Long. "Black Infinity: Slavery and Freedom in Hegel's Africa." *Journal of Speculative Philosophy* 32.3 (2018): 414–25.

Copjec, Joan. "May '68, the Emotional Month." *Lacan: The Silent Partners.* Ed. Slavoj Žižek. New York: Verso, 2006. 90–114.

Fanon, Frantz. *Black Skin, White Masks.* New York: Grove, 2008.

Freud, Sigmund. *Beyond the Pleasure Principle.* 1920. *The Standard Edition of the Complete Psychological Works of Sigmund Freud.* Trans. and ed. James Strachey. Vol. 18. London: Hogarth, 1955. 1–64. 24 vols. 1953–74.

———————. *Civilization and Its Discontents.* 1930. *The Standard Edition.* Vol. 21. 1955. 57–146.

———————. "Constructions in Analysis." 1937. *The Standard Edition.* Vol. 23. 1955. 255–70.

———————. *The Future of an Illusion.* 1927. *The Standard Edition.* Vol. 21. 1955. 1–56.

———————. "The Future Prospects of Psychoanalytic Therapy." 1910. *The Standard Edition.* Vol. 11. 1955. 139–52.

———————. *The Interpretation of Dreams.* 1900. *The Standard Edition.* Vol. 4. 1955. ix–627.

La Boétie, Étienne de. *The Politics of Obedience: Discourse on Voluntary Servitude.* Trans. Harry Kurz. Auburn: Mises Institute, 2015.

Lacan, Jacques. *Encore: Feminine Sexuality, the Limits of Love and Knowledge: The Seminar of Jacques Lacan Book XX.* Ed. Jacques-Alain Miller. Trans. Bruce Fink. New York: Norton, 1999.

———————. *The Ethics of Psychoanalysis: The Seminar of Jacques Lacan Book VII.* Ed. Jacques-Alain Miller. Trans. Dennis Porter. New York: Norton, 1997.

———————. *L'insu que sait de l'une bévue s'aile à mourre.* Seminar XXIV. Unpubl.

———————. *The Other Side of Psychoanalysis: The Seminar of Jacques Lacan Book XVII.* Ed. Jacques-Alain Miller. Trans. Russell Grigg. New York: Norton, 2007.

———————. *The Psychoses: The Seminar of Jacques Lacan Book III.* Ed. Jacques-Alain Miller. Trans. Russell Grigg. New York: Norton, 1993.

Lipovetsky, Gilles. *L'Ère du vide: essais sur l'individualisme contemporain.* Paris: Gallimard, 1983.

López, Quispe. "Zoom Banned Virtual Orgies: Here's How Sex Parties and Orgy-seekers Are Getting around It." *Insider* 29 Apr. 2020. https://www.insider.com/zoom-banned-orgies-heres -how-people-are-getting-around-it-2020-4.

Marriott, David S. *Lacan Noir: Lacan and Afro-pessimism.* New York: Palgrave, 2021.

———————. *Whither Fanon? Studies in the Blackness of Being.* Stanford: Stanford UP, 2018.

Miller, Jacques-Alain. *La Psicosis ordinaria: La convención de Antibes.* Buenos Aires: Paidós Ibérica, 2003.

Nancy, Jean-Luc, and Philippe Lacoue-Labarthe. "The Nazi Myth." Trans. Brian Holmes. *Critical Inquiry* 16.2 (1990): 291–312.

Terada, Rei. *Metaracial: Hegel, Antiblackness, and Political Identity.* Chicago: U of Chicago P, 2023.

Weber, Max. *The Protestant Ethic and the Spirit of Capitalism.* Trans. Talcott Parsons. London: Routledge, 2001.

Inviting Catastrophe:
The Welcoming of the Act in Psychoanalysis

*T*his essay will approach the problem of the act from the perspective of psychoanalysis, which teaches us that the fear of the act as catastrophic—and especially as a mortal threat to the social bond—is often synonymous with the repudiation of the unconscious itself, whether by the individual subject or by the collective. To understand how an act of the unconscious can be received as catastrophic, whether by the actor or by others, we first have to consider both the resistance to the act at the level of the ego and its censorship by culture and civilization. For this we need to be more explicit about the nature of the act with which psychoanalysis is concerned, which is very different from other kinds of acts.

Which Act?

In everyday language, of course, an act can be almost anything a person or a people does, any kind of action or undertaking whatsoever. In the most common uses of the term, an act is generally understood as the result of a conscious and voluntary decision or deliberative process. For example,

Volume 34, Number 3   DOI 10.1215/10407391-10898199

we speak of legislative acts, the "action items" that define a group's priorities and agenda, or more generally the importance of adopting an active rather than passive stance with regard to one's life goals and commitments. All of these acts have specific and identifiable aims, which may be creative or destructive, liberatory or repressive. It is at this level that we can speak about something like a terrorist attack as an act: it deliberately deploys violence against a target to achieve specific aims. Even when an act is spontaneous and unscripted, as is often the case with political acts—for example, a mass demonstration in response to police violence, the recent storming and occupation of the presidential palace by angry crowds in Sri Lanka, or even Rosa Parks's refusal to move to the back of the bus—it is generally related to specific ends that can be identified, named, and defined, even if the actors involved do not do so in advance. These examples cannot be considered apart from language and consciousness, therefore, even if other factors are also in play (for example, the feelings and emotions that motivate actors in a political demonstration).

A second set of examples is more closely related to what we are dealing with in psychoanalysis, because they attest that an act may or may not be conscious or directed by a specific intention or aim and may or may not be related to something that could be expressed in language. The arena of performance foregrounds something that is implicit, if not always obvious, in the preceding examples, namely, that acting necessarily involves the body. In dramatic or comedic acting, the acts of the body may be placed in the service of a script or express a conscious decision on the part of the actor. As dance and musical performance make clear, however, this subordination is in no way inevitable and can never be absolute. What acts in and through the body exceeds what can be expressed in language or made to serve a meaning or narrative. Such acts therefore underscore the dimension of the aesthetic as such: the "purposiveness without purpose" that for Kant defines the beautiful (173), or "the presentation of the unpresentable" that is enabled by the feeling of the sublime.[1] The aesthetic appeals to something in the subject that transcends self-interest, taste, or pleasure, or even—in the case of the sublime—survival or self-preservation. The link between the act and aesthetics is not limited to works of art, however. It comes into play whenever the subject acts without regard for its own interests on behalf of something that is more important than its own survival, for example, by lunging in front of a speeding car that is bearing down on a child or running into a burning building to save someone who is trapped. This aesthetic dimension can also be present in acts that are conscious and deliberate, but only on the condition that they give expression to, or create a space for, something that didn't exist previously: for example, a new manifestation of the people or a new social contract. (The importance Jacques Rancière accords to the aesthetic dimension of political speech acts is just one well-known elaboration of this possibility: politics attests to the emergence of something that was not perceptible in the prior "distribution of the sensible," a subjectification that cannot be placed with respect to available identifications).[2]

In psychoanalysis, however, the act also names something more specific that is not captured by these other usages and examples. An act gives expression to an unconscious mental presentation or a censored experience that cannot pass through language and that is therefore either inscribed in the erogenous zones of the body (in the form of fixations or symptoms) or staged in the real through failed acts (*actes manqués*) or episodes of acting out (*passages à l'acte*) wherein the conscious intention of the actor is subverted by an unwilled action or behavior that fulfills an unconscious aim. The act thus understood is never the result of an intention or plan, therefore. For the same reason, it isn't something that could be the object of a collective enterprise. Because it gives expression to something that is inscribed in the erogenous body, an act is necessarily specific to a singular subject.

When the current issue of *differences* interrogates the effect of catastrophic acts on the social bond, and especially those acts that turn away from language and interpersonal relations and are inimical to the symbolic sphere, it seems to be this type of act that is at issue. But while these acts may be unwilled and unwelcome, both for the individual who commits them and for the social and cultural context in which she lives, they are not necessarily catastrophic. At a minimum, we would have to ask: under what conditions is an act of the unconscious catastrophic? And catastrophic for whom, or what?

Etymologically, a catastrophe is an "overturning" or a "sudden end" (from the Greek *kata*, "down," and *strophē*, "turn"). When an act is received as catastrophic, therefore, what does it overturn or bring to an end? And what emerges or becomes ascendent as a result? Inasmuch as it overturns the actor's conscious intent and pays no heed to the norms and ideals that regulate the social sphere, the act is often received as catastrophic both by the ego and by the social bond (where it is not only feared or unwelcome but often treated as something requiring behavioral modification or pharmacological control).

Like the acts in the previous set of examples, however, an act of the unconscious is never *only* a source of symptoms, failures, ruptures, or threats. This is because it gives expression to something that cannot pass through language and cannot manifest itself in any other way. That expression will necessarily be disruptive in a way that may be experienced as violent (an unwelcome intrusion or sudden break) but that may also be judged aesthetic inasmuch as it makes a space for something that couldn't be expressed previously, something that others will find to be either beautiful or sublime. These two divergent outcomes—violence or aesthetics—are already internal to the word *catastrophe*, which entered the English language in the aesthetic context of tragedy to describe "the conclusion or final event of a dramatic work" and was later adopted, in the eighteenth century, to speak about such "devastating events as earthquakes and violent eruptions" ("catastrophe, n."): the very manifestations of "natural might" that Kant would later describe as preeminent occasions for the experience of the sublime, in which the subject discovers its highest calling—that of having to supply a presentation for the unpresentable. While an analysis will inevitably deal with the disruptive effects of the act in the subject's life, and in some cases its violent consequences for others, its aim is not to contain that force or require that it submit to the symbolic, but rather to allow it to find an aesthetic expression through which the subject may bring something new into the world and stamp humanity with its unique signature.

The Act in the Analytic Experience

Before describing the role of the act in the unfolding of an analysis, I want to begin at the beginning. For the subject who decides to undertake an analysis, the act is almost invariably an object of profound ambivalence. On the one hand, the analysand—and the neurotic analysand in particular—often speaks of being blocked at the level of action and aspires to be capable of an act that would break through the impasses in which she or he is mired. From this perspective, the act is something to aspire to, the key to the subjective liberation the analysand has until now sought in vain. Consciously, therefore, the subject wants very much to be capable of an act. Importantly, however, she generally conceives of this capacity for action as something that would be in the service of her conscious intentions and goals.

An act of the unconscious, however, is anything but. This act isn't the result of a conscious decision procedure on the part of the individual, but something that arrives unbidden, from an "elsewhere" that is alien to the social link in which the ego searches for approval, love, and success. Far from helping the analysand to take action or make progress on her conscious life goals, it frees something that creates a rupture in her life and in her relations with others. This kind of act is probably all too familiar to the analysand, even if she is unlikely to use that word to talk about the problems that are plaguing her life. As the analysis gets underway, it becomes clear that she isn't only stalled at the level of action but also suffers from the insistence of acts in her life that she blames for all of her troubles and impasses: unwelcome repetitions or repetitive failures, symptoms in her relations with others, acts of self-sabotage or self-harm. The analysand has probably never thought of these as "acts," but rather as behaviors or tendencies she would like very much to control or eliminate altogether. These are precisely the acts that interest the analyst, however.

So while the analysand is right when she imagines that undergoing analysis will result in the freeing of an act, it is generally not the act she anticipates or hopes for. Because the act is not under the control of the conscious aims or intentions of the actor, it is inimical to the ego and the unified body image that is its foundation. This is why an act often takes the form of a *failed* act that overturns or waylays the actor's conscious will or intent. This dimension of failure is key and helps to explain the dread of the act (and of the unconscious more generally) on the part of the ego.

So why, for psychoanalysis, is the act not only *not* catastrophic but something the analyst waits for and welcomes? As counterintuitive as it may seem from a therapeutic perspective, the analyst is allied with the act and the failures it engenders, and not with the patient's ego. This is because while the *intended* aim of the act fails, something else succeeds at the same time. If this is sometimes experienced by the analysand as a catastrophe, it is because the aims and ideals of the ego will necessarily be subverted and overturned by an unconscious aim, a quest acting in the subject—and therefore in the body—that runs counter to the aims of the social link in which she lives and can only be experienced as a violent intrusion. (In the first phase of an analysis, the surging forth of the unconscious that is provoked by the transference is often figured in dreams as an overflowing toilet or as a destructive flood or earthquake that invades the dreamer's home or causes the walls to collapse.)

The act is solicited and provoked by the transference and advances the analysis by giving expression to something that cannot pass through language—which can then become an object of work in the session when the analysand is invited to speak about what is acting. However, it is important to understand this operation not as implying the superiority of talking over acting or as implying that what is acting must be submitted to or contained by language. Indeed, the centrality of language to the analytic experience is often overstated or misunderstood—a point I will return to in more detail below. While *speech* is certainly crucial, it is not just any speech that matters, but only those rare acts of speech that manage to evoke or metaphorize the censored experience or fantasy that is staged or enacted in the form of repetition compulsion, bungled actions, or episodes of acting out: an experience for which there is no name and that has never been conscious.

Freud's "Wolf Man" case offers one excellent illustration of the function of the act in the unfolding of an analysis. The fantasy of the primal scene leaves traces in the subject's life, informing his life choices, dictating the repetition of certain painful experiences and episodes of acting out, and determining the choice of a specific symptom—the constipation whose treatment is central to the final phase of the analysis—that inscribes the fantasy in the body. When Freud manages to treat the symptom psychoanalytically, much to his patient's astonishment, he writes with satisfaction that his bowel "began, like a hysterically affected organ, to 'join in the conversation,'" furnishing a response to the analyst's questions there where the patient's own associations were unable to ("From the History" 75). At this point a new phase of the transference begins, in which the response of the bowel—as the erogenous zone implicated in the fantasy of the primal scene—acts to confirm or refute the accuracy of the fantasy's construction. Crucially, however, that fantasy will never become conscious for the Wolf Man. It cannot be remembered, therefore, but only *constructed* by means of the transference that calls on the bowel to produce acts in response to Freud's desire to know about the unconscious enjoyment of the fantasy. The censored returns "in the real" in the form of an act or an affect with no ideational content. It does not take the form of a thought or a phrase that can be identified through the undoing of distortion, but of a staging or enactment of a drive presentation.

The Freudian Unconscious

Through this case and others, Freud discovers that the act has not only a "local" meaning or function in the analysis—that of staging or enacting something that couldn't be spoken about the day before—but is at the same time the vehicle through which the subject of the unconscious itself becomes manifest. Beginning around 1914, Freud begins to theorize both the fantasy and the death drive. At this point he becomes increasingly interested in the unconscious not simply as a repository of memories and thoughts that have been rejected from consciousness but as a "force" at work in the life and in the body of the patient that gives rise to mental presentations that are entirely inaccessible to consciousness. This force is expressed through actions rather than words. The corollary is that the act is what ultimately moves the analytic process forward, and not the restoration to consciousness of a forgotten or rejected history.

In "Remembering, Repeating, and Working-Through," Freud formulates very well the inadequacy of any psychoanalytic technique that focuses on memory or consciousness alone. He begins by breaking down into three distinct periods the evolution of the technique and the aims of psychoanalysis. In the early days of psychoanalysis, the cathartic method pioneered by Freud's colleague Josef Breuer used hypnosis to bring "directly into focus the moment at which the symptom was formed"; it endeavored "to reproduce the mental processes involved in that situation, in order to direct their discharge along the path of conscious activity" (Freud, "Remembering" 146). During this period, Freud and Breuer's guiding assumption was that "hysterics suffer mainly from reminiscences" (*Studies* 7): memories that could be called up, made conscious, and so stripped of their traumatic charge. As a technique, hypnosis promises something like a full recovery of those memories. It "brings into focus" a triggering situation or event in the manner of a cinematic flashback, thereby allowing the thoughts and feelings associated with it to be relived and spoken about.

When hypnosis fell out of favor, a new technique came to the fore, which consisted in "discovering from the patient's associations what he failed to remember" ("Remembering" 146). Here the emphasis was still on the "situations which lay behind the moment at which the illness broke out," but these were arrived at through free association—and therefore with the aid of speech—rather than through the pseudoscientific technique of hypnosis. In comparison with the cathartic method, the analyst now placed less emphasis on "abreaction," the catharsis associated with reliving an experience in order to purge or release the energy associated with it. The focus instead shifted to circumventing the patient's *resistance*, which was understood to be responsible for the content undergoing repression in the first place. That resistance was now conceived primarily in ethical terms, as a refusal on the patient's part to confront something that was painful, unpleasant, or at odds with her own morals or ideals.[3]

Finally, Freud describes "the consistent technique used today in which the analyst gives up the attempt to bring a particular moment or problem into focus." Instead, he "contents himself with studying whatever is present for the time being on the surface of the patient's mind" (146). A striking feature of this latest technique is that the interest in reproducing the mental processes associated with a past event that could be understood as the exciting cause of the illness, which had been central to the first technique in particular, diminishes in importance or even falls away altogether. Instead, the analyst presumes a psychic continuity between what is present right now on the patient's mind and the symptoms, affects, or behaviors that brought him into treatment.

One important consequence is that the unconscious can no longer be understood as a set of "memory traces," but as something that is expressed through acts. As an example of the latter, Freud cites several "psychical processes" that are not susceptible to being remembered: "[P]hantasies, processes of reference, emotional impulses, thought-connections—*which, as purely internal acts, can be contrasted with impressions and experiences*, must, in their relation to forgetting and remembering, be considered separately. In these processes it particularly often happens that *something is 'remembered' which could never have been 'forgotten' because it was never at any time noticed—was never conscious*" (147; my emphases). Here it isn't a matter of a lost memory suddenly popping into the patient's head or being recalled in a specific connection, as with the restoration of a link that has been severed by repression. Nor is the memory or rejected thought represented in distorted form or by means of a substitute. Rather, something is "remembered" only in the form of an act, whether that act is "internal" (a fantasy, a feeling) or external (a repetitive behavior, a staging, or an episode of acting out). It acts in and through the subject in a way that does not enter into consciousness and is not dependent upon it.

Freud then observes that "[t]here is one special class of experiences of the utmost importance for which no memory can as a rule be recovered. These are experiences which occurred in very early childhood and were not understood at the time but which were *subsequently* understood and interpreted. One gains a knowledge of them through dreams and one is obliged to believe in them on the most compelling evidence provided by the fabric of the neurosis" (148). Before the child speaks, he has experiences that are out of language. These are not only beyond his understanding, therefore, but inaccessible to the consciousness that language founds. The footnote to this passage explains that the reference is to the Wolf Man case. The experience at issue there, which Freud calls the "primal scene," was completely unconscious. This is true not only because it dates from a period when the child did not speak, or because he didn't have the maturity and the knowledge of human anatomy to understand what he was seeing:

for example, to grasp that what he witnessed was a sexual act and not a violent castration, or to understand that the mother was being penetrated in the vagina and not the anus. More importantly, the experience was *never* available to perception-consciousness. This is because the child experienced something more, or something different, than what he "witnessed" when he lay in his crib in the parents' bedroom. He experienced the effects of a fantasy—a mental presentation—that emerged in response to that witnessing. It is this fantasy that continues to act upon the patient throughout his life, driving a compulsion to repeat that takes the form of behaviors that are not under his conscious control and inscribing itself in the erogenous zones of his body.

Freud concludes that "the patient does not *remember* anything of what he has forgotten and repressed, but *acts* it out. He reproduces it not as a memory but as an action; he *repeats* it, without, of course, knowing that he is repeating it." It follows that "[a]s long as the patient is in the treatment he cannot escape from this compulsion to repeat; and in the end we understand that this is his way of remembering." "We may now ask," Freud continues, *"what it is that he in fact repeats or acts out.* The answer is that he repeats everything that has already made its way from the sources of the repressed into his manifest personality—his inhibitions and unserviceable attitudes and his pathological character-traits" (149). He also repeats "all his symptoms in the course of the treatment," which explains the "deterioration during treatment" that is often an unavoidable response to the analytic work. It therefore becomes clear, Freud concludes, that "the patient's state of being ill cannot cease with the beginning of his analysis, and that *we must treat his illness, not as an event of the past, but as a [still active] force*" (150; my emphasis).

What is enacted in repetition belongs neither to the past nor to the present, therefore, but is an always active "force" in the patient's life that is called forth by the transference and asked to show itself. More importantly, however, what is acted out is now conceived not merely as a "mental process" that has undergone repression, but as something like the crux of the patient's unconscious subjectivity. Unlike the unwelcome thought or psychic conflict at stake in repression, whose avoidance is at the origin of the patient's illness, the act is concerned with a quest in the subject that cannot be reduced to a pathology requiring treatment. Accordingly, writes Freud, the analysand "must find the courage to direct his attention to the phenomena of his illness. *His illness itself must no longer seem to him contemptible, but must become an enemy worthy of his mettle, a piece of his personality, which has solid ground for its existence and out of which things of value for his future life have to be derived"* (151; my emphasis).

At the end of the essay Freud speaks of the transference as a "playground" in which the compulsion to repeat is allowed to expand in complete freedom:

> *The main instrument [. . .] for curbing the patient's compulsion to repeat and for turning it into a motive for remembering lies in the handling of the transference. We render the compulsion harmless, and indeed useful, by giving it the right to assert itself in a definite field. We admit it into the transference as a playground [Tummelplatz] in which it is allowed to expand in almost complete freedom and in which it is expected to display to us everything in the way of pathogenic [drives] that is hidden in the patient's mind. (153)*[4]

This wonderful expression underscores the centrality of the act to a psychoanalysis, where it is never simply a problem to be solved but the engine driving the analytic experience. Even as Freud calls on the compulsion to repeat to display the "pathogenic drives" hidden in the patient's mind, he makes clear that what is acting in repetition cannot be conceived merely as a threat to the patient's health that could be cathected or abreacted and so stripped of its power, but as a force that is creative as well as destructive and that has "the right to assert itself" in the field of the transference. The latter is not only a field for the identification and treatment of pathogenic material, therefore, but a space for the manifestation of the subject as such.[5]

The unconscious is now conceived as the site where what remains outside of language, unrepresented, continues to be repetitively staged and enacted and to work on the body. It is this unconscious that interests Freud, writes Lucie Cantin, because "it is the censured, the unnamed, that is the 'still active force' at work in the life of the patient, pushing her to act without regard for the wishes of the ego and seeking a path for itself through the symptom or acting-out—no matter the consequences for the organism or the ego in the social link" (28).

Untreatable

Willy Apollon, in his most recent contributions to the Freudian metapsychology, significantly develops this fundamental insight by conceiving the act not only as the means through which something that is otherwise inaccessible is brought into the analysis, but as giving expression to the fundamental "quest" of the subject (his development of the concept of desire). This force that acts in the subject—this "enemy worthy of our mettle," in Freud's words—is the essence of the subject of the unconscious as Apollon understands it. He observes that every analysand is sooner or later confronted with the disquieting realization that "the object of his quest [is at the same time] the object of all his misfortunes. He can neither rid himself of it nor require that it be healed, unless it is by the negation of his very existence as a subject" ("Untreatable" 37).

The "untreatable" is the name Apollon gives to this unconscious quest from which the subject will not be derailed, no matter the consequences. This term captures in an ingenious way the vicissitudes of the analysand's attitude toward the act over the course of an analysis. What he initially experienced as something terrifying, loathsome, or shameful that he aspired to be rid of is in time recognized and affirmed as the very core of his subjectivity, something that could never be "cured" or eliminated. "Untreatable" translates the French *intraitable*, which means not "incurable" (as in the case of a disease for which there is no cure), but rather "intractable, inflexible, uncompromising." It exceeds the treatment framework implied by illness, which presumes at the same time the possibility of a cure. It is this untreatable object that Apollon has in mind when he suggests that the end of an analysis articulates the analysand to what constitutes his or her "signature in the social link," the mark of the subject in its refusal of all concessions ("La passe").

The "untreatable" can be understood as Apollon's take on the object *a*, the "object-cause of desire" that Lacan locates at the heart of the fundamental fantasy. In the reception of Lacan's theory, the object *a* is sometimes understood either in very abstract and formal terms or treated as the ultimate prize or treasure—the holy grail of the subject's quest, as it were. In contrast, Apollon's "untreatable" has the virtue of underscoring how the object-cause of our desire is inseparable from the things we most despise or fear about ourselves: and, in the case of the neurotic in particular, urgently seek to be unburdened of.

One analysand spoke of the fear that there was something toxic in her that might even endanger the life of her partner if he were exposed to it—a "something" she eventually comes to recognize as her own desire, which exceeds the framework of what her culture recognizes as acceptable for a woman. Another analysand, who was entering the final phase of his analysis, spoke of something being "freed" in his life. In this connection, he was reminded of an Ursula Le Guin novel where something breaks into another world through a dream, after which nothing will ever be the same again. In the novel, however, this effraction is figured as something destructive, a violence done to this world from which it might not recover. The association underscores the trepidation that often accompanies the freeing of the act for the analysand, including fear of its potential to be disruptive or deadly for others. What the analyst recognizes as a liberation of the subject's desire can at first be experienced with ambivalence by the analysand, as an untethering that is alternately thrilling and terrifying because it puts the analysand on uncharted terrain where there are no longer any models or ideals to guide him. In this untethering we recognize the "unbound" character of the drive in all its dizzying potential.

These examples capture something fundamental about the act, the fact that it necessarily disrupts the subject's relations with others. This disruption doesn't have to be violent, however, but can also be transformative: the introduction of something new that didn't exist before and that advances the cause of the human. A colleague shared with me an act of her own that illustrates very well this second possibility. When she was in the final weeks of her analysis (although she didn't yet know it), she walked into her analyst's office and immediately sat down in *his* chair, rather than lying down on the couch as usual. This unintended act expressed something of her position as a subject that she wasn't yet conscious of or able to speak about: namely, that she had stepped into the position of the analyst.

Speech Acts

Thus far I've addressed the repudiation of the act on the side of the analysand, and the perhaps surprising fact that the analysis not only doesn't help to control the offending act but actually retriggers it—precisely because it is through the act that one enters into communication with the subject, as opposed to the ego. Now I want to speak to the rejection or censorship of the act that is central to the very constitution of the social bond, which also goes to the heart of what is at stake in speech, as opposed to language and the symbolic.

Why do we act in the first place? What causes us to act in ways that are without parallel in the animal world and consistent neither with the instincts that allow the living being to survive in a natural environment nor with the norms of behavior that regulate the social sphere? For Apollon, the act is the consequence of the effraction of the neurophysiological limits of the living organism by the human mind or spirit [*l'esprit*],[6] which sets it on a quest for something other than the survival of the species or the advancement of the group. This effraction, which Apollon calls *real castration*, results not only in the loss of the object and the displacement of the instincts by the drives that is so central to the Freudian metapsychology but in the emergence of the quest of desire. This is because the spirit is characterized by its capacity "to conceive something that doesn't exist, to want it, and eventually to create it" ("Psychanalyse"). The mental space that emerges through this effraction, and in particular the acts to which it gives rise, are therefore the source of all creativity and all novelty, the paths through which something new enters the world and transforms it.

For the same reason, however, they are also threatening to the survival of the group. Precisely because the act gives expression to a quest that is outside of language and alien to the norms and ideals that regulate social coexistence, it presents a threat to the collectivity. Apollon advances that every culture is founded upon a censorship of the mind or spirit in each human being that allows it to guarantee its own material and ideological reproduction. This censorship has four different manifestations: first, a refusal of the inviolability and autonomy of the human being, with the violence it supposes; second, the collective possession of the objects of speech through language; third, the introduction of a cultural construction of the sexual wherein sex is conceived solely as an organ pleasure, and therefore as a means through which every culture produces the man and the woman that it needs to reproduce itself; and fourth, the constitution of the Other as the guardian of the limits of the receivable through the structure of the address that founds the social link ("Psychanalyse").

We often treat language, speech, and address as if these belong to the same field. For example, I want to speak to you about something, and to do so I address you in the language we have in common. For Apollon, however, these three dimensions are distinct and often in tension. As counterintuitive as this may seem, speech for Apollon actually *precedes* language: there is a speaking being (a *parlêtre*, in Lacan's neologism) long before there is language. Apollon evokes the "human *thing* that speaks," or the "thing that speaks in the human" ("Subject" 6), formulations that recall Freud's *Es* (the "it" or id) and Lacan's *ça parle*, "it speaks." Speech isn't something we "have" or "use," therefore, but something that erupts within us without our volition or consent. Like the act itself, therefore, speech is driven by the effraction of the psychic apparatus by the mind or spirit.

Homo sapiens emerged three hundred thousand years ago. Language, on the other hand, is a relatively late acquisition of human beings, dating to only about fifty thousand years ago. Apollon hypothesizes that it emerged at a moment in human history that was defined by the need for human beings to band together in larger and larger groups in order to survive in a hostile environment. This claim by itself is not particularly novel, of course. As Apollon understands it, however, language is not primarily a tool that allows humans to communicate with one another more effectively, or to conceive and execute collective projects. Instead, it is the means through which the collective suppresses the quest that acts in the individual—a quest that necessarily takes him or her far beyond the limits of the collective and even the instinctual aims of survival and reproduction—in order to press him or her into the service of the group and its reproduction ("Subject" 8–9). Through language, the collective takes possession of the objects of speech to subordinate the quest acting in each individual to the shared reality that language founds. Henceforth, only those things that can be said in the language of the group are deemed to be real. One consequence is that the object at stake in speech "seems to withdraw if not disappear as language is installed," both in the history of humanity and in the life of the child (2).

This argument helps to explain why the act is often aligned with catastrophe from the perspective of the social tie. Because it is concerned fundamentally with what cannot be said, the act necessarily shatters the structure of the address: and, with it, the reduction of the human being to the man and the woman that culture requires. It therefore dissolves the glue of the cultural construction and its grip over the human subjects who make up the group. At the limit, Apollon argues, this rupturing of the structure of the address threatens every culture with the possibility of its disappearance. What if young girls were to pursue their own subjective quests, for example, and not to accept their status as sexual objects or as resources controlled by a culture in the interest of its own reproduction? The violent resistance that cultures all over the world are currently mounting against that possibility, whether through forced marriages, the banning of abortion, or the prohibition of education, are evidence of the threat that true subjective desire represents. The suicides of girls who refuse to be pressed into this material and ideological reproduction of culture must therefore be understood as true acts, however tragic they are.

If the structure of the address that founds the social link constitutes the Other as the guardian of the limits of the receivable, then there is an important part of the subject's experience that cannot pass through language and is not receivable in culture. The characterization of the psychotic's delusion as "insane," and as a danger to the social bond that necessitates involuntary treatment or even arrest, would here be paradigmatic. But we can also think about the experience of the child, whose reality—peopled by imaginary friends and monsters under the bed—is much more capacious than that of the family or society in which he lives. When the child enters into the language of the social link, these experiences undergo censorship: the child literally stops seeing and hearing certain things. And when this censorship does not occur—as in the case of the psychotic—participation in social life can become difficult if not impossible precisely because the subject attests to a real that is outside the boundaries of what the group recognizes as reality. This does not mean, however, that censorship is either necessary or desirable.

To privilege language and the social over the act is to adopt the perspective of the social bond and of the culture whose first priority is its own ideological reproduction. Without language there is certainly no possibility of a social bond. Language is not everything, however, and it excludes and renders mute and invisible important dimensions of human experience without which humanity—as distinct from a given culture or civilization—cannot advance and continue to create.

Symbolic castration is the name Apollon gives to this subordination of the human quest to the language and the shared reality of the collective. The reality imposed by language nevertheless leaves a part of this quest untouched, which "escapes communal consciousness and subverts the life of the adolescent, for whom desire will follow paths that go against the paths that are traced out by the expectations of culture" ("Subject" 12). This untouched part of the quest thus "constitutes the real object that maintains, at the heart of the human being, the irreducible desire to create something else." The aim of a psychoanalysis, therefore, is to establish a space for the speech that sustains this quest, "beyond the stakes of civilization, in service to the human and its future" (13).

Which speech, though? If language is fundamentally in the service of censorship, then what is the specificity of the speech with which psychoanalysis is concerned? And what does it do if not bring something into the social sphere as an object of shared consciousness and collective negotiation?

If speech precedes the development of language by 250,000 years, then it is clear that speech is not limited to the use of language. Instead, early speech would have taken the form of acts: a fact whose ongoing significance is confirmed by Freud when he discovers that the symptom, repetitive behaviors, and the *acte manqué* are all forms of unconscious speech that do not involve language. When speech does make use of language—for example in the condensations and displacements of the dreamwork, slips of the tongue or the pen, or the metaphors and figures of speech that manage to evoke something of an experience that is out of language—it is because the quest acting in the subject of the unconscious has managed to wrest words away from language, forcing them to say something other than what they are supposed to mean in the shared reality of the social link. As the author Elfriede Jelinek put it, "language must be tortured to tell the truth." Only very rarely is language speech, therefore, and speech only occasionally makes use of language.

Apollon writes that when Freud decided to let the hysteric do all the talking, he effectively broke with the structure of the address that defines and delimits what can or cannot be said to another person ("L'humain"). By remaining silent and neither responding to nor validating or invalidating what the analysand says, the analyst empties out the place of the Other whom the patient addresses, rupturing the structure of the address that defines the social tie in order to create a space for speech that is no longer constrained by the receivable. (The function of the analyst as absent Other is thus completely opposed to that of the psychotherapist, who is explicitly positioned as an Other who guarantees the limits of the receivable. The therapist is an interlocutor whom the client addresses in the language of the social link and appeals to for help in being successful within its constraints.) In speech, the subject attempts to evoke something that is not observable, to which others have no access. Its function is therefore very different from the language of the collective.

Whereas language founds the social link and determines the limits of reality in order to subordinate the human quest to its own reproduction, speech (*la parole*)—and especially what Lacan calls "full speech" (*la parole pleine*)—is an *act* that gives expression to that part of the censored human quest that continues to work upon the body. An act, writes Apollon, "supposes an effraction of the organism or of the psyche that has been repeated and inscribed: a writing." It is precisely for this reason, he continues, that speech is an act: "[I]t supposes the letter of an inscription not only in the body of the subject who speaks, but in that of the Other who is addressed. An act surges forth because something was inscribed [that] couldn't be said," an inscription that constitutes a part of the body ("L'humain").

In sum, therefore, we must be wary of any application of psychoanalysis that affirms language or the symbolic over the act. While psychoanalysis is certainly oriented around the importance of finding a speech that is adequate to the mental presentations and the drives that have been inscribed in the body in the form of symptoms or acts, it should not be understood as involving the colonization or control of what is acting, its submission to language and social norms, or its stabilization through signifiers that would be accessible to and shared by other members of the group. The subject of the unconscious is a subject that is out of language, and this does not change after a psychoanalysis.

■

The act necessarily interferes with or even ruptures the subject's relations with others. But while that rupture may be experienced as violent, this isn't an inevitability: it may also be judged aesthetic, as something that the person thus affected would never accept to lose or that confronts him with something more important than his own life. Because what acts in the subject is singular and unique, it necessarily contributes something to the human that didn't exist before.

Even violence, moreover, is not necessarily catastrophic. When an act is received as violent, especially by the status quo of a social order, we have to question both the object of that violence and its consequences. I am reminded of the famous words of Jesus to his apostles: "Do not think that I have come to bring peace upon the earth. I have come to bring not peace but the sword. For I have come to set a man against his father, a daughter against her mother, and a daughter-in-law against her mother-in-law; and one's enemies will be those of his household" (*New Oxford Bible*, Matthew 10.34–42, Luke 12.49–53). Jesus doesn't hesitate to evoke a weapon of war in his attack not only on the social tie, but on the family itself. This is not a gratuitous violence waged against innocent victims for selfish aims, however, but an attack on the forms of social organization that stand in the way of a recognition of the sanctity of the human as such, above and beyond the models of the human that each culture promotes.

Walter Benjamin's notion of "divine violence" captures very well the stakes of such a violence, which targets "what is" in the name of what could be. It is a "law-destroying" violence whose concern is for the human and whose aim is justice (248). The object of divine violence is not "mere life," but the power of the mythic order and the "law-preserving" violence that sustains it. While it is "annihilating," therefore, divine violence often takes the form of nonviolence. Greta Thunberg's Fridays for Future movement is a perfect example of such nonviolent violence. By refusing to go to school on Fridays in protest of government and societal inaction on climate change, schoolchildren reject the way that industrialized societies perpetuate themselves—and above all their economies—without regard for the future of humanity. Ingeniously, their violence takes as its most immediate object the system of compulsory education for children, which society uses to manufacture the adults it requires to reproduce and perpetuate this inhumanity.

Earlier I distinguished the act of a terrorist from the acting-out at stake in psychoanalysis, arguing that the former is not the unconscious manifestation of a singular subjective quest but of a deliberate effort to achieve specific aims—aims that the preceding development allows us to identify as those of a particular culture or civilization. The terrorist act is in the service of a specific ideological agenda or civilizational program, to which the actor—the suicide bomber would here be paradigmatic—sacrifices not only his own life but his humanity inasmuch as it invariably exceeds that project and cannot be contained by it. Such forms of violence have the "power making" and "boundary-preserving" character that Benjamin associates with "mythic" or state violence (248–49), since they work on behalf of a culture or civilization to police and control which iterations of the human will be tolerated and to eradicate those that are not. The terrorist who wages war on the infidel or the white nationalist who seeks to overturn a lawful election or criminalize teaching about institutionalized racism defends one specific iteration of the human as the best, the only one that must be allowed to survive. While such acts of terror cannot be considered as subjective acts from a psychoanalytic perspective, they are excellent examples of what Freud calls the group psychology, where the members of the group unite around a common leader or idea precisely in order to repress, through identification, the fragmented body of the drives and the singular mental presentations that are the foundation of human subjectivity (*Group*). The individual actor must affirm and take responsibility for what acts in the body if its repudiation is not to serve as an excuse for the worst acts of "mythic" violence, which the privileging of the collective above all else too frequently enables.

TRACY MCNULTY is a psychoanalyst in private practice in Ithaca, New York, as well as a professor of comparative literature and Romance studies at Cornell University. She is the author of *The Hostess: Hospitality, Femininity, and the Expropriation of Identity* (University of Minnesota Press, 2007) and *Wrestling with the Angel: Experiments in Symbolic Life* (Columbia University Press, 2014), as well as numerous essays on psychoanalysis, political theory, contemporary philosophy, and literature. Currently, she is completing two book manuscripts: "Libertine Mathematics: Perversions of the Linguistic Turn" and "Emancipation by Relay: Unconscious Transmission and the Transindividual Subject."

Notes

1   Jean-François Lyotard offers this formula as a gloss of the Kantian sublime in an essay of the same name (64).

2   "Any subjectification," Rancière writes, "is a disidentification, removal from the naturalness of a place, the opening up of a subject space where anyone can be counted since it is the space where those of no account are counted, where a connection is made between having a part and having no part" (*Disagreement* 36). See also *Politics*.

3   Freud's early claim that hysterics "suffer mainly from reminiscences" and his emphasis on restoring "memories" that have been "forgotten" situate the subject's symptoms and impasses as the result of a failure to face up to reality, to take responsibility for what is or is not possible (for example, Lucy R. acknowledging that she has no future with her employer) (*Studies* 121). Reality has not yet become a mere "principle" for Freud, as it will later on, but functions here as a hard limit: the neurotic is someone who has trouble facing up to (social, interpersonal) reality and needs to confront and take responsibility for that limit.

4   In my citations of the *Standard Edition* I have consistently substituted "drive" for "instinct" wherever *Trieb* or *Triebe* is used in the German text.

5   Or, put another way, the drives are "pathogenic"—creating problems for the analysand in the form of symptoms or difficulties with social adaptation—only to the extent that they have no field in which they can assert themselves, no other means of finding expression.

6   *Spirit* is a word that is rarely used in English outside of a religious or supernatural context. The French *esprit*, on the other hand—like the German *Geist*—is a very common noun that is used in many different contexts and can be translated in a number of ways. The most obvious is *mind*, but only if we distinguish the mind from the brain and from the psychic apparatus that all animals possess (Hegel's *Phenomenology of Spirit*, for example, is sometimes translated *Phenomenology of Mind*). *Esprit* can also be rendered as liveliness, spirit, humor, intelligence, or wit; a *mot d'esprit* is a joke. To describe someone as *spirituel(le)* is to say that he or she is spirited, quick-witted, lively or intelligent, and not spiritual in the religious sense. "Ghost in the machine" is a phrase coined by the British philosopher Gilbert Ryle to express the mind/body dualism in Descartes (22). The latter does not speak of a "ghost," of course, but of *l'esprit*—which animates the living being but does not belong to the biological organism. In short, *l'esprit* really characterizes what is uniquely human in us, our imaginative and creative capacities.

Works Cited   Apollon, Willy. "La passe conclusive à l'École freudienne du Québec." Sept. 2014. Unpubl.

——————. "L'humain en question." *La psychanalyse face au devenir de l'humain*. Ed. Lucie Cantin. Quebec: Gifric, 2023.

——————. "Psychanalyse et mondialisation." Lecture series in Quebec City, Quebec. 2020–2021. Unpubl.

——————. "The Subject of the Quest." Trans. Daniel Wilson. *Penumbr(a)* 2 (2022): 1–14.

——————. "The Untreatable." Trans. Steven Miller. *Umbr(a)* 1 (2006): 23–39.

Benjamin, Walter. "Critique of Violence." *Selected Writings 1913–1926*. Vol. 1. Ed. Marcus Bullock and Michael W. Jennings. Cambridge, MA: Harvard UP, 1996. 236–52.

Cantin, Lucie. "The Drive, the Untreatable Quest of Desire." Trans. Tracy McNulty. *differences* 28.2 (2017): 24–45.

"catastrophe, n." *Merriam-Webster Dictionary*. https://www.merriam-webster.com/dictionary /catastrophe (accessed 12 May 2023).

Freud, Sigmund. "From the History of an Infantile Neurosis." 1918. *The Standard Edition of the Complete Psychological Works of Sigmund Freud*. Trans. and ed. James Strachey. Vol. 17. London: Hogarth, 1955. 1–124. 24 vols. 1953–1974.

——————. *Group Psychology and the Analysis of the Ego*. 1921. *The Standard Edition*. Vol. 18. 1955. 65–144.

——————. "Remembering, Repeating, and Working-Through." 1914. *The Standard Edition*. Vol. 12. 1958. 145–56.

——————. *Studies on Hysteria*. 1895. *The Standard Edition*. Vol. 2. 1955. i–305.

Jelinek, Elfriede. "Sidelined." Trans. Martin Chalmers. 7 Dec. 2004. Nobel Prize Speech. Transcript. https://www.nobelprize.org/prizes/literature/2004/jelinek/lecture/.

Kant, Immanuel. *Critique of Judgment*. Trans. Werner S. Pluhar. Indianapolis: Hackett, 1987.

Lyotard, Jean-François. "Presenting the Unpresentable: The Sublime." Trans. Lisa Liebmann. *Artforum* 20.8 (1982): 64–69.

The New Oxford Annotated Bible with the Apocrypha. Ed. Bruce M. Metzger and Roland E. Murphy. New York: Oxford UP, 1991.

Rancière, Jacques. *Disagreement: Politics and Philosophy*. Trans. Julie Rose. Minneapolis: U of Minnesota P, 1999.

——————. *The Politics of Aesthetics: The Distribution of the Sensible*. New York: Continuum, 2004.

Ryle, Gilbert. *The Concept of Mind*. London: Hutchinson, 1951.

Black Transmission: Toward a Hieroglyph-Analysis

These undecipherable markings on the captive body render a kind of hieroglyphics of the flesh whose severe disjunctions come to be hidden to the cultural seeing by skin color. We might ask if this phenomenon of marking and branding actually "transfers" from one generation to another, finding its various *symbolic substitutions* in an efficacy of meanings that repeat the initiating moments?
—Spillers

Any materiality abstracted as a formal element from the erotogenic body deserves to be called a letter, identifiable in its singularity. This letter is, as such, capable of being reproduced, re-evoked, repeated in some way, so as to scan and articulate the chant of desire.
—Leclaire

Psychoanalytics Experimentation

*T*he question Hortense Spillers raises is so magisterial in its reach and precise in its diagnostic that one experiences answering it as a Lacanian "loop of desire"—incessantly encircling an unobtainable answer, without reprieve or success, but undeterred in the quest for decipherment.

This meditation, entrapped in an orbit of intellectual desire, is a thought experiment of an affirmative response: yes, blackness does, indeed, repeat and transfer its hieroglyph in various symbolic substitutions and undecipherable symptoms. We might call this repetition and transmission a *black Pass*, resembling the psychoanalytic Pass in that the initiating moment of traumatic violence "is not an event of the past, but a present-day force," according to Freud (150). It is a force that incessantly works on and through the body, transmitting its unsaid (its unrepresentable) to black others. The primary concern of the Lacanian Pass, according to Tracy McNulty in "Untreatable," is to open a path for "[s]omething that exceeds the signifier, and that therefore passes through the body. This real object, transmitted by

Volume 34, Number 3   DOI 10.1215/10407391-10898213

an act of the unconscious, is what Lacan calls the object *a*. It is not an object of conscious observation or recording, but instead something that is at once *transmitted* by a body and *received* by a body, depositing itself in the bodies of the two passeurs without their knowledge" (229). The Lacanian Pass transpires during the retelling of an analytic experience (by the "passant," a candidate for analytic certification), while two witnesses, or "passeurs," listen to this experience but leave with "something more," a transmission of that experience into their bodies. This "something more" is what Lacan calls object *a*—the object cause of desire. So, what is passed between the participants is an unconscious force, a remnant of the drive, that activates itself within the body.

Returning to Spillers, we can think of this hieroglyph as a historical-traumatic force: not necessarily an object *a*, but a collective, unrepresentable marking resembling the psychoanalytic object in its transfer between black generations. It constitutes a singularity that, indeed, might be untreatable but that shares similarity across deep space and time. Spillers considers such resemblance (or "poaching," in her words) a psychoanalytics, a project that "unhook[s] the psychoanalytic from its curative framework and [tries] to recover it in a free-floating realm of self-didact possibility that might decentralize and disperse the knowing one" ("All the Things" 427). This poaching experiment is distinct from psychoanalysis proper in that the hieroglyph is not completely consigned to the unconscious but occupies an interstice between conscious/unconscious, requiring a protocol that psychoanalysis might not recognize as legitimate or efficacious. This, for Spillers, is the consequence of a cultural analysis of the captive body's repetition within an antiblack world of transferential structures. Thus, concepts and language obfuscate more than clarify, given this heuristic use of psychoanalysis (as if my essay is analyzing itself), but this intellectual impediment and distortion is an inevitable symptom of psychoanalytics.

Despite this conceptual distortion and revision, and the caution black psychoanalytics assumes concerning wholesale application and uncritical appropriation of psychoanalysis, I still find the Lacanian Pass an indispensable heuristic in thinking through repetition, transmission, and the body for blackness, especially since the unconscious is "the site where what remains outside of language, unrepresented, continues to be repetitively staged and enacted and [works] upon the body" (McNulty, "Untreatable" 228). The work of the hieroglyph is what concerns this meditation, and although its status is liminal for Spillers (as an unconscious/conscious interstice), this work isn't completely conscious and is unrepresentable, generationally, as an enacted and repeated symptom. Thinking with the psychoanalytic Pass and erotogenic body provides a generative framework for addressing Spillers's question and the work marking blackness as nihilistic.

Transmission and Black Nihilism

Does the "phenomenon of marking and branding actually 'transfer' from one generation to another, finding its various *symbolic substitutions* in an efficacy of meanings that repeat the initiating moments?" (Spillers, "Mama's" 216). This question—ironically, both a desire to decipher the undecipherable and an implicit demand, as an Other (black thought) within discourse—opens another scene of blackness, one often disavowed. The urgency of the question (often codified as "crisis") and the inescapability of this scene presents blackness with two major concerns with psychoanalytic resonance: repetition and transmission. If what is repeated and transmitted is undecipherable, resistant to transparency and sense making (deciphering), then obtaining knowledge of this "phenomenon" and presenting a protocol of address is crucial. Indeed, without such knowledge and protocols, blackness suffers from the rhetorical symptoms and reenactments often considered irrational, self-destructive, and loveless.

In *Race Matters*, for example, Cornel West attempts to answer this question by misreading hieroglyphics ("an angst resembling clinical depression") and offering a reaffirmation of humanity ("a politics of conversion") as a solution, instead of pushing the symbolic substitution (the marking *as* symptom) beyond its limits, beyond its pleasurable humanism. West terms this symptom "black nihilism": "Nihilism is to be understood here not as a philosophic doctrine that there are no rational grounds for legitimate standards or authority; it is, far more, the lived experience of coping with a life of horrifying meaninglessness, hopelessness, and (most important) lovelessness. The frightening result is a numbing detachment from others and a self-destructive disposition toward the world. Life without meaning, hope, and love breeds a coldhearted, mean-spirited outlook that destroys both the individual and others" (23). West differentiates nihilism as a philosophy contesting rational grounds and ultimate legitimacy (that is, Nietzsche's philosophy) from black nihilism, which he defines as a self-destructive posture toward life and the absence of meaning, hope, and love within experience. Thus, black nihilism, for West, is a repertoire of disturbing behaviors and fatalistic perspectives.

We might say that West, despite his nauseating moralism and uncritical humanism, (mis)names a drive within black experience—something that, as Lucie Cantin describes it, "pushes the human being to go too far, to seek out that Thing that goes beyond the reasonable, that exceeds the needs of the living being, and that falls outside of the limits of pleasure and unpleasure. It runs counter to norms and laws, having no regard either for morality, for the notions of good and evil, or for whatever culture allows in the way of satisfaction" (25). This "(self-)destructive disposition" repeats and transmits an excess, a beyond the humanistic mandates of black vitalism and its unbridled optimism. Meaninglessness, hopelessness, lovelessness, numbing, and self-destruction instantiate this hieroglyph, actually repeating the initiating moment of black subjection in the New World, rather than a contumacious disregard for living. Black nihilism, then, is not a collective depression; rather, it is an analytic space within which the hieroglyph is passed between blacks (interior intersubjectivity) and the work of the drive cuts the "captive body" (a collective body) into undecipherable parts.[1]

West, in a nostalgia for a black *Gestalt* (a fantasy object), avers that "cultural structures of meaning and feeling" once sustained black existence and warded off the nihilistic threat in black life—preventing suicide, ultimately (24). This sense of wholeness, however, constitutes the narcistic image of blackness, before the Real of the hieroglyph ruptures it (the black body returned in "bits and pieces").[2] In other words, West disavows the fragmentation of black life throughout history, the various ways the hieroglyph manifested as sorrow, slaves jumping overboard ships, sharecroppers worked to death, the unavoidable anxiety of lynching, and so on. This romanticization of black life (before the sixties, we are told) is more a disavowal of repetition and transmission than a retrieval of an authentic moment in time and history. A *black life principle*, then, structures West's reading of nihilism, distorting the message of the hieroglyph, or what in black life is repeated because it is unrepresentable and without language. Perhaps, if anything, West is witnessing the symptom *intensify*—not because institutions are disappearing or dysfunctional, but because blackness is now *open to the knowledge*, the undeciphered message, of the hieroglyph. Much like, for psychoanalysis, the analytic process attempts to free the act and provide a short-circuited avenue of expression, black nihilism *pushes* blackness beyond its various defenses and resistances, opening, or clearing, a path for the expression of historical trauma.

In his reading, West misrecognizes surplus pleasure for hedonistic pleasure (market-value living). This capitalist market–driven pleasure "has little to do with the past and views the future as no more than a repetition of a hedonistically driven present" (26). Hedonistic repetition is severed from "the past" and endlessly repeats the present as the future. Although this repetition appears to acknowledge the Freudian act, in which the repetition is a force of the present, the Freudian act actually displaces temporality, such that the force is impervious to temporal distinctions (there is neither a past to romanticize nor a future to reclaim). In other words, a hopeful temporality disciplines and extinguishes hedonistic pleasure for West (for example, a present worth living, a past to preserve, a future of unbounded possibilities). Hedonistic pleasure, then, is a mere repetition of consumer influences and interests; blackness is not condemned to repeat this pleasure if it abandons its nihilistic orientation, according to his interpretation. Contrary to West's black vitalism, surplus pleasure pushes blackness beyond mere satisfaction and cupidity; it intensifies this beyond life and pleasure in nihilistic behavior. To put this more directly: the hieroglyph is not the product of hedonistic capitalism; it is the repetition of the "marks" of captivity, those lacerations, traumas, agonies, and despairs. West has observed *an act*, a black Pass, rather than mere hedonism or insouciance. We might, however, acknowledge that capitalism (as the transatlantic slave trade) provided the ground for hieroglyphic marking (a *white* hedonism)—but this ground is neither sybaritic behavior nor willful embrace of consumerism for blacks. It is a violence unending and inescapable.

What is the solution to black nihilism for West? The return of the nostalgic (but not the repressed), the politics of conversion "proceeds principally on the local level—in those institutions in civil society still vital enough to promote self-worth and self-affirmation. It surfaces on the state and national levels only when grass-roots democratic organizations put forward a collective leadership that has earned the love and respect of and, most important, has proved itself *accountable* to these organizations. This collective leadership must exemplify moral integrity, character, and democratic statesmanship within itself and within its organizations" (West 30). A vital black institutionalism, much like ego psychology, purports to refashion the "black self" into a worthy and affirming subject within its mirror of moral integrity, character, and democratic statesmanship. How institutions repair a broken self or restore life to the socially dead is not addressed, other than to assume our romantic past (before the sixties) possesses the answers and these answers are applicable to the contemporary moment. Nostalgia for community, a wholeness untainted by nihilistic imperatives, however, is not unique to West; even Spillers expresses "nostalgia for the lost love-object

[that] cannot be entirely laid down, I suspect, to the affects of anxiety's displacements alone, but relates as well to *dispersal* of community" ("All the Things" 384). Nostalgia for community and its fortified institutions, it seems, provides a defense against the hieroglyphic's brutal repetition. Nostalgia, of course, protects the child from the trauma of difference, in psychoanalysis, freezing time in a nostalgic plenitude of sameness (but also requiring a fetish to concretize the task of disavowal).[3] But nostalgia, as disavowal, fails to contend with what repeats unrepresented (community, in this sense, is the institutionalization of black representations in various forms).

If what we desire is a protocol of healing, as Spillers avers, such a protocol would require an analytic of the hieroglyph. Political conversion is not analysis; its moralizing and condescending diagnosis does nothing more than fetishize "hope and love" *against* the hieroglyph's message. We might charge West with *fetish hedonism*, the rapture of disavowal and addiction to fantasy objects, as he misdiagnoses the black nihilist with impressionability and immaturity. But exchanging charges won't accomplish the aim at hand: to develop a protocol of deciphering the hieroglyph and freeing its action for more generative expression.

This meditation will fail to obtain this object of desire, the ultimate answer; it will, instead, encircle it unsatisfyingly. But perhaps "understanding" the contours of the hieroglyph, attempting to discern its act, might provide the opening we need.

Hieroglyphics and the Captive Body

Our task, here, is impossible but necessary: we must attempt to render the opaque transparent and subordinate the repetition to signifiers. This intellectual desire, as a quest for clarity, will disappoint us along our circuit, encountering contradictions, impasses, and aporias—but this is unavoidable when analyzing the act.

What is the hieroglyph? From our preliminary investigation, we can describe the Spillerian hieroglyph as the unrepresentable and undecipherable mark of antiblack violence on the captive body. Such markings are tralatitious and replicable (enacted but not representable). What, then, is the act? The repetitive act is the disruption of the body and severing of the flesh—the way violence unravels, unmakes, and disassembles the body and produces a gap between flesh (cosmological orientation) and body (a legal construction, commodity form). The *act* of disrupting and severing leaves the body in bits and pieces as a commodity form: a slave. The hieroglyph, then, emerges from this disruption/severing; it locates the initiating force, too overwhelming to introduce into language. The body of the hieroglyph is not the Ancestral body transmogrified into the captive body. Much like the erotogenic body differs from the organism for psychoanalysis, the captive body differs from the body of ancestry, or what Spillers describes as a body that "focuses a private and particular space, at which point biological, sexual, social, cultural, linguistic, ritualistic, and psychological fortunes converge. This profound intimacy of interlocking detail is disrupted, however, by externally imposed meanings and uses" ("Mama's" 206). The body is an "interlocking" of various vectors—biological, sexual, social, cultural, linguistic, ritualistic, and psychological. Let's call this ancestral body a *heuristic*. Exceptional brutality pulverizes this body, and the aim of this violence is to disarticulate this ancestral body, deform it through pain and torture ("externally imposed meanings and uses"), concomitantly producing a captive body. The hieroglyph emerges through the "cut" of antiblack violence (resembling the emergence of the Lacanian subject through the cut of the signifier). Continuing our psychoanalytics experimentation, we could suggest that the (de)creation of the ancestral body (producing hieroglyphs, the captive body is its composition) resembles the (de)creation of the organic body (producing letters, the erotogenic body is its composition). The analyst, then, develops a protocol, or orthography, to spell out and decipher the message of the Real, locating the site upon which the Real works on and through the body. The captive body, the composite of various hieroglyphs, is still in search of such a protocol, an empowered orthography. Spillers, then, turns to the psychoanalytic, unhooking it from its curative framework, for such an orthographic procedure.

Continuing this resembling and poaching experimentation, we observe how various characteristics of this captive body mirror the erotogenic body in psychoanalysis. According to Spillers:

> *1) The captive body [is] a source of an irresistible, destructive sexuality; 2) at the same time—in stunning contradiction—it is reduced to a thing, to being for the captor; 3) in this distance from a subject position, the captured sexualities provide a physical and biological expression of "otherness"; 4) as a category of "otherness," the captive body translates into a potential for pornotroping and embodies sheer physical powerlessness that slides into a more general "powerlessness," resonating through various centers of human and social meaning. ("Mama's" 206)*

This fractured, disassembled captive body constitutes a destructive sexuality, irresistible to the captor. This body is both an object of a white drive and a source of destruction for the captive, since "powerlessness," "otherness," and "pornotroping" foreclose subjectivity and impose meaning on various locations of this body. This meaning, "hidden to the cultural seeing through skin color," is another name for *hieroglyph*. The meaning imposed on the disassembled body, after the cut of this violence, finds its efficacy in symbolic substitutions, repetitive acts.

For Serge Leclaire, the erotogenic body, the composition of fixated letters, is also an other for the subject—inscribed at the site of *jouissance*:

> *[T]he letter has now been situated in its psychoanalytic sense as a trait that constitutes and marks in a place on the body the surfacing of* jouissance *in the immediacy of an exquisite difference. [. . .] [T]o take the body literally is, in sum, to learn to spell out the orthography of the name composed by the erotogenic zones that constitute it. It is to recognize in each letter the singularity of the pleasure (or the pain) that the letter fixates, and to identify by the same token the series of objects in play. (52–53)*

This psychoanalytic body, produced through inscription, is analogical to the captive body, produced through imposed meaning and violence. What distinguishes a hieroglyph-analysis from a psycho-analysis, however, is that the hieroglyph is without a grammar/orthography of translation: this is the psychic definition of black suffering. Because it is impoverished of language (Spillers argues blacks have been barred from language), or even foreclosed to the Symbolic, it can only be passed down and repeated. If for psychoanalysis the object *a* is transmitted during the analysis as a constitutive aspect of the work, a hieroglyph-analysis, void of sufficient language, must find a protocol to decipher the repetition of the hieroglyph singular to each subject (what Spillers calls the One—both a collective and singular simultaneously). Blacks continue to pass the hieroglyph between themselves, without a language of decipherment (or an analytic interpretation).

∎

The repeating captive body (the composite of traumatic hieroglyphs at the site of antiblack severing/disruption) might appear destructive, irrational, loveless, and hopeless to critics like Cornel West and others invested in black vitalism/optimism. Repetition and transmission encode catastrophic acts with a meaning to be deciphered. Such a deciphering procedure, a hieroglyph-analysis, is undeveloped but desperately needed. In *Post Traumatic Slave Syndrome: America's Legacy of Enduring Injury and Healing*, for example, Dr. Joy DeGruy-Leary understands this repetition and transmission as a "syndrome" embedded in structural inequality, intramural violence, and damaging behavior. She argues that "varying levels of both clinically induced and socially learned residual stress-related issues were passed along through generations as a result of slavery" ("Post Traumatic"). DeGruy-Leary identifies vacant esteem, a marked propensity for anger and violence, and racist socialization as the root of this syndrome. This study steers us in the direction of a "protocol of healing," although self-esteem itself (her proposed solution) isn't enough to decipher what generational stress is communicating and how transmission can be addressed. The work of hieroglyph-analysis is difficult and without easy answers. A psychoanalytics, as I hope I've demonstrated, might provide insight into the act of repetition and transmission, the way the hieroglyph returns to the same place, despite our frustration or disgust.

If Freud was correct and the event is not past, but an active, present force, then black nihilism names this present force, the repetition of severing and disrupting. Rather than thinking about black nihilism as a pathological, destructive disposition, we might recast it as the *analytic setting of blackness in the New World*. In this setting, the hieroglyph passes from black to black in an efficacy of meaning we work hard to interpret. This brief meditation was designed as an opening to further development of this analysis—a psychoanalytics in action.

CALVIN WARREN is an associate professor of African American studies at Emory University. Duke University Press published his first book, *Ontological Terror: Blackness, Nihilism, and Emancipation* (2018). He is currently working on a second project, "Onticide: Essays on Black Nihilism and Sexuality," which unravels the metaphysical foundations of black sexuality and argues for a rethinking of sexuality without the human, sexual difference, or coherent bodies.

Notes

1 For an analysis of black nihilism as philosophical orientation, see Warren.

2 For a racialized reading of Lacan's "body in bits and pieces," see Silverman.

3 McNulty articulates the relation between time, freezing, and perverse fetishism in her essay "Unbound." The child must freeze the moment of sameness, before the trauma of difference, using a maternal phallus, a speculative fetish.

Work Cited

Cantin, Lucie. "The Drive, the Untreatable Quest of Desire." Trans. Tracy McNulty. *differences* 28.2 (2017): 24–45.

DeGruy-Leary, Joy. *Post Traumatic Slave Syndrome: America's Legacy of Enduring Injury and Healing.* Milwaukee, OR: Uptone, 2005.

——————. "Post Traumatic Slave Syndrome." University of California, Santa Barbara. 8 Nov. 2019. https://campuscalendar.ucsb.edu/event/post_traumatic_slave_syndrome_joy _degruy.

Freud, Sigmund. "Remembering, Repeating, Working-Through." 1914. *The Standard Edition of the Complete Psychological Works of Sigmund Freud.* Trans. and ed. James Strachey. Vol. 12. London: Hogarth, 1958. 145–56. 24 vols. 1953–74.

Leclaire, Serge. *Psychoanalyzing: On the Order of the Unconscious and the Practice of the Letter.* Trans. Peggy Kamuf. Stanford: Stanford UP, 1998.

McNulty, Tracy. "Unbound: The Speculative Mythology of the Death Drive." *differences* 28.2 (2017): 86–115.

——————. "Untreatable: The Freudian Act and Its Legacy." *Crisis Critique* 6.1 (2019): 227–51.

Silverman, Kaja. *The Threshold of the Visible World.* New York: Routledge, 1996.

Spillers, Hortense. "'All the Things You Could Be by Now, If Sigmund Freud's Wife Were Your Mother': Psychoanalysis and Race." *Black* 376–427.

——————. *Black, White, and in Color: Essays on American Literature and Culture.* Chicago: U of Chicago P, 2003.

——————. "Mama's Baby, Papa's Maybe: An American Grammar Book." *Black* 203–29.

Warren, Calvin. "Black Nihilism and the Politics of Hope," *CR: The New Centennial Review* 15.1 (2015): 215–48.

West, Cornel. *Race Matters.* New York: Vintage, 1994.

Divine Violence Today: The Question of *First Reformed*

The Film

*I*n 2017, Paul Schrader released the film that put into practice his theory of the "transcendental style in film," which he had offered to the world of film theory in 1972, had recently revisited, and would republish in 2018. The film was *First Reformed,* starring Ethan Hawke, Amanda Seyfried, and Philip Ettinger—in my opinion, his masterpiece.

Hawke plays the Protestant pastor of a historic church with a dwindling congregation in upstate New York that is being taken over by a smooth-operating fellow Calvinist megachurch, the Church of Abundant Life. The megachurch dwells in a modern, sleekly functional structure of shiny industrial plywood, beige and white surfaces, large television screens, and biblical passages covering many of its walls in an artsy, advertising style. With its many spaces (megasized sanctuary, group therapy and Bible class rooms, cafeteria, recreation rooms, and so on), the new structure has far outstripped First Reformed Church—"built in 1801 by settlers from West

Volume 34, Number 3   DOI 10.1215/10407391-10898227

Friesland," we read on its plaque at the start of the film—which it seems to be holding financially afloat only for its last breath, namely, a "Reconsecration" on its 250th birthday. This, we quickly gather, will be the First Reformed Church's last stand before being completely devoured and digested by the megachurch, which is in turn essentially owned by Balq Industries. Thus, according to the same plaque, Balq Industries already owns First Reformed ("An Abundant Life historic church") as well.

The pastor's name is Ernst Toller (more on that name later), a former army chaplain racked with guilt for the death of his son Joseph—whose enlistment he had encouraged—in Iraq. Soon we see that he is ill, urinating blood, not eating, drinking whiskey (at one point he mixes his whiskey with pink Pepto Bismol), and struggling to learn to pray again by writing, longhand and on paper, in a journal, "writing every word out so that every inflection of penmanship, every word chosen, scratched out, revised, is recorded. To set down all my thoughts and the simple events of my day factually and without hiding anything," Toller's voiceover tells us. Schrader shows some of his cards with this voiceover, revealing his most important influences (some of which he also discusses in his book on the "transcendental style"): Robert Bresson's *Diary of a Country Priest* (1951) and *Pickpocket* (1959) (for the journal writing and the voiceover); Ingmar Bergman's *Winter Light* (1963) (for the church exteriors and interiors, the static camera, and its deep commitment to recording the Eucharist); Yasujirō Ozu's 1950s films about everyday family life (for its dedication to the objects and spaces of ordinary life); and even aspects of Schrader's own 1976 *Taxi Driver* (in particular Travis Bickle's voiceover and his chronicling of his preparations for his final act). Toller's reference to the recording and contemplation of "the simple events of my day" as the common denominator between these films reveals to us some of his theology. The sanctification via contemplation of everyday gestures, rituals, and acts was a dominant feature of the lives of the early, not yet institutionalized Christians, as it is also the dominant feature of transcendental cinema (Schrader 61).

From the start of the film, the precarity of First Reformed Church poignantly reveals itself to the viewer. The first few shots of the film immediately set up this presentation of the Church, which appears like a living organism asking to be recorded and preserved: in a dolly shot, the camera approaches the perfectly white and geometrically simple and pleasing, small, and poignant structure of the First Reformed Church, its steeple always pointing to the sky even when the shot angle changes in order to accommodate the camera's approach. The camera gets so close to the church that the perspectives and the geometric angles shift and transform right before our eyes, until the structure alone fills the frame, its geometric lines and shapes changing, bending, almost bursting, and yet still hanging together.

Reverend Toller's own life is also strained by crisis. He is likely seriously ill, his church is on its last leg, there are five parishioners in the pews on Sundays, and breezy Abundant Life parishioners pass by the church mainly to acquire souvenirs of a place whose history few people care about and no one will miss. One detail of its history, we learn, is that in the nineteenth century it functioned as a link in the Underground Railroad, providing shelter in its cellar for runaway slaves. We see, in passing, Toller giving a tour of the church to a group of schoolchildren and their teacher—a very different group from the typical tourists who show up here and there, one man actually pressing a couple of dollars into Toller's hand as he leaves—as these young visitors are shown something more meaningful than a future postcard of what once was: Toller opens up for them a hidden trapdoor to the cellar that otherwise remains invisible and covered by a rug. The historic organ is usually out of order but will be fixed—paid for by Abundant Life—only because of the upcoming ceremony. Toller lives alone in an almost empty house attached to the church, surrounded by only the most rudimentary of objects: a table, a chair, a bed, a toilet. In his personal life he is pursued by the Abundant Life choir leader Esther whom, as he tells her, he "despises." And finally, he has lost the ability to pray and hopes that his journal writing will help restore it.

One Sunday after mass, Reverend Toller is approached by one of his parishioners, Mary, who attends on Sundays with her husband Michael. Mary tells Toller that Michael was in jail in Canada for his activities with Green Planet, an activist environmental group, and was released when the couple learned Mary is pregnant. She is worried about Michael: "He thinks it's wrong to bring a child into this world. He wants to kill our baby." Would Reverend Toller speak with him? When Toller meets with Michael, the latter is eloquent in explaining why bringing children into this world as we head toward climate catastrophe is evil, a fact that, Toller agrees, can rationally be met only with despair. But, Toller argues, despair without hope is sinful. In fact, despair cannot be despair without hope. Michael mentions environmental activists who, "like the early Christian martyrs," are "killed every day" for wanting to protect and preserve the earth. What silences Michael, ending their back-and-forth after hours of conversation, is Toller's statement that the despair accompanying the act of bringing a child into a world heading for self-destruction can never equal the despair upon a child having been taken from it, meaning his son, Joseph, "the boy thrown down the well [. . .] the dreamer [. . .]. Courage is the solution to despair," not reason, Toller concludes. The image that is floated by the two, of the "dreamer boy" sitting underground in a well, can be aligned with the image of the underground runaway slaves hiding in the church's cellar (that shot occurs about halfway through the film), as well as with the image of Christian martyrs, conjured by Michael, hiding and being buried in underground catacombs. Together, the three images combine the well's preservation of the ultimately politically victorious "dreamer" (Joseph) with the preserving tunnels for escaped slaves and the survival or martyrdom of early Christians. At the end of his dialogue with Michael, Toller declares, "Wisdom is holding two contradictory truths in our mind simultaneously. Hope and despair. A life without despair is a life without hope. Holding these two ideas [survival and terror] in our head is life itself." It is a sort of Benjaminian "dialectical image," to which I will return.

Though the two plan to meet again, before they can do so, Mary tells Toller that she has found a suicide vest in their garage. Shortly thereafter, Michael asks Toller to meet him in the woods. When Toller arrives, he finds Michael, who has shot himself with his shotgun, and with that a first violent tear appears in the film, as Mary, adopting Christian iconography, is now left alone with child. Michael, as both the sword-wielding archangel and the other "Joseph" figure, Mary's husband, has ejected himself from the scene. As the link between this family, now in a state of dissolution, and the larger community, Toller will come to partially stand in for Michael. He is a symbolic "Father" as pastor and as such he represents the larger social bond. Yet we know how precarious this position is: as a real father, he is so lacerated and perforated by guilt that his symptom has become perforation itself: his diet is almost entirely liquid and alcoholic. The social bond he is to represent, uphold, and nourish as symbolic Father—the repeated scenes of the Eucharist ritual emphasize this function—is clearly in a state of crisis and dissolution.

There follows a grotesque and desperate funeral, scripted by Michael in his last will and testament to take place at a polluted superfund site, cluttered with rusty dead barges and other industrial waste, where Mary will dump Michael's ashes into the polluted water (a further image of paternal liquefaction), and where the Abundant Life Choir, whom we had heard and seen practicing earlier at the gimmicky, smile-filled Abundant Life, now sings Neil Young's song about a despairing, dying Earth, "Whose Gonna Stand Up." The four choir members vocalize and harmonize exactly as they had done at practice in the megachurch, their expressions neutral and vacant (they will sing anything, anywhere), the harmonizing mastered with total ease, a well-oiled machine. The same emotional vacancy will characterize Esther singing the hymn at the end of the film, in the First Reformed Church for the Reconsecration: a monotonous, seemingly endless hymn set on an infinite loop as a soundtrack to the literal violence, passion, death, rebirth, and ecstasy being enacted in the pastor's living quarters next door unbeknownst to anyone in the church.

Following Michael's suicide, Toller begins surfing the websites Michael had visited on Michael's laptop and reading about individual big polluters. He learns that Balq Industries, the company that owns Abundant Life, First Reformed, and everyone in them, and who is underwriting the Reconsecration, is a major local polluter. Ed Balq will soon begin attacking Toller for having carried out Michael's funeral instructions that were nothing but, he claims, a provocative demonstration for the media. The disdain is mutual, and soon Reverend Jeffers, the leader of the megachurch, summons Toller for a meeting in which he paternalistically criticizes Toller for being "always in the Garden," advises him to "lighten up" and cease his activism, and promises him Abundant Life's "help" with rehab following the Reconsecration, or "maybe" for Toller to "go to Nicaragua and preach the gospel or build houses." Ed Balq, he adds, will play a large part in the ceremony and will be introduced by the governor of New York. The program is clear: a new "reconsecrating" social bond, based on mutual brand boosting between the corporate, the political, and the religious powers that be, will be inaugurated at First Reformed Church. This newly forged "Abundant Life" will seek obscenely to fill or swallow the hole torn by Michael's suicide into the "holy family," and thereby negate its precarity. This new bond, with its glossy, infinite-loop, readymade programming of superficial ritual that has, insanely, made nature and natural life dispensable, frames for Toller his own new position: learning more about ecological abuse, images of devastation and information partially shared with us, Toller begins to study, tend, mend, and wear Michael's suicide vest when he is away from Mary. We also see him trimming barbed wire from the dilapidated fence around the church's cemetery (another "Garden"), to which he tends as well.

We begin to hear from Toller about his newly forming intentions to act after he shows the schoolchildren the trapdoor to the "Underground Railroad," the place that concealed and preserved escaped slaves. Toller's private voiceover declarations begin to take on a whole new intensity that contrasts sharply with various actual discursive failures—his conversations with Jeffers, with Balq, with God, and his first and only one with Michael. Toller's meaning begins to echo Travis Bickle's in *Taxi Driver* and signals, perhaps announces and precipitates, the looming violent act. But something else happens before any fateful *passage à l'acte* takes off: an entirely different form of communication—visual, embodied—comes into being between Toller and Mary. This is a miracle[1] that the viewer is allowed to witness. It is the only supernatural moment in the film. The scene begins with Toller, alone, recording his "struggle against torpor" in his journal and reemphasizing this struggle with "I must set pen to paper," as the stationary camera records his painstaking writing activity at the table in his almost empty, unadorned, and weakly lit house. Then Mary knocks at his door. She is anxious, suddenly in dark despair, and she describes to Toller the "Magical Mystery Tour" that she and Michael used to enact together: fully clothed, they would lie one on top of the other, as many points of their bodies as possible touching. "We'd have our hands out and we would just look straight into each other's eyes and move them in unison . . . and then we would breathe in rhythm." Toller says, "Show me," and they enact the ritual. They lie on the wooden floor, their arms outstretched, tentatively forming the shape of the cross, Mary on top of Toller, and look into each other's eyes. Some of Mary's long hair drops down off her shoulder, forming a sort of curtain between the viewer and their profiles. The camera slowly pulls away, and when it is able to show the full length of their bodies, we see them begin to levitate. The camera now slowly circles around (at the end of the movie this circling will be repeated, intensified) their floating bodies somehow placed in space and among the constellations. With their two bodies never leaving the frame, the camera, with the viewer, now flies above them and within pristine, sublime, natural settings—snow-covered mountains, oceans, corals, deep green coves and orchards. The intensity of the natural scene brings to mind not only Creation itself but also the Book of Job, when God displays his transcendence of human constructs and realities, their attempts at structure and control, by insisting on the continuity of his power and violence as destructive and creative at the same time ("Can you tie the chains of the Pleiades or loose the straps of Orion?" [Job 38.31]). Then the camera seems to slightly pull their cruciform bodies down by their feet, just barely tilting their cross on its vertical axis, almost standing but not quite, still floating, and we see Toller, whose face has until now been hidden below the back of Mary's head, move the curtain of Mary's hair out of the way, fraying it, to allow his anxious face to peer out. He looks despairing (and no longer at Mary), and at that moment the phantasmagoria changes into a catastrophic nightmare vision:

traffic, mountains of discarded tires, polluting factories, endless mountains of trash mixing in with shantytowns, wildfires, and then the superfund site where Michael's funeral took place.[2]

There is an abrupt cutaway to the scene involving the Underground Railroad I have mentioned: Toller lets the children into the sanctuary, opens the trapdoor, and has the kids peer inside as he urges them to imagine what it would be like to sit in the dark, the heat, shaking with fear, alluding once again to Joseph in the well and to other stories of underground terror. Immediately after, we cut to a scene of leave-taking: Mary is moving away, talking about returning for the Reconsecration, and Toller sharply asks her not to come. Reluctantly she agrees. "Be strong in the Lord and in His mighty power," he then reads in voiceover, presumably writing once he is alone again. "Put on the full armor of God," we hear, as we see him finishing his mending of the suicide vest, "so that you can take your stand against the devil's schemes. For our struggle is not against flesh and blood, but against the rulers, against the authorities, against the powers of this dark world," he reads at his most gnostic and also, weirdly, his most Travis Bickle–like, as, donning the vest, he looks at himself in the mirror. While in *Taxi Driver* the camera shows us the mirror reflection of Bickle, here the camera points at the "flesh and blood" Toller himself.

There follows a montage of individual actions that Toller performs, almost as if he were performing them in order to record and collect them: he goes on a group tour of Balq Industries; he stops for "miso and fish, such a simple pleasure"; driving at night, he sees a large overweight man bully a young child; he revisits the superfund site of Michael's funeral. We see him there as he reads to us, "Every act of preservation is an act of creation." He stays there until the sun begins to rise, a shot of immense, harsh beauty, the silhouettes of the ghostly discarded rusty ships against the background of a purple sky: "I have found another form of prayer," he says in this garden of Gethsemane.

The juxtaposition of this shot against the next one of the ugly modern beige building of Abundant Life with the inscription, "I am come that they may have abundant life, and might have it abundantly (John 10.10)," speaks for itself. Toller now has the meeting with Jeffers, who reprimands him for being always "in the Garden"; the two argue about the role of religion and church in the face of climate disaster and Jeffers mocks Toller for being "a minister at a tourist church that no one attends." He also suggests that perhaps we just can't see "what God has in mind" regarding climate change. "You think God wants to destroy his creation?" Toller says, crying in exasperation, at which point Jeffers promises Toller Abundant Life's "help," rehab, and "Nicaragua," "doing something in the real world."

The next shot takes us into the day of the Reconsecration at First Reformed. It is being simulcast to Abundant Life, the Church company determined to suck the last dregs of life out of its foster child. Jeffers and entourage arrive at the church in what is a very different kind of media event compared to Michael's funeral: the rich and powerful step out of their black shiny SUVs and wave to the cameras as security guards escort them into the church. Then we cut to another "Travis Bickle" shot: Toller in front of the mirror, buttoning up the loaded suicide vest. Throwing on his black cassock, he walks briskly to his window and sees people arriving at the church. The camera now enters the church and we see the Jeffers family seated and Ed Balq arriving with his.

When Toller looks out the window a second time, he sees Mary walking into the church and goes into a tailspin. He whimpers and screams, even as the people filling the church grow restless. While Jeffers angrily knocks on Toller's door, Toller is frantically moving through his house, gathering the barbed wire he had trimmed off the cemetery fence, grunting as he wraps it around his bare chest. He does not hear Jeffers' knocks, and the latter, returning to the church now, asks Esther to begin the service. Now begins the hymn that she will sing, alone on the dais, on an infinite-loop setting that will last through the film's ending, the maddening and monotonous hymn, "Leaning on the Everlasting Arms."[3] The camera mechanically zooms in on Esther (by way of *Night of the Hunter* she is identified as a predator) and the shot is perfectly framed, dominated by a matte white and beige interior, her face and body both totally motionless, vacant, neutral. As she sings the refrain, "Leaning, leaning," we cut to Toller's mirror image, his face contorted in pain as he presses the barbed wire into his bare torso, blood running down his body. He gasps, his eyes opening wide; we hear his skin and flesh being pierced, as the automaton's voice sings on about "leaning, safe and secure, from all alarms." The camera then cuts back to Esther, a full frontal shot now, as she stands perfectly centered and balanced before the altar, the top of her head continuing the vertical line of the perfectly centered large cross hanging on the wall behind her in the greyness and beigeness of the shot. That same line continues down along the front of her body and connects in space with the vertical line of the microphone she is singing into. Given the context, the result is "a ridiculous image," as Pastor Ericsson says of the Throne of Mercy hanging on the church wall in Bergman's *Winter Light* (see below). With the line "Oh, how sweet to walk," we are visually back with Toller, who is now wearing a white cassock covered in blood stains, as the blood oozes through. On "Oh how bright the path, grows from day to day," Toller tosses the whiskey from his glass and fills it with Drano. With the refrain of "Leaning, leaning on the everlasting arms," we get an extreme close-up of the thick Drano filling the glass. Then: "What have I to dread, what have I to fear," and, as he raises the glass to his lips, Toller turns toward the door, and there stands Mary. She says, "Ernst." "I have blessed peace," sings Esther. Toller drops the glass, and suddenly the rule of the stationary camera that has completely dominated the film in a sequence of perfectly boxed and static shots is euphorically and ecstatically broken: Toller turns and rushes toward Mary and she toward him, they embrace and kiss (in a clear reference to the end of *Ordet*, following the resurrection of Inger), and the camera circles around them, around and around, while the hymn continues in its refrain, "leaning, leaning, on the everlasting arms," until the film abruptly breaks rather than ends, by cutting off in the middle of the word "lean-."

Breaking, Bleeding, Feeding

One of the gifts Schrader gives to a discerning viewer is that through his film, we can return to and understand better the "transcendental" films of the 1950s and 1960s—Dreyer's *Ordet*, Bresson's *Diary of a Country Priest* and *Pickpocket*, Bergman's *Winter Light*—that are introjected in *First Reformed*. *First Reformed*'s action, following the geometrically transforming and intensifying shot of the church building at the start of the film, begins with Sunday mass: Reverend Toller is breaking bread, enacting the ritual of the Eucharist in an echo of the first magisterial scene of mass and Communion in Bergman's *Winter Light* (with Gunnar Björnstrand as the pastor, Max von Sydow as the despairing parishioner, and Ingrid Thulin, exmistress and scapegoat to the pastor and his despair).[4] It is no coincidence that Schrader establishes the connection between the two through the image of breaking bread. Breaking, in my reading of *First Reformed*, is its central trope. The beginnings of these two films mutually illuminate one another dialectically; each one fills out, almost to the bursting point, the other. In *Winter Light*, the despairing and soon suicidal parishioner Jonas cannot come to terms with his era's apocalyptic nightmare: the threat of nuclear catastrophe. As happens to Toller, Pastor Ericsson's own despair is kindled and fueled by the anguish of his parishioner who, like Michael in *First Reformed*, also commits suicide after their first conversation. Both pastors are struggling with their faith: Toller is attempting to discipline himself into relearning how to pray, while in *Winter Light* there is the striking moment when the Pastor looks up briefly at the "Throne of Mercy"[5] hanging on the church wall and says, "What a ridiculous image," almost in passing, deflating the ponderousness of his officiating of the mass. Loss of faith, despair, suicide, both pastors' illnesses, their cruelty to their former mistresses, the apocalyptic horizons that both films invoke, all of this is about a social bond *in extremis*. In essence it's what both films "are about": a dissolving social bond and the question of what action to take in face of it.

The cutting humiliation of the "Throne of Mercy" by Pastor Ericsson as just a "ridiculous image" seems extreme—as is Toller's plan to suicide bomb First Reformed Church. Both denote the end of an order, perhaps a civilization. Suicide and murder-suicide are a *passage à l'acte*, and one of the problems that both Bergman and Schrader take on is the suicidal element in Christianity itself, a paradox and madness that Pastor Ericsson seems to imply in his dismissive comment. Christianity has always carried within itself its own suicidal *passage à l'acte*, which lies at the very heart of the salvation faith promises. When Toller, despairing because he cannot bomb the church because Mary is in it, turns to "at least" self-destruction, he does it as a suffering lamb of God, as Jesus on the cross, as he wraps the barbed wire around his body and pours the "cup of poison," the Drano. But Toller's script has already been written for him and he merely acts it out, suggesting that there is no *passage à l'acte* here, though I will return to that question. Toller predominantly remains stuck in what Walter Benjamin thought of as the heaviness of guilt and myth, unmovable and eternal law, sacrifice ("Critique"); Toller's fate is Christian. But it is not only that; this is not simply Christian masochism. He had planned something more collective, so to speak, something unregulated, unscripted, that would erupt as "divine violence." Instead, he is forced to "diminish" this instance and turn it on himself alone. An element of live, unformed divine violence has nevertheless risen to the surface. Repressed lethality in Christianity, one might say, is symptomatic in Communion (hence the latter's pervasive appearances in the film), that posttraumatic consolation in blood and flesh and symbol of the Christian social bond whose origins tend to be forgotten. Repressed within Christianity's suicidal heart is this deeper repression of an even more original divine violence ("Critique" 249), to use again Benjamin's term, to which I will return below. Toller's rage at a corrupted Christianity seems to open up access to a deeper origin, a purer messianic intensity.

Returning to *Winter Light* with *First Reformed* in mind enables one to experience consciously the poignancy and precarity that lie at the heart of the Communion ritual. The ritual repeats connection and bonding while it also, post-traumatically, opens the wound again and again. What at first seems overbearing, heavy, and patriarchal in Pastor Ericsson's enactment of it is, in *First Reformed*, revealed as precarious, broken, and corrupted in the extreme, releasing a messianic force that appears in our era, depressingly, as rusty fencing and Drano. By returning to *Winter Light*'s heavy symbols and the black-and-white clarity of the age-old ritual objects through a viewing of *First Reformed*, the sense of oppressive and dominant tradition in the first is undermined and potentially transformed (this, too, functioning as a dialectical image) even as it is faced with a potential catastrophic liquefaction. Toller's agency doubles down on its own Christian dogmatism, its own mythical, that is, hegemonic, force. While early on we watch him enacting the Communion ritual, he asks in voiceover, "What is the only comfort in life and death? That I, with body and soul, both in life and death, am not my own, but belong unto my faithful Savior Jesus Christ, who with his precious blood [. . .]." This giving of one's own body, its flesh and blood, and one's own soul, Toller intimates, is the essence of both Communion and communication, and both lie at the heart of the religious social bond. Perhaps, paradoxically, breaking and commingling are to bind the community. But what happens when this bond has become either too liquid (Toller's suicidal alcoholism) or mute, sticky, overfed, dulled, undead? In a voiceover to the same Communion scene, Toller writes and reads from his journal: "This journal is a way of speaking, of communication from one to the other," and what is communicated is a recording of the everyday ("give us our daily bread"); both are a form of prayer, a form of eating and feeding, of sustenance, a giving of oneself. The language of God, writes Benjamin, communicates communication itself ("On Language" 63), giving of the self, which we no longer know how to do. *First Reformed* ends with a Toller who wants literally to "give" his flesh and blood, bloody body fragments, to the parishioners, to mix it with their flesh and blood, all commingling in a final devastation—or is it salvation? Throughout the film, the relationships between meaningful action, Communion, and communication (forming the basic structure of the social bond) are close to nonexistent, savage and glib, breaking and feeding, conflated with consumption, cannibalism, and endless waste. Moreover, were the community of Abundant Life actually to blow up, we get the sense that no one would actually care much, even as, simultaneously, the black shiny SUVs arriving for the Reconsecration are clear indicators of the correlated obsession of our era: security.

These implicit and interwoven references to breakage, liquefaction, consumption, and communication also include another, even more latent, trope in the film. During a first meeting between Toller and Reverend Jeffers in which they discuss the need to fix the organ for the Reconsecration, Jeffers tells a tired Martin Luther joke concerning the hymn, "A Mighty Fortress Is Our God": "Did you know that Martin Luther wrote that in an outhouse?" He then imitates the hymn's first line, sung as if he were straining on the toilet. Toller's response, after a polite chuckle, is "I think every seminarian knows that one." "Oh man, I cannot get that image out of my mind," Jeffers drags it out, "I mean, whenever I see that song going on, I can look around the congregation and I know everyone is thinking the same thing." The conversation ends on the note that Toller should spend more time away from "the souvenir shop" (that is, First Reformed Church) and put some variety into his life/diet. The constipation theme persists in the following scene, in which Toller has lunch with Esther in the Abundant Life cafeteria. Esther is overbearing, invasive, suffocating in her supposed care of Toller, worrying about his lack of appetite, offering unwanted maternal eyes. With her greedy "caring," she is the perfect embodiment of the megachurch that stuffs its children with too much of everything. In a Lars von Trier–like shot, they sit facing one another, and we see them both from the side, their silhouettes against the backdrop of a wall that has Gospel verses printed on it in a large font. The passage they sit in front of reads, ". . . one place and shared everything they had. They sold their property and possessions and shared the money with those in need. They worshiped together at the Temple each day and met in homes for the . . . Supper . . . shared meals with great joy . . ." Their bodies hide much of the rest. The text describes daily hours of learning and sharing of resources of the early Christian period that contrasts sharply with the dystopian-utopian megachurch, filled generally with healthy-looking, though emotionally vacant, brawny teenagers, and a pervasive emotional constipation embodied by Jeffers, the "counselors" who lead group sessions, and at first even Toller.

In a later scene, Toller sits in on a youth group rap session in which he responds to one girl's voiced anxieties about the emotional state of her father who has been unable to find work. Toller is asked to respond, and he begins by saying that Jesus stood for the poor, not for the prosperous whose faith, material wealth, and prospects for salvation turbocharge one another (though he doesn't put it this way). He is immediately shut down by another of the teenagers, almost, as Toller later tells Jeffers, "as if I had taken a shit on the American flag." Before that, though, and following his lunch with Esther, we see Toller walk into his own church's parish toilet with Drano and toilet plunger and get to work unclogging the toilet. "Discernment intersects with Christian life at every moment," Toller writes-reads.[6] When the fecal clog dislodges, the voiceover achieves its insight. "Discernment": analysis, sorting out. And as he pours Drano down the toilet in a finale we hear: "Listening and waiting for God's wish what action must be taken."

Action, Acting Out, Passage à l'acte

What kind of action—in this world both overfed and clogged with waste, as oblivious humans stand stupidly by—is being suggested here? There is the Benjaminian "attentiveness" of discernment, but this is merely preparing the ground. We can only begin to see the contours of action. The Drano obviously links this moment to the spectacular murder-suicide Toller plans at the end.

Toller is named for Ernst Toller, a German Jewish Expressionist playwright who, as a soldier in wwi, suffered a mental collapse. After the war, he served as the president of the Bavarian Soviet Republic and then led its army, which offered violent resistance to the German government in Berlin. For this he served five years in prison. He died in 1939 by suicide in New York, where he had lived in exile from Nazi Germany.[7] Ernst Toller's biography, with its reference to violent resistance, brings to mind yet another cinematic influence on *First Reformed,* namely Steve McQueen's film *Hunger* (2008), related to *First Reformed* thematically and tropologically. Both films might also indirectly invoke the story "The Hunger Artist" by Kafka, who, like *First Reformed*'s Toller, cannot accept collectively organized food, feeding habits, or consumption, and dies of hunger. Schrader's Toller is repulsed by the megachurch, and everything it stands for, that wants to feed him (this explains his verbal assault on Esther). Both films ruminate on the question of action, especially violent action. In *Hunger,* Bobby Sands, leader of the ira hunger strike in Maze Prison in 1981, claims that political violence becomes inexorable under certain conditions: when a foal breaks its leg, he says, and recovery is impossible, putting it out of its misery requires shooting it; standing by and doing nothing is not an option. *Hunger* starts off with a fecal attack by the political prisoners on the prison authorities in their "no wash protest," in which they smear the walls and themselves with human waste. Toller's metaphor, perhaps even his symptom, for action is dissolving the clog in the toilet, which stands for the contemporary social bond, a clog of excrement, that he will attempt to plunge, dissolve (with Drano), and flush.

The toilet flush is a nice metaphor for the *passage à l'acte,* defined by Lacan as a subject abruptly and radically leaving the (symbolic) "scene" (111), the scene of social interpersonal relationships—in other words, the social bond. "Leaving" involves a sudden act that puts an end to verbalization, discourse, and possibly prayer; it is extreme and usually violent. Lacan's visualization of the *passage à l'acte* is helpful for understanding it: he references Freud's case of the "homosexual woman" who throws herself suicidally onto the railway tracks when she encounters the disapproving gaze of her father, who sees her walking with her female companion. Lacan claims that one of the necessary conditions for the *passage à l'acte*—a "letting oneself drop" (111) *out of* the scene—to take place is a moment of "supreme embarrassment," a mortification extreme enough to trigger a radical physical movement and self-disappearance. The *passage à l'acte* is categorically different from acting out, which does not involve a total exit from the scene and, even though it rejects verbal communication in the moment, is still a form of symbolic communication. In *First Reformed* Toller and Mary engage in an extraordinary acting-out session when they enact their miracle of levitation to conquer Mary's anxiety. Their levitation does not leave the scene; in fact, it presents as a moment of the most intense experience and communication, even though, already here, in the shape of Toller moving the curtain of Mary's hair away from himself, he seems desperate to leave the scene. The later murder-suicide act via suicide vest certainly would be leaving the scene; it is open to debate where the end actually falls.

We can imagine situations where a passing out of the symbolic and social networks and into violent and dissolving action takes place (first instances of suicidal terrorism, such as American school shootings and Freud's patient). I would add another famous one, visually striking, which continues to fascinate: Ulrike Meinhof, cooriginator of the German Baader-Meinhof group, leaving the scene (*untertauchen* in German, "submerging") when she aided in Andreas Baader's escape from prison when the two were allowed to meet for an "interview" at the Berlin *Zentralinstitut* in 1970. On an impulse and in a split-second decision, Meinhof followed Baader's climb out the window to disappear underground, leaving behind her life as *engagé* journalist, activist, and mother ("Ulrike"). The *passage à l'acte* violently tears open symbolic textures and produces terror. Ironically, however, the instances I have just listed have already been coopted, scripted. School shootings occur regularly, we can list them like a rosary. Meinhof's leap out of the window has become an icon of cool. We can consider such events to be instances of a *passage à l'acte* given that they involve a "fall" or a "drop" out of the networks of social meaning and visibility, tearing a hole as they do so. Freud's "homosexual woman" dropped herself onto the railroad tracks; when Meinhof made her decision, she "dropped" out of the window. Lacan makes clear that this "being dropped is the essential correlate of the *passage à l'acte*." And thus, "[i]t is then that, from where he is—namely the locus of the stage where alone, as a fundamentally historicized subject, he is able to maintain himself in his status of subject—he rushes and topples off the stage, out of the scene" (115). Schrader's predecessor films similarly depict such falls or drops: at the end of Bresson's *Diary of a Country Priest*, the priest dies and literally falls out of the scene, before the camera slides toward and focuses on the (empty) crucifix; in *First Reformed*, at the moment that Mary appears in the doorway, Toller drops the glass of Drano. But Schrader then does something interesting: in a moment of irresolvable ambiguity, he allows for a visualization to transform Toller's *passage à l'acte*, or passage-to-death, into an ecstatic affirmation of life. Of course, this, too, has been scripted, lies at the heart of the great Script, the gospels themselves. I wonder, though, whether this affirmation of life can't be read in other ways, too.

"Life"

What makes *First Reformed* a successful work of art in addition to being a religious meditation—and possible terrorist manifesto—is that, to speak with Heidegger, it folds the viewing subject into the ontological precarity that takes over Toller's existence following his meeting with Michael, which also brings to the surface again the senseless loss of his own son in Iraq. The ontological interpellation is enhanced aesthetically by the purple sky shot at the superfund site, where the beauty and serenity of the first part of the levitation scene is smashed. At night, Toller, "in the Garden," gathers together at this moment his era's catastrophic mode of being in the world: the earth is dying, while the purple sky reflects this destruction, mixing sky blue with blood red; Toller is dying, urinating blood; he is torn apart by his memory and despair and is awake, though the gods "have fled" (Heidegger, "What" 91).[8] This shot in this location is the gathering point where Toller decides to pass to the violent act. Toller writes-reads, "Every act of preservation is also an act of creation." Bombing the church is breaking the bread, bleeding the lamb, for the sake of salvation. Heidegger claims that through "building" comes "caring" (for earth, sky, humans, and divinities) and "preserving." But "building," like founding acts in general, implies violence ("breaking ground," "tilling the soil," and so on).

The planned church scene (at this point only a fantasy on the part of the viewer, who knows what to expect) can be read in an entirely Christian, as well as Heideggerian, way: breakage and bleeding inside the church for the sake of salvation. "Reconsecration" will build faith and salvation in the same way that to cultivate the soil, the earth must be broken open, plowed, then cared for. Breakage and bleeding of the people collected in the church can be seen as a necessary act for shaking awake the oblivious for the sake of preserving the earth.

A non-Christian but messianic reading of the film's violence that may have even more relevance are moments in the Benjamin of 1938–1940, in his writings about history and messianism. A context similar to the one in which Benjamin formed and formulated his "theological" thinking calls on us as well: the rise of fascism. Benjamin's concept of divine violence, however, was formed earlier, in his famous "Critique of Violence" of 1921, addressed to Carl Schmitt's far-right theorization of "political theology" that produced the legal theory for Hitler's movement and party to accede legally to dictatorship. Both Benjamin and Schmitt attempted to reconceive "life" as distinct from and in excess of "mere life" (Benjamin, "Critique" 251; Schmitt, *Concept* 78). Both wrote from within a dismal context of clogged possibilities and both entangled themselves in thinking about renewal and regenerative social and political life and action—in their case, in the Weimar Republic—Schmitt to found a new living order and Benjamin to smash the inertia of conditions that prepared the ground for fascism. Schmitt's thinking was foundational and Benjamin's was anarcho-messianic. While Schmitt theorized the state of exception for the dictator who would suspend constitutional law in order to instate a new but not entirely unknown order, Benjamin's divine violence would transform the sclerotic structures of the law as we know it, that mythical system of obligation and domination, in an emancipatory and as of yet unfathomable direction. In other words, Benjamin's divine violence would demand a dropping out of the scene entirely. Both Schmitt and Benjamin would tear the world open to something radically different. While for Schmitt the exceptional dictator would be the medium to new (but imaginable) life, for Benjamin divine violence was linked to categorical exceptionality. Both would be positing an emergent new social bond, but for Schmitt the emergency was of the dictator's newfound decisionism (*Dezisionismus*). Benjaminian divine violence is a wiping clean of the slate, a smashing of the very conditions for the scene of this fascistic production of new life on the European stage.

First Reformed works with a counterimage to the images of a scene in which the only possible political act that would spit in the face of the order of turbocapitalism, ecological disaster, and so on, would be blowing up the church and/or drinking Drano. That counterimage takes the shape of a hole in the ground connected to a verbal description of fear and courage, the relic of the Underground Railroad. The question is, can this image and its historical significance ever translate into the present era? The other dominant scenario of *First Reformed,* closer to our own scene, is the one that bears similarities to Benjamin's 1940 claustrophobic view of his own historical context, where catastrophe is the order of the day: "that things go on *status quo,*" he writes in his "Central Park," "*is* the catastrophe" (184). His insight (in his Thesis VIII of the "Theses on the Philosophy of History"): "[T]he tradition of the oppressed teaches us that the 'state of emergency' in which we live is not the exception but the rule. We must attain to a conception of history that is in keeping with this insight" (257).

The scene is catastrophic also from a Heideggerian point of view. Our era is the era in which things, places, other lives have all become alienated: *Gestell* (see Heidegger, "Question"). In Abundant Life things and beings are neither distant nor near, just sickeningly all the same and stockpiled—human life flat, identical, and meaningless. What will *not* happen, what can no longer happen, is Heideggerian "authenticity," the possibility of building a meaningful way of being in the world by way of the claims that time (past and future) makes on us and by way of our active relationships to other beings. In explaining authenticity (*Eigentlichkeit*) Heidegger constructs the term *Jemeinigkeit* (*Sein* 43). Perhaps one of the most untranslatable of Heidegger's word-creations, it suggests ways in which "self" is created *not* as enduring essence, but by establishing "belonging" through movements, steps taken ("je"), actively, through time and space, each step a moment of self-possession that never endures as such. Such an experience of self would be "authentic," whereas "inauthentic" is the perverted and alienated capitalistic modality of possessiveness and property. In the following quote, imagine the "bridge" as the self that strives to belong to itself in time and space and by relating to and drawing in other beings:

> *The bridge swings over the stream "with ease and power." It does not just connect banks that are already there. The banks emerge as banks only as the bridge crosses the stream. The bridge designedly*

> *causes them to lie across from each other. [. . .] It brings stream*
> *and bank and land into each other's neighborhood. The bridge*
> gathers *the earth as landscape around the stream. [. . .] The*
> *bridge* gathers *to itself, in its* own way, *earth and sky, divinities*
> *and mortals. ("Building" 152–53)*

Toller's final acts are preceded by what looks and sounds like such a moment of "gathering," as in the "Garden" moment under the purple sky. But such a pathetic gathering has of yet little persuasive power, and Heidegger's phenomenology cannot help us much (yet) in terms of thinking of the very possibility of a *political* act that escapes all of us. We have no idea about how to envision political action when the only disrupting explosiveness around us are the AR-15s shooting up schools and the attempts by far-right militias to lynch people of color and instate a dictator. Toller makes a decision toward apocalypticism, even messianism, and even at this moment of self-destructive violence in the film one may experience a massive injection of life. But does this injection transcend traditional Christian dogma? What are the sorts of actions that Schrader allows one to imagine? Arguably he presents Benjaminian divine violence as justified, even appropriate in our historical context. Early on, Michael compares his own acts to those of the early Christian martyrs, and the roaring Toller in his blood-stained white cassock is an enraged prophet. Both Michael and Toller commit suicide, but both had planned something different. *First Reformed* does not end like Bresson's *Diary of a Country Priest*, where the priest falls out of the picture, dead, the camera ending up with a shot of the empty cross, even though Toller is indeed in the middle of a radical *passage à l'acte*. What we get instead is the ending of Bresson's *Pickpocket* and Dreyer's *Ordet*. At the very end of *Pickpocket*, after a lifetime of calculated action, Michel, during his prison visit with Jeanne, in a radical transformation suddenly breaks into an ecstatic kiss with her; *Ordet* ends with a similar kiss and an ecstatic affirmation of life, following Inger's (literal) resurrection. *First Reformed* ends with a soul-churning kinetic lunge on the part of the camera when Toller suddenly sees Mary standing in the doorway, calling out "Ernst!" (indicating that this is a vision, as she never calls him by that name). They rush toward each other and kiss as the camera turns and turns around them, after having been quite still for the entire film. Schrader combines here the "falling away" of the apocalyptic *passage à l'acte* (murder, suicide, or both) as the glass of Drano falls out of Toller's hand with the ecstatic ending of *Ordet* and *Pickpocket*: life and death both. We know that, despite the vision,

Toller "in reality" "falls out of the scene"; *still*, that "fall" tumultuously and ecstatically lights up. What kind of final passage is this?

Passage à l'acte: *What Sorts of Acts?*

It is helpful to view Toller's catastrophic acts against the claustrophobia-inducing image of the shiny black suvs arriving at First Reformed Church, an image that suggests the totalizing and apparently unmovable conjunction of state, religion, and capital. The three major forces that the film displays are the all-devouring and mind-numbing savagery of the power of capital, the destitution of subjective agency, and the destruction of nature. I have focused on tropes of breakage, on representations of transformation (from chatter to prayer, from traumatized muteness to expression, from apathy to rage), on ecstatic negation (the final scene), and on Toller's particular *passage à l'acte* and its possible significance. All conjure for me a set of Benjaminian ideas that illuminate what may be the significance of Toller's *passage à l'acte*. These are ideas that came into ever sharper focus for Benjamin as fascism and Nazism were closing in on him: most dramatically, in his "Theses on the Philosophy of History," composed in 1940.[9] And these ideas may speak to us today as well. Benjaminian "theology" and messianism, in the shape of his life-long preoccupation with "origins," "dialectical images," and allegory, describe the nature of acts—human, messianic, and political—that harshly interrupt and potentially transform in some way the inert sameness of things-as-they-are, as well as impoverished and scripted ideas of what official history allows one to imagine as far as modes of being are concerned. While Benjamin attacks "historicism" as a "positive" sequential narrative of "how it actually was" in Thesis VI ("Theses" 255), his own conception of how the "historical materialist" should interact with history if they wish to rescue something that is truly living (what he calls "happiness," as we will see) demands "blasting," an explosive baring of "origin."

I turn to Benjamin's esoteric "Theological-Political Fragment" to look at the relationship between theological and political acts as Benjamin sees it; to his concept of the "dialectical image" in his *Passagenwerk* [*Arcades Project*] as a set of instructions for performing a reading of history that opens up space for action; and to a brief description of the "mortificatory," strangely expiatory acts of the allegorist who identifies with the refuse of history, its waste matter. The "acts" I attempt to bring to the surface here are intimately related and all in some way include catastrophic acts operating in different but parallel dimensions: the ontological, spiritual, political, and psychoanalytic.

In Benjamin's thinking, *theology* is a force that can open profane history up to categorical revolutionary change. It does not directly make change but is the name of the force behind the political and emancipatory principle as such, the redemptive lightning bolt that creates the caesura for political acts as such. Its force is messianic: "the Messiah himself completes all history," he writes. Benjamin's Messiah's act of "completion," for which humanity must set the stage, would seem to correlate with a collective *passage à l'acte*.[10] It never correlates with religious dogma, cannot be formalized by religious institutions, and, crucially, eschews any sort of theocracy: "[T]he secular order cannot be built on the idea of the Divine Kingdom, and theocracy has no political, but only a religious meaning" ("Theological" 305). Thus, Benjamin's theology is categorically distinct from all literalist political theology, such as that of fundamentalist evangelism.

Profane history can never bring about the "Messianic Kingdom," cannot "become" itself messianic; nor can the former ever lead into the latter. Instead, for Benjamin, the messianic is a force that blasts "the continuum of history" open, eschewing all utopian content but unleashing the sheer potential for something transformed and new. The two registers, the profane and the messianic, affect each other indirectly. Moments of intense "happiness," appearing on the scene at utterly unplanned instances of *Jetztzeit* ("now-time"), clear the space for the theological intensity, while religion, for Benjamin, obscures and belies messianic intensity because it is always on the side of mythical eternity. Redemption in Benjamin is defined precisely by its corrosion and breakdown of myth. Without a messiah (utterly alien, unhistorical intensity), there can be no change, no new event: "Only the Messiah himself completes all history, in the sense that he alone redeems, completes, creates its relation to the messianic" ("Theological" 305). Historical change depends on a messianic interruption of things-as-we-know-them, and a historical human being can both echo and open up space for the messianic call. Moments of "happiness," which burst through the mythical ordering of institutions, and the messianic bring each other into being. Or one might put it this way: theology is the revolutionary force that cannot be codified; at any moment the messiah can appear. As Benjamin writes in Thesis XVIIIB of his "Theses on the Philosophy of History," "[T]he future did not, however, turn into a homogeneous and empty time for the Jews [who were not allowed to look into the future]. For in it every second was the narrow gate, through which the Messiah could enter" (264). The flame of theology, the intensity the messianic carries, is destructive and constitutes the essential violence of the divine in Benjamin's thinking. The Messiah's act of throwing religion into disarray *is* theology, and theology thus conceived *is* a political act insofar as it smashes mythical might and operates in parallel with human happiness.[11]

If theology shatters, interrupts, destructively breaks open, how can the Messiah also actively "redeem and complete history," as Benjamin puts it in the "Theological-Political Fragment"? Perhaps he can because what is destructive upon the historical realm inversely also throws, instantaneously, the potential for something new and living into a particular historical constellation. A crisis moment in history flashes up as a moment both catastrophic and potentially redemptive. When, in the view of the dweller in history thirsty for rescue, a historical moment flashes up in an instant of crisis and insight simultaneously, an intimation of and a potential for changing course opens up as well. The apocalyptic "end" that is the messianic is an absolute caesura that shatters myth, mythical violence, and empty prattle. A particular moment in history can set the stage for the messiah to appear; the "end" of history would be the "consummate" messianic act. Catastrophe and human suffering themselves provide the openings, the messianic portals for redemption.

Neither the "Messianic Kingdom" nor "happiness" can be codified or institutionalized or made to endure. Consequently, for Benjamin, nature is messianic and is so in its very transience, its coming and going: "The spiritual *restitutio in integrum*, which introduces immortality, corresponds to a worldly restitution that leads to the eternity of downfall, and the rhythm of this eternally transient worldly existence, transient in its totality, in its spatial but also in its temporal totality, the rhythm of messianic nature, is happiness" ("Theological" 306). Consequently, the destruction of nature opens up the possibility for an everlasting hell.

I read Schrader's "consummation" of Dreyer's *Ordet* at the end of *First Reformed* along the lines of Benjamin's understanding of messianic intensity as destructive and redemptive simultaneously. It is as if the inertia and looping sameness of the Reconsecration ceremony in the church next door is blasted open by the ecstatic kiss, around which the camera, for the first time, actively joins the scene by moving, thus coming alive. Even as Toller has, in the profane order, abruptly dropped out of the scene in a suicidal *passage à l'acte*, reading the scene in conjunction with Benjamin's "Theological-Political Fragment" makes a case for resurrecting a Benjaminian understanding of theology as an ontological, maybe even political, tool.

In Convolute N of his *Arcades Project* Benjamin ruminates on methods of perceiving and recording history[12] that would instantaneously not only "resurrect" in images and in writing discarded objects and the promise they formerly held but also reveal "in a flash" what has gone wrong in their history (insofar as they are discarded, dead) and in history in general (*Arcades* 473 N9, 4). For this work Benjamin conceives of the construction of "dialectical images": "The dialectical image is an image that emerges suddenly, in a flash. What has been is to be held fast—as an image flashing up in the now of its recognizability. The rescue that is carried out by these means—and only by these—can operate solely for the sake of what in the next moment is already irretrievably lost" (473 N9, 7). We are, in Schrader's film, watching how First Reformed Church appears in its last moments of life, before being devoured by Abundant Life; in the film's very first shot, the church, and what it stands for, appears as if it is about to blast apart. In Benjamin's theory, the momentary resurrection of an image, the positive moment, is "lost" when, in the montage with and against another image, the two images act corrosively and dissonantly one upon the other. This corrosion, however, is preceded by a momentary insight that the clash has produced. Such moments in the historian's gaze at history's artifacts—be they images or objects—break open the seemingly linear moment of history by juxtaposing images torn out of their own chronologically linear sequences. The effect is a sudden caesura, a destruction of context that nevertheless produces a flash of insight: "To thinking belongs the movement as well as the arrest of thoughts. Where thinking comes to a standstill in a constellation saturated with tensions—there the dialectical image appears. It is the caesura in the movement of thought" (475 N10a, 3).

Benjamin's act of creating dialectical images—the task, for him, of the historian, the visual artist, the educator—are acts of profane revelation and insight. At work are simultaneity of rescue, insight, and loss, a rhythm of revelation and loss that reproduces nature's transience, the rhythm of natural history. It is the potential political effect of the intellectual, even emotional, dissonance that makes the process of the montage of the dialectical image into a potentially redemptive act. How can such moments be invoked? They occur in ordinary, "profane" moments of seeing; everywhere there could open up a tiny portal through which the messiah will come. Benjamin calls such moments "presence of mind as a political category" (477 N12a, 1).

In *First Reformed*, a good example of a dialectical image is the productive friction between the biblical image of Joseph preserved in the well against his envious and murderous brothers, enabling him to forgive, teach, and in turn transform them for the sake of the future.[13] A second image, brought into conjunction with the first, is Toller's son Joseph, simply blasted to bits in Iraq, essentially for nothing but a lie. The friction between the two produces insight about former hopes and their failures. It shows us what we have lost.[14]

Benjamin: Natural History and Allegory

First Reformed's purple sky scene is affecting in a number of ways: the shot is a montage that is thick with biblical reference: Gethsemane and death, Eden, life and loss, while the sun is rising (the coming and going of nature). I associate with it Benjamin's understanding of natural history (defined by "transience" and enframed by theology, as we saw), which subtends the vision of the allegorist both in Benjamin's book on the baroque *Trauerspiel* (*The Origin of German Tragic Drama*) and in the massive history of nineteenth-century Paris in his *Passagenwerk*. The shot itself, the dark corroded ruins of ships and barges against the purple sky of the rising sun, is a manifestation of natural history as described in the *Trauerspiel* book: "The word 'history' stands written on the countenance of nature in the characters of transience. The allegorical physiognomy of the nature-history [. . .] is present in reality in the form of the ruin. In the ruin history has physically merged into the setting" (*Origin* 177).

In Benjamin's understanding, the allegorist does his cultural and historical work by undoing the schizoid relegation of historical artifacts to the garbage bins of history once their function and monetary value have been devoured and exhausted. The allegorist (as historian and as artist) rescues the broken and discarded objects of history by opening and raising them up (like the Eucharist), by liberating the time, labor, and care they contain as opposed to delivering them up to a dissociated forgetting. At the same time, the allegorist is not a symbolist; in other words, he sees nature not as static and essential, but as structured by transience, that is, a coming-and-going, life and death drives.

In our own time, we may see the superimposition of history on nature as a sort of death's head (Benjamin often describes allegorical activity as imprinted with a death's head), promising, with its supposed "progress" of technology and capitalism, to become ever more savage, to blot nature out entirely and to continue reducing human agency and acts to merely acquiescing to be devoured by digital code ("allowing 'cookies,'" for example) and to suicide.

Benjamin's reader of natural history breaks open symbolic aspirations to eternity, convenient historical telos-driven narratives, empty incessant chatter, and, for us, the deadening glue of digital code and supposed connectivity. His allegorist works by fragmenting these frozen, fossilized, and dissociated falsifications of meaning ("myth," for Benjamin) and releasing (allowing for "completion," according to the "Theological-Political Fragment" [305]) the bits and pieces of life and "origin" suppressed and undead in language and redeeming them. Benjamin's allegorist is, like his messiah, bound to origin: in the *Trauerspiel* book, "origin" is the force that precedes the "individual," always necessarily egotistical and deluded.[15] "Origin" is its own withdrawal, negativity as such, abyss, the flame under the subject, always necessarily destitute and driven. *"Ursprung ist das Ziel,"* Benjamin writes, quoting Karl Kraus, "origin is the end" ("Theses" 261). In this way, the allegorist is also tied, by way of this binding, to the drives and to the unconscious. We are in danger of losing contact with both. The allegorist strips the layers of history and reads them, digging up and releasing (at least partially) unconscious material that it is then up to the rest of us to see and take in, enfolding it and hopefully enriching the bonds between us, before this meaning, these bits of origin, disappear again. Such must be our acts. These are acts that would attempt to recover the power and depth of the negative. Toller tries, but fails: he remains glued to the Christian script, and his death by Drano is pitiful, though his act can tell us what our acts must be. But where? In psychoanalysis, in our relationships with children, students, the coming generation, and, finally, in the survival and resurrection of the humanities and students' exposure to history, to ways of reading history, to the unconscious dimensions of word and image, and to recovery of the power of the negative. Without them, we are lost.

ELIZABETH STEWART is an associate professor of English at Yeshiva University, the author of *Catastrophe and Survival: Walter Benjamin and Psychoanalysis* (Continuum, 2010), and translator and editor of *Lacan in the German-Speaking World* (State University of New York Press, 2004). She is currently working on a book on intergenerational relations from a psychoanalytic and philosophical perspective in German society and culture during the twentieth century, with a focus on the postwar period. She is a contributor to *Understanding Lacan, Understanding Modernism*, edited by Thomas Waller, which will appear in 2024 (Bloomsbury), and has contributed chapters to several edited volumes.

Notes

1   This is Schrader's partial homage to Carl Theodor Dreyer's *Ordet* (1955), which realizes, in an equally measured yet persuasive way, a resurrection, leading to that film's ecstatic ending.

2   It could be an apt echo of Walter Benjamin's Angel of History: "A

Klee painting named 'Angelus Novus' shows an angel looking as though he is about to move away from something he is fixedly contemplating. His eyes are staring, his mouth is open, his wings are spread. This is how one pictures the angel of history. His face is turned toward the past. Where we perceive a chain of events, he sees one single catastrophe which keeps piling wreckage and hurls it in front of his feet" ("Theses" 257).

3   The quotation of *Night of the Hunter* here is brilliant: "It's a hard world for little things," says Rachel (Lillian Gish) in that film, who embodies "good" vs. the evil of Pastor Powell, when she witnesses an owl pouncing on a rabbit in the night scene outside where the predatory serial killer and religious fanatic Pastor Powell is hovering and singing this same hymn.

4   Possible acknowledgment of the allusion to *Winter Light* is Toller's cough during the ritual, a cough that is entirely gratuitous in *First Reformed*; Pastor Ericsson in *Winter Light*, however, is coming down with the flu, coughs throughout the morning, and his illness is a theme of conversation.

5   The "Throne of Mercy" is the representation in Western Christian art of God the Father seated and holding the (smaller) dead or dying Christ between his legs.

6   Here he echoes, in my mind, what Benjamin called in his essay on Kafka "attentiveness," often misquoted as "attentiveness to the creaturely." What Benjamin actually writes is "'the natural prayer of the soul': attentiveness. And in this attentiveness he included all living creatures, as saints include them in their prayers, to the creaturely" ("Franz" 143).

7   The figure of the historical Toller leads me to associate him (and also Schrader's Toller) with the figure of John Brown, the leader of his abolitionist army against the slavers, and all three figures with Kleist's Michael Kohlhaas, who cannot find justice for the mistreatment and starvation of his black horses by the Junkers and sets half of the German states on fire.

8   A world from which the gods have fled is the technologized world in which we no longer know how to communicate with each other or the gods: "Not only have the gods and the god fled, but the divine radiance has become extinguished in the world's history. The time of the world's night is the destitute time, because it becomes ever more destitute. It has already grown so destitute, it can no longer discern the default of God as a default" (Heidegger, "What" 91).

9   Tragically, of course, 1940 was also the year of Benjamin's suicide.

10   Such as, for example, the outbreaks of Jewish messianism led by Sabbatai Z'vi following the Khmelnitsky pogroms. See Scholem's *Sabbatai Zevi*.

11   It also rises to the surface in the martyr-kings in the *Trauerspiel*, as those figures begin to leak something that is corrosive to symbolic wholeness. The martyr is the negative version of "happiness," however, and carries corrosive force.

12   In this work, Benjamin planned a massive history of industrial and capitalist modernity perceived through the lens of the "lives," so to speak, of the microcosmic cultural and industrial objects of nineteenth-century Paris.

13   The image brings with it the image of slaves being hidden and preserved in the Underground Railroad as well as images of early Christian resistance in the catacombs.

14   Other examples of moments that could be conceived of as dialectical images are the image of the nineteenth-century Underground Railroad cellar (image of escape, preservation, future) and the twenty-first-century suicide vest (immediate annihilation, no future).

15   It is difficult not to also see Schelling's influence on Benjamin here, the Schelling of the *Weltalter* (1813) where he describes God as half mad, torn between himself as the churning "abyss," always in motion, always in change, and himself as the God of creation. Matter emerges out of this abyss of pure potentiality, spins outward from the vortex, is thrown, spewn out, and in its subsequent self-imposed fixity, struggling to hold itself fast, it invariably obscures its own origin: "In a series from time immemorial, each era has always obscured its predecessor," Schelling writes (121). Matter wants to endure, and thus creation leads to fixity, to myth, and to ossification and falsity. To reveal the origin as endless flux, potentiality, time itself, the various strata must be parsed and mortified: read. While the abyss is true and potentiality is constant, a will to live repeats and signifies itself insistently—but, unavoidably, in its quest for eternity, it ossifies, thus also becoming its own death drive. Thus, God is torn between the two drives: the functioning of the psyche itself.

Works Cited

Benjamin, Walter. *The Arcades Project.* Trans. Howard Eiland and Kevin McLaughlin. Cambridge, MA: Harvard UP, 1999.

——————. "Central Park." *Selected Writings, 1938–1940.* Vol. 4. Ed. Michael W. Jennings, Marcus Bullock, Howard Eiland, and Gary Smith. 4 vols. Cambridge, MA: Harvard UP, 2003. 161–99.

——————. "Critique of Violence." *Selected Writings, 1913–1926.* Vol. 1. Ed. Marcus Bullock and Michael W. Jennings. 4 vols. Cambridge, MA: Harvard UP, 1996. 236–52.

——————. "Franz Kafka: On the Tenth Anniversary of His Death." *Illuminations* 111–40.

——————. *Illuminations: Essays and Reflections.* Ed. Hannah Arendt. Trans. Harry Zohn. New York: Schocken, 1968.

——————. "On Language as Such and on the Language of Man." *Selected* Vol. 1. 62–75.

——————. *The Origin of German Tragic Drama.* New York: Verso, 2009.

——————. "Theological-Political Fragment." *Selected Writings, 1935–1938.* Vol. 3. Ed. Howard Eiland and Gary Smith. 4 vols. Cambridge, MA: Harvard UP, 1996. 305–6.

——————. "Theses on the Philosophy of History." *Illuminations* 253–64.

The Bible. Authorized King James Version. Oxford: Oxford UP, 1998.

Diary of a Country Priest. Dir. Robert Bresson. Brandon Films, 1951.

First Reformed. Dir. Paul Schrader. A24, 2017.

Heidegger, Martin. "Building Dwelling Thinking." *Poetry* 143–61.

——————. *Poetry, Language, Thought.* Trans. Albert Hofstadter. New York: Harper Colophon, 1975.

——————. "The Question Concerning Technology." *The Question Concerning Technology, and Other Essays.* Trans. William Lovitt. New York: Garland, 1977. 3–35.

——————. *Sein und Zeit.* Tübingen: Max Niemeyer Verlag, 1967.

——————. "What Are Poets For?" *Poetry* 89–142.

Hunger. Dir. Steve McQueen. Film4 Productions, 2008.

Kafka, Franz. *A Hunger Artist and Other Stories.* Oxford: Oxford UP, 2012.

Kleist, Heinrich von. *Michael Kohlhaas (aus einer alten Chronik).* Stuttgart: Ernst Klett Verlag, 1979.

Lacan, Jacques. *"Passage à l'acte* and Acting Out." *Anxiety: The Seminar of Jacques Lacan Book X.* Ed. Jacques-Alain Miller. Trans. A. R. Price. Malden: Polity, 2014. 114–30.

The Night of the Hunter. Dir. Charles Laughton. United Artists, 1955.

Ordet. Dir. Carl Theodor Dreyer. A/S Palladium, 1955.

Pickpocket. Dir. Robert Bresson. New Yorker Films, 1959.

Schelling, Friedrich Wilhelm Joseph von. *Ages of the World* [*Die Weltalter*]. 1813. *The Abyss of Freedom/Ages of the World.* Slavoj Žižek and Friedrich Wilhem Joseph von Schelling. Trans. Judith Norman. Ann Arbor: U of Michigan P, 1997. 105–82.

Schmitt, Carl. *Concept of the Political.* Trans. George Schwab. Chicago: U of Chicago P, 2007.

——————. *Political Theology: Four Chapters on the Concept of Sovereignty.* Trans. George Schwab. Chicago: U of Chicago P, 2005.

Scholem, Gershom Gerhard. *Sabbatai Ṣevi: The Mystical Messiah, 1626–1676.* Trans. R. J. Zwi Werblowsky. Princeton: Princeton UP, 2016.

Schrader, Paul. *Transcendental Style in Film: Ozu, Bresson, Dreyer.* Oakland: U of California P, 2018.

Taxi Driver. Dir. Martin Scorcese. Writ. Paul Schrader. Columbia Pictures, 1976.

"Ulrike and Andreas." *New York Times* 11 May 1975. https://nyti.ms/3JRC4vH.

Winter Light. Dir. Ingmar Bergman. Janus Films, 1963.

ANTHONY C. WEXLER

Pedagogy in Gray: Primo Levi as Teacher

I

*P*rimo Levi, perhaps the most well-known Western witness to the Holocaust, lived with a heightened sense that civilizations were vulnerable. As an inmate in Auschwitz, Levi was immersed in a world in which the "last trace of civilization had vanished," and the experience left him unable to forget Paul Valéry's famous dictum that civilizations, like people, were mortal (*Survival* 171).[1] In the years that followed, the Italian survivor became increasingly aware that a similar sense of vulnerability—if largely unacknowledged—ran through the lives of all modern Europeans, thanks, in large part, to the invention of the atomic bomb. Europeans, Levi claimed in a 1985 essay, lived with an "obscure unease"—a feeling of menace that permeated daily life, but one that they struggled to name.[2] He described how this feeling could activate an "inborn tendency of ours towards the radical" (*Other* 2250): a tendency to see the future as a script that has already been written, one over which we have no control.[3] When faced with such a future, people tend to overlook the middle ground, ignore possible contingencies, and stop asking the question "What is to be done?" In an effort to shield themselves from catastrophe, they invest their hope in prophets and charismatic

Volume 34, Number 3   DOI 10.1215/10407391-10898241

leaders. And wherever such a "delirious handover of responsibility" takes place, Levi warns his readers, we create the conditions for another Auschwitz (*Other* 2250). But making his readers aware of this vulnerability, and the havoc it could wreak on social bonds, was no easy task, and one that became increasingly complex with the passage of time.

Part of the challenge was an effect of time's impact on memory. In the forty years between the end of the war and his presumed suicide in 1987, Levi, the aging survivor, watched as the destruction of Europe's Jewish civilization was being transformed into "a repository of 'lessons' about 'man's inhumanity to man,' a metaphor for victimization in general, a rhetoric for partisan politics, [or] a cinematic backdrop for domestic melodrama" (Rosenfeld, *End* 11). And Levi felt these changes with special intensity when visiting classrooms across Italy to talk with students about the Holocaust—visits, as we will see, that forced him to reckon with the limits of his testimonial project.

How could Levi, a survivor losing control of the events that defined his life, leverage his own experiences to help his young readers "defend" their "souls" when "a similar test should once more loom before us?" (*Drowned* 40). How could he make the young understand the connection between their own personal lives and the survival of their civilization? What kind of pedagogical approach could generate such awareness? This essay attempts to answer these questions. The first half of the essay considers the challenges Levi faced while visiting classrooms across Italy between the late 1960s and the mid-1980s: visits mentioned by Levi's biographers but largely overlooked by scholars. These classroom encounters exposed Levi to the challenges facing not just survivors but Holocaust educators of all stripes, especially as we move farther from the event in time. The second half of the essay considers how Levi responded to these emerging challenges by cultivating a pedagogical approach that encourages young readers to focus on the very thing they most want to forget: the sense of vulnerability—or "essential fragility" as Levi will call it—that leads people, in ways conscious and unconscious, to collude with power and to seek privileges (*Drowned* 69).[4] To do so, I argue, Levi turns to the space that separates the victims from the persecutors, what he calls the "gray zone," and to the figures that inhabit that "zone"—most notably the duplicitous figure of Chaim Rumkowski, a figure who so powerfully embodied this zone. In the process, I hope that the image of Levi as a gifted teacher—as someone deeply interested in, and responsive to, his young readers and students—will come into greater focus.[5]

Levi recognized the power of the classroom, but not exclusively as a force for good in the world.[6] In his last work, *The Drowned and the*

Saved, published less than a year before his death, Levi locates the origins of the Holocaust in the classroom.[7] In a remarkable passage, he describes the Germans who followed Hitler as people who had been "badly reared": they were a group of people, he says, that had all "been subjected to the terrifying miseducation provided for and imposed by the schools created in accordance with the wishes of Hitler and his collaborators" (202). Here, Levi blames the miseducation provided in German schools—as opposed to an innate drive for violence—for preparing a generation to carry out the most heinous of crimes.[8] But if a form of "miseducation" could lead to Auschwitz, then a different form of education could lead people away from intolerance and violence. What such an education might consist of—and this is a topic of ongoing concern for Holocaust educators and others—is much debated and hard to pin down. It was a question that Levi, a survivor who saw memory as a duty, never stopped asking in the years after his liberation. Yet Levi's pedagogical approach—and his role as a teacher more generally—has been routinely overshadowed by other aspects of his identity, and for obvious reasons.

Levi's diverse body of work has shaped—and continues to shape—how generations of readers imagine Auschwitz and the Holocaust more generally. An impressive group of writers and scholars name Levi as their preferred guide to the horror; and he is seen by many as a wise man in possession of important messages for humanity. Since his death in 1987, Levi's reputation has only continued to grow, and the publication of *The Complete Works of Primo Levi* in 2015—a three volume collection featuring an introduction by Toni Morrison—helped solidify his legacy as one of the most important writers of the second half of the twentieth century.[9] Much of the scholarly work on Levi focuses on Levi the witness, Levi the writer, and Levi the chemist. These identities—writer, witness, scientist—have become central categories for thinking about Levi's life and work, and the key terms used by various editors to organize essay collections on his work.[10] Perhaps not surprisingly, far less critical attention has been paid to Levi's career as a teacher, despite the fact that he visited over one hundred and thirty schools between the late 1960s and mid-1980s, and that a strong didactic element runs through much of his work. This didactic element links his science fiction stories that consider the dangers of new technologies to his teacherly essays that explore a diverse group of subjects ranging from the biological need to yawn to the function of the intellectual in Auschwitz (Thomson 29). Moreover, the role of teaching—and scenes of teaching, more specifically—play an important role in a number of his works, including his 1978 novel *The Wrench* and his last work, *The Drowned and the Saved*.

Readers of Levi's first work, *Survival in Auschwitz*, may well remember that some of the most famous scenes in that work are presented under the sign of teaching. In scenes where inmates begin to adapt to life in the camps, they learn to slough off their civilized education and to return to more primitive states. Life in the Lager forced them to unlearn and relearn how to survive in a place governed by absolute irrationality (Rosenfeld, *Double* 57). And for this reason, Alvin Rosenfeld refers to Levi's first work as a "reverse *Erziehungsroman*, a narrative of *mis*education" (57). But other scenes of teaching from that work address the ongoing desire to protect civilization against collapse, to find ways to import a measure of rationality, of culture into an otherwise chaotic environment. Consider, for example, the scene where an inmate named Steinlauf administers a "complete lesson" to Levi on the importance of daily washing, a ritual that must be performed regularly even in the "turbid water of the filthy washbasins" (41). Here, an older inmate instructs his younger counterpart about the importance of moral survival within the degraded universe of the Lager. The younger Levi quickly recognizes that the ritual was part of a larger effort to "save at least the skeleton, the scaffolding, the form of civilization" (*Survival* 41). The individual act of washing—an act that serves no practical purpose within the camp—has collective implications for the survival of civilization.

The most often-quoted scene of teaching from *Survival in Auschwitz* operates along similar lines. In "The Canto of Ulysses" chapter, Levi endeavors to teach Italian to Pikkolo, a young Alsatian inmate. Levi, having received a robust education in the classics, turns to the twenty-sixth canto of Dante's poem as a source text for his first language class in Auschwitz. The lesson takes place as the two men struggle to transport a soup cauldron. The selection of "The Canto of Ulysses" chapter, which deals with the uniquely human quest for knowledge and excellence, speaks to Levi's larger effort to create a point of contact between Dante's literary world and the world of the Lager. And teaching Pikkolo, like the act of washing, becomes part of a larger effort to preserve the scaffolding of civilization: to ensure the transmission of values across time and place, and to impose a measure of control and order on the chaotic universe of the Lager. In this instance, the act of teaching establishes a form of transhistorical continuity that allows Levi to "reestablish a link with the past," and to save "it from oblivion," a process, he says in his last work, that helped to reinforce his identity (*Drowned* 139).[11] The act of teaching, at least in this moment, functions as a form of salvation— "after all," says Victor Brombert, Levi "claims to have 'saved' (*salvato*) a given line on Dante from oblivion" (*In Praise* 116). But this optimistic vision of teaching as a force linking people from radically different cultures into a chain of tradition would be seriously challenged over the course of Levi's life. And that challenge, at least in part, was due to technological innovations and the rise of mass communication.

Levi was powerfully attuned to the impact that these developments would have on the transmission of knowledge and how they would make it increasingly difficult for members of older generations to communicate with their younger counterparts. The French anthropologist Claude Lévi-Strauss took up the issue in an essay that Levi—with the help of his sister—translated into Italian in the early 1980s. In the "Belated Word about the Creative Child," an essay published in *The View from Afar*, Lévi-Strauss offers the following account of the impact of mass communication on the transmission of knowledge: "[Knowledge] no longer filters down slowly from one to the next within a family or a professional milieu but is propagated at disconcerting speed in a horizontal direction and at levels with ruptures between them. Henceforth, each generation will communicate more easily with its members than with the generation that precedes or follows it" (270). According to Lévi-Strauss, mass communication has disrupted the flow of knowledge down through the generations. And this disruption threatens to render obsolete the traditional function of the school, which has long served as "a relay station between past and present." This disruption, says Lévi-Strauss, has turned educators into anthropologists of a "society that is other than the one to which apply the methods they once learned" (271). Levi, who praised this essay in a personal letter to Lévi-Strauss, came to see himself as an anthropologist of sorts, as someone whose words—whose teachings—were not being received by his young readers.[12]

In interviews from the early 1980s, Levi would come to echo the concerns articulated by Lévi-Strauss. Levi describes feeling ashamed in front of the young people with whom he interacted in educational settings. These young people, Levi said, "use calculators with nonchalance" and "learn from television things I never learned," and he came to feel "inferior" to them as a result (*Voice* 230). His struggle to communicate with them pointed toward a larger challenge for someone in his position. If mass communication was making it impossible for the school to act as a "relay station between past and present in a vertical direction," then how could Levi, during his classroom visits, hope to educate these young people about what had taken place? How could he bridge this growing intergenerational chasm? The question would move from the margins to the center of Levi's consciousness between the late 1960s and the mid-1980s, the years during which he was visiting classrooms across Italy. And it is toward those visits that I now want to turn.

II

Levi spent considerable time in classrooms during the last two decades of his life. By the late 1960s, Levi's second book, *The Reawakening*, was already an established text in Italian schools; many of the students he met with would have been familiar with the book's wonderful account of his circuitous trip home from Auschwitz.[13] In these years, Ian Thomson, Levi's most meticulous biographer, says that "talking to the young became Levi's 'third profession' effectively, after chemistry and writing" (322). But when he started visiting with students in the late 1960s, students related to him primarily as a writer and not as a Holocaust survivor; in those days, they were not primarily interested in the content of Levi's testimony.[14] Instead, they wanted to discuss the nature of Nazism in relation to the war in Vietnam and the current American civil-rights movement. Levi, eager to talk with the young, was happy to oblige. Initially, he drew strength from these visits, and he expressed a sense of pride in his ability to reach the young through these classroom visits and his writing. His books were being passed from children to parents, and Levi enjoyed the fact that a whole new demand for his books was being "born from below" (Thomson 322). We know that Levi was an engaging conversationalist with students, the kind of teacher who was able to involve even the quietest students in the discussions. Feruccio Maruffi, a survivor of the Mauthausen camp who accompanied Levi on a number of class visits, was most impressed with Levi's humility: "If a pupil was writing an essay on *Survival in Auschwitz,* Primo would invite him into his house to discuss it with him. Where today could you find such a readily available writer?" (qtd. in Thomson 323). Over the years, however, students would begin to interrogate this "readily available" writer more critically.

In a 1983 interview, Levi describes a scene during a school visit when two brothers questioned him directly about his decision to continue talking about the Holocaust: "Why are you telling us all this stuff, after forty years, after Vietnam, after Stalin's gulag, Korea and all the rest? What for?" (*Voice* 230). The questions left Levi feeling "cornered, on the ropes, trapped in my role as returnee." At that moment, his pedagogical talents and rhetorical skills, his long career of witnessing, seemed useless. Was he simply privileging his own experiences over those of others? Why should he continue to speak about these events when there had been more recent genocides? He told the brothers that he spoke about the events he had experienced first-hand and that if he had lived through different events, he would have discussed those instead.

Students kept asking the same questions, and Levi, in various essays and afterword's, kept responding with the same answers. These students wanted to know why so few Jews escaped, rebelled, or failed to leave Europe sooner. Some of his Catholic students wanted to know why he refused to "forgive" his tormentors, while others, influenced primarily by a series of POW adventure movies, started to filter the facts of the Holocaust through the lens of entertainment (Thomson 323). There were also students who directly challenged the facts of what had taken place. In 1986, for example, the Socialist journalist Carla Perotti asked Levi to meet with her wayward son, Emanuele. The boy turned up at Levi's apartment with doctored photos of Auschwitz that "showed" that the gas chambers were false (488). The boy wanted to know why Levi was lying about what took place, and no amount of information to the contrary could sway the boy. Levi eventually asked the boy to leave, but the experience did little to lift to his mood.[15] According to Thomson, Levi "allowed a spoiled, misguided youth to have a disproportionate influence over him." And from that day on, Levi "completely shuttered his heart to Italy's young—neo-Fascist or otherwise" (488). In the mid-1980s, Levi decided to stop visiting classrooms, but the desire to communicate with the young would play a key role in his last work.

The Drowned and the Saved, a work that reflects repeatedly—almost obsessively—on the risks and rewards of intergenerational communication, can be read against the backdrop of the struggles he encountered in classrooms across Italy. "For us to speak with the young becomes ever more difficult," Levi says in the conclusion of that book. "We see it as a duty and, at the same time, as a risk: the risk of appearing anachronistic, of not being listened to" (199). These risks coalesce in a remarkable scene of failed pedagogy that Levi includes in his last work. It's a rare scene in Levi's oeuvre, one of the few places where he offers a glimpse into a classroom visit. The scene, quoted below in its entirety, dramatizes one of the central challenges facing the aging survivor.

> *I remember with a smile the adventure I had several years ago in a fifth-grade classroom, where I had been invited to comment on my book and to answer the pupils' questions. An alert-looking little boy, apparently at the head of the class, asked me the obligatory question: "But how come you didn't escape?" I briefly explained*

to him what I have written here. Not quite convinced, he asked
me to draw a sketch of the camp on the blackboard indicating
the location of the watch towers, the gates, the barbed wire, and
the power station. I did my best, watched by thirty pairs of intent
eyes. My interlocutor studied the drawing for a few instants,
asked me for a few further clarifications, then he presented to me
the plan that he had worked out: here, at night, cut the throat
of the sentinel; then, put on his clothes; immediately after this,
run over there to the power station and cut off the electricity, so
the search lights would go out and the high-tension fence would
be deactivated; after that I could leave without any trouble. He
added seriously: "If it should happen to you again, do as I told
you. You'll see that you'll be able to do it." (157)

The scene, which entwines tragic and comedic elements, exposes the sharp
contrast between the content of the survivor's testimony and the ways his
testimony was interpreted—and ultimately misinterpreted—by the young boy.

Since the scene unfolds under the sign of teaching, and because
it so powerfully illuminates the challenges Levi faced in the classroom, I
often discuss it with my own students. And I've been surprised on a few occasions when my students challenge, at least initially, my attempts to analyze
the scene in any kind of depth. After all, they tell me, the boy is only in fifth
grade; why should we expect a youngster to relate to Levi's testimony with
understanding or compassion? If the boy had been older, then his response
would warrant a closer reading. Anticipating their pushback—and because I
want them to take the scene seriously—I start with a simple question: why, I
ask them, does Levi remember the scene with a smile? And here they don't
hesitate. Levi's smile, they tell me, stems from the child's willingness to
invert the student/teacher hierarchy. The boy, after all, places himself in
the role of teacher, while Levi, the survivor, is cast in the role of student.
In the role of teacher, the young boy doesn't get hung up on the horrors of
daily life in the concentration camp; instead, he confidently instructs Levi
on how to act in the event of another Holocaust. When I ask them why Levi
might be interested in this scene, the discussion usually veers toward the
issue of miscommunication and to the "missed encounter" between Levi
and the student.

From here, it doesn't take us too long to arrive at the same reading of the scene that Levi goes on to develop. Levi says that the scene illuminates the "gap that exists and grows wider every year between things as they were 'down there' and things as they are represented by the current imagination" that has been fed by "books, films and myths" (*Drowned* 157). Levi not only names the slippage between raw memory and representation, but he also describes this as a fatal slide "towards simplification and stereotype." He then positions his last work as a bulwark against this slide. But Levi also suggests that this experience in the classroom is continuous with a much more general phenomenon: the difficulty we face when trying to perceive the experiences of others, especially at a distance of years. We are prone to assimilate the experiences of others to those we can understand. And this process, Levi says, leads people to assume that "the hunger in Auschwitz was the same as that of someone who had skipped a meal, or as if escape from Treblinka were similar to an escape from an ordinary jail." Importantly, this assimilation process, dramatized through the scene of failed pedagogy, threatens to render the survivor obsolete.

At this point, I usually ask my students to reflect on their own thought process when it comes to the Holocaust. How do they imagine the event? To what extent do they interpret the event through the lens of the present? These questions move us away from that initial temptation to ignore the boy's response (to blame it on his age), and to consider instead how his response is part of a larger phenomenon—one that extends to their own understanding of the events. At this point, we turn our attention to *how* the young boy interprets Levi's testimony, and to his specific commitment to the idea of escape. Levi raises this question in an afterword to *The Reawakening*, offering the following response: "Today's young people feel that freedom is a privilege that one cannot do without, no matter what. Consequently, for them, the idea of prison is immediately linked to the idea of escape or revolt" (216). Young people, inspired by a host of literary and cinematic sources, have come to understand the concept of escape as a moral duty. In films like *I Am an Escaped Convict*, *Hurricane*, and *Papillon*—all of which Levi mentions by name in his last work—the typical prisoner is presented as a man of integrity, full of physical and moral strength, and capable of overcoming any barriers placed before him. The hero never loses the power to act, and the experience of imprisonment, no matter how challenging, never seems to jam his moral compass. As Levi explains: "In the universe of the cinema the unjustly (or even justly) incarcerated hero is always a positive character, always tries to escape, even under the least credible circumstances, and the attempt is invariably crowned by success" (*Drowned* 152).

This way of thinking causes the young student to misrecognize the dehumanized, worn-out inmate of Auschwitz, a figure for whom escape was not an option, as a hero-in-waiting: a man who, in the event of a second Holocaust, would be able to escape with the right information—the right teacher. In the child's imagination, the Holocaust functions as a cinematic backdrop against which the "hero" can express his demand for freedom. Here, then, we come back to the inversion of the teacher/student hierarchy that my students were quick to point out, but we can now see *why* the survivor appears like someone in need of an education. From the boy's perspective, the survivor's testimony appears like a script that can be more effectively interpreted—more effectively acted out—by someone who was never in a camp. And from the vantage point of the young boy, the survivor is the one who needs help understanding his own testimony, who must be taught how to escape by someone who was never interned. The survivor, it seems, is the one in need of an education, and no amount of testimony can alter the situation. No wonder, then, that Levi came to feel like some kind of obstacle in the presence of these young students.

A similar sentiment was powerfully articulated by Jean Améry, another Holocaust survivor who died by suicide in 1978 and a figure with whom Levi is routinely compared.[16] Améry imagined a coming world in which the survivors would be perceived as standing in the way of progress: "We, the victims, will appear as the truly incorrigible, irreconcilable ones, as the anti-historical reactionaries in the exact sense of the word, and in the end it will seem like a technical mishap that some of us still survived" (80). Given the situation, how could Levi continue bearing witness? How could he teach these young students and readers about the ongoing threat posed by Auschwitz? In the next section, I consider how Levi's focus on the gray zone, especially in an essay from his last work, can be read as a kind of educational response to the challenges he faced in the classroom, a way of temporarily stripping his young readers of their simplistic—and cinematic—ideas about the Lagers and the Holocaust more generally. And a way of offsetting any kind of easy identification with the victims. How the gray zone functions pedagogically, and the role that Chaim Rumkowski plays in that process, is the subject of the next section.

III

Levi's long-standing interest in the space that separates victims from persecutors extends back to his first book, but his most formal analysis of this zone takes place in a chapter from his last work titled "The Gray Zone." The gray zone is a space of violence and ambiguity within the camps in which victims and perpetrators were "bound together by the foul link of imposed complicity" (*Drowned* 54). Distinctions between victims and persecutors seethe and collapse within the gray zone, and the collapse of those categories can be disorienting for readers. Critics, of course, have made much of the gray zone, and it's been interpreted in many ways beyond the domain of Holocaust studies. Giorgio Agamben famously universalizes this zone of violence and ambiguity, imagining it "as the hidden yet constant paradigm for modern civilian life" (qtd. in Sanyal 6). Agamben describes it as a space "where the oppressed become oppressor and the executioner in turn appears as victim" (21). In this "zone of irresponsibility," he says, we see how "good and evil and, along with them, all the metals of traditional ethics reach their point of fusion" (21). My intention, however, is not to take issue with the ways that the gray zone has been interpreted by others; instead, I want to consider how the gray zone can be read as a kind of educational response to that scene with the young boy I focused on in the previous section—how, in other words, he seems to deploy the gray zone with his young students in mind.

My reading of the gray zone begins, like the chapter itself, not with a description of the actual zone—that comes slowly and in pieces—but with the curious admission of failure that opens the chapter. "Have we," asks Levi, "we who have returned—been able to understand and make others understand our experience?" (*Drowned* 36). Levi's aim here is not to blame the survivors (the "we" in this case) for failing to make others understand; instead, he wants to focus readers' attention on the meaning of the term *understanding*. The problem, Levi goes on to say, stems from the fact that the act of "understanding" requires a "profound simplification" (35). Without such simplifications, Levi says, we would experience the world as an "infinite, undefined tangle that would defy our ability to orient ourselves and decide upon our actions" (36). Levi then links this need for simplification with the way that history is taught in schools. In schools, complex historical phenomena are reduced to simplistic accounts and easy lessons that avoid "half-tints and complexities" (37). And Levi, perhaps not surprisingly, aligns this propensity for "Manichaean" thought with youth: "The young above all demand clarity, a sharp cut; their experience of the world being meager, they do not like ambiguity." This demand for clarity—and certainty—is what leads the young, says Levi, to experience with such intensity "the need to separate evil from good, to be able to take sides, to emulate Christ's gesture on Judgment Day: here the righteous, over there the reprobates." But while the desire for simplification is justified, says Levi, it "does not always apply to the simplification itself, which is a working hypothesis, useful as long as it is recognized as such and not mistaken for reality."

Interestingly, the gray zone chapter doesn't open with a discussion of the Holocaust per se; instead, Levi begins by talking about the young, their resistance to ambiguity, and the ways that history is taught in schools. He focuses on how the act of "understanding" relies on a process of simplification. And if this process of simplification is presented as a kind of educational problem at the start of the chapter, then the description of the gray zone that follows can be read as a kind of educational solution. More specifically, Levi exposes his young readers to this zone of radical ambiguity and moral disorientation in order to temporarily destabilize their simplistic and stereotypical lines of thought when it comes to the Holocaust—a way of thinking about the event that leads the young boy, in that fraught classroom encounter, to educate Levi on life in the Lager. The gray zone, in other words, targets a way of thinking that Levi associates with his young readers.

The actual description of the gray zone begins with a comparison between the young and the "newcomers to the Lagers, whether young or not" (*Drowned* 37). These newcomers, Levi tells us, arrived in the camps armed with conceptual models that left them ill equipped to deal with the fiercely individualistic realities of camp life. They entered the camps, says Levi, hoping to find a terrible but decipherable world "in conformity with that simple model which we atavistically carry within us—'we' inside and the enemy outside, separated by a sharply defined geographic frontier" (38). But instead of a world organized around an easily recognizable set of oppositions, the new arrival discovered a disorienting world that did not conform to any models. The inmates who were unable to adapt were unlikely to survive, and many of them soon became part of the faceless mass of men called the *Muselmänner*: the "anonymous mass" of men who formed "the backbone of the camp" (*Survival* 90). Those who made themselves amenable to more powerful people had a better chance of surviving. And by suggesting that the survivors benefited from some form of privilege—a claim Levi makes in his last work—he casts a pall over the survivors, himself included.[17]

Over the course of the chapter, Levi passes from the extreme example of the Sonderkommandos, the Jews who were in charge of running the crematoria, through a series of events and people who occupy positions along the "gray band, that zone of ambiguity which radiates outwards from regimes based on terror and obsequiousness" (*Drowned* 58). Levi is clear that the need for a complication of judgment is not an argument for the eradication of judgment. Ultimately, it is essential that we not confuse the murderers with their victims, for to do so is, he says, "a moral disease or an aesthetic affectation or a sinister sign of complicity, above all, it is a precious service rendered (intentionally or not) to the negators of truth" (48–49). And yet, despite the warnings, the development and style of the chapter are both eccentric and disorienting, and it seems clear, based on the chapter's beginning, that Levi turns to the zone in an effort to challenge and revise his readers' simplified rendering of events.

At the end of the chapter, Levi introduces the chapter's protagonist: Chaim Rumkowski, a man whose life and death illuminates the central themes of the gray zone. Levi began writing about the duplicitous figure of Chaim Rumkowski in the mid-1970s. A short article on Rumkowski published in the Italian newspaper *La Stampa* in 1977 called "King of the Jews" was republished as "The Story of Coin" in Levi's 1981 book, *Moments of Reprieve*.[18] And he would return to the figure of Rumkowski in the penultimate essay of what would become his last work, where he imagines the man as an avatar of the gray zone. The story of Chaim Rumkowski, he writes, "sums up in itself the entire theme of gray zone" (*Drowned* 66). Through this figure, who stands in for the zone as a whole, Levi found a way to embody in the experience of a single individual what might otherwise remain too abstract for his young readers to understand.

Rumkowski was a failed industrialist who, fueled by a pathetic sense of pride, seized the opportunity to assume control of the Lodz ghetto. An "energetic, uncultivated, and authoritarian man" who "passionately loved authority," Rumkowski, a Jew, clung to his position as president of the ghetto despite the fact that his administrative efforts had disastrous consequences for his fellow Jews (*Drowned* 62). He organized a police force within the ghetto, delivered speeches in the oratorial style of Mussolini and Hitler, and had songs written to honor him. After helping the Nazis liquidate the ghetto, he, too, was sent off to the camps. "Drenched in duplicity" and intoxicated with power, Rumkowski was a degraded figure who clung to any sign of privilege, hoping that it might ensure his own survival and the survival of others (65). But Rumkowski was not a monster, and he should not be judged as one. He was simply a man who sought to save himself and his family by collaborating with the enemy; a man whose life dramatized the ways that political coercion gives birth to an "ill-defined sphere of ambiguity and corruption" (66). And this is the thread that Levi follows in the chapter's final pages.

Levi's interest in Rumkowski extends beyond what the man did to preserve a modicum of power within the ghetto. He also focuses on

Rumkowski's inner life and reflects on the kind of self-delusion that seemed to protect him from shame. Levi suggests that Rumkowski probably saw himself as "a messiah, a savior of his people, whose welfare, at least at intervals, he must have certainly desired" (64). Even though he was constantly mistreated by the Germans, he probably thought of himself "not as a servant but as a lord." He was, Levi tells us, addicted to power, and the addiction led to all sorts of problems: a "distorted view of the world, dogmatic arrogance, the need for adulation, convulsive clinging to levers of command, and contempt for the law" (67). Levi goes out of his way here to draw attention to the misalignment between Rumkowski's perception of himself as a great leader and savior of his people and the way that others perceived him as a pathetic figure being pulled through the ghetto by an ailing horse.[19] Levi was fascinated by the intensity of Rumkowski's self-delusion, and he wanted his readers to find their own "corrupted shape"—their own capacity for self-delusion—mirrored in the figure of Rumkowski (Lara 123). As Levi says at the end of the chapter: "We are all mirrored in Rumkowski, his ambiguity is ours, it is our second nature, we hybrids molded from clay and spirit" (69). Importantly, Levi doesn't suggest that his readers are interchangeable with Rumkowski or that they are guilty of his crimes, but rather that they can locate in his life—and in the ambiguity under whose sign he lived—a reflection of their own attraction to power and prestige. Through the figure of Rumkowski, Levi humanizes the gray zone: he transforms it from a "space" into a way of being, and he invites his readers to recognize their own willingness to inhabit, albeit imaginatively, that way of being.

Levi goes on to point out the amnesia that follows from Rumkowski's addiction to power: "Like Rumkowski, we too are so dazzled by power and prestige as to forget our essential fragility" (69). But what, exactly, does Levi mean by "essential fragility"? In an effort to shed light on this state of forgetfulness, Levi draws two fascinating comparisons: first, he likens Rumkowski's "fever" to the fever of "Western civilization that 'descends into hell with trumpets and drums,' and its miserable adornments are the distorting image of our symbols of social prestige." Next, he compares Rumkowski's self-delusion to Isabella's description of mortal man in Shakespeare's *Measure for Measure*. In the play, Isabella refers to mortal Man as someone "Dressed in a little brief authority, / Most ignorant of what he's most assured" (qtd. in *Drowned* 69). In these examples, the failure to reckon with one's vulnerability, a fragility we share as humans, produces a kind of comedic spectacle in which the viewer is encouraged to recognize a form of delusional hubris—or "fever," as Levi calls it—in each of the actors.

Rumkowski, a man who so willingly elevated himself over others, was defined by this hubris. And while Levi holds up Rumkowski as a negative example, he doesn't offer his readers an alternative path or a way out of the problem. Instead, he asks his readers to reflect on what the act of remembering one's "essential fragility" might mean: how it might lead to a state of humility in which one recognizes a shared sense of vulnerability; and how an awareness of that vulnerability, or essential fragility, might make one less susceptible to the trappings of power and prestige. In the chapter's last lines, Levi extends a thread from our attraction to power to the ever-present threat of Auschwitz: "We make our deals with power, willingly or not, forgetting that we are all in the ghetto, that the ghetto is walled in, that outside the wall are the lords of death, and that not far away the train is waiting" (*Drowned* 69).

The themes that come together in the figure of Rumkowski—addiction, the illusions sustained by addiction, the connection between individual acts of forgetting and the collapse of civilization—have a long history in Levi's work. These themes enable Levi to explore the interplay between individual states of being and the impact of those states on the survival of civilization. Consider, for example, his science fiction short story titled, "Trattamento di quiescenza," which literally means "acquiescence treatment" but that has been translated as "Retirement Fund."[20] The story, published in 1966, focuses on a device called the Torec (for "total recorder"), a proto virtual reality machine that grants "users" access to the experiences of others (both human and animal), experiences that would otherwise be off limits. The possible benefits of the Torec are quickly eclipsed by the risks it poses to the users. Simpson, the recently retired salesman in possession of the Torec, quickly becomes addicted to this form of immersive entertainment. When he's not "using" the Torec, he feels "oppressed by boredom vast as the sea, as heavy as the world" (*Sixth* 124). Simpson ends up sacrificing everything of meaning in his life—"his peace, his work, his sleep, wife and books"—to continue using the Torec.[21]

The narrator, a stand-in for Levi, zeroes in on the state of Simpson's self-deception, much like he does with Rumkowski in his last work. In the story's final lines, Simpson mistakenly compares himself to the aged King Solomon, the assumed author of Ecclesiastes and a figure known for his legendary wisdom. "In Ecclesiastes," Simpson tells the narrator, he sees a reflection of "himself and his condition" (*Sixth* 124). But where Simpson compares himself to the wise king, the narrator sees an addict in a delusional state. After all, Solomon's legendary wisdom "had been won over a long life of work and responsibilities," where Simpson's wisdom is the "fruit of a complicated electronic circuit and eight-track tapes and he knows and is ashamed of it" (125). To escape the shame, the narrator tells us, Simpson plunges back into the Torec.

In the story, Simpson's addiction to technology functions analogously to Rumkowski's addiction to power: both lead to a radical divergence between how these figures see themselves and how they are perceived by others. And like Rumkowski, Simpson's addiction contains a larger, civilizational threat. After experimenting with the machine, the narrator says that it encourages a solipsistic, solitary life—a way of life that presents a direct challenge to our social order, our civilization: "No machine that was ever invented contains so great a threat to our habits and our social order. It will discourage all initiative, indeed, all human activity: it will be the last great step after mass entertainment and mass communications [. . .]. But who will have the willpower to escape a Torec spectacle? It seems much more dangerous than any drug: who would ever work again? Who would still take care of his family?" (111). Here, then, the Torec functions as an "emblem of humanity's demise," despite the fact that Simpson, like Rumkowski, remains oblivious to the link between his way of life and the end of the social order.

I linger on this science-fiction story because it explores, in narrative form, many of the same themes as the gray zone chapter: addiction, self-delusion, the link between individual action and the collapse of civilization. The difference, however, is that Levi, in the gray zone chapter, makes all of these connections explicit, transcribing them from a literary universe into a more explicit kind of teacherly essay. He doesn't just present Rumkowski as someone addicted to power; he wants his young readers to see their own willingness to collude with power and to forget their essential fragility reflected in Rumkowski's corrupted image. Where readers relate to Simpson as a literary character maneuvering within a literary universe, in Levi's last work, readers are asked to locate themselves in the gray zone through the figure of Rumkowski. In this way, he deploys the gray zone and the figure of Rumkowski to destabilize the categories his readers use to make sense of the world and to force them into a state of uncertainty regarding the events in question. No longer can Levi's readers imagine the Holocaust as a simple story about Nazi monsters and innocent victims—a story that grants them a measure of emotional and psychological distance from the events. And no longer can they imagine the Holocaust as a cinematic backdrop against which the "hero" can always express his desire for freedom. Here, then, Levi acts like a teacher trying to open his students' eyes to a new set of possibilities, to a way of seeing themselves and their own appetites and fears that they would rather ignore. He wants them to see the heights of delusion people will sustain to avoid reckoning with their own fragility. And the ability to generate this kind of uncertainty within his readers—uncertainty about themselves, the world, their understanding of the past—is precisely what Levi's pedagogy in gray aims to achieve.

In this way, we can see how Levi's version of a Holocaust education moves beyond the exclusive realm of Holocaust history or memory, and how, instead, Levi uses that history as a kind of backdrop to help his young readers reflect on their own moral armature: the strength and quality of their own characters. And he does so, it seems, as part of a larger effort to guide his young readers from a state of hubris to one of humility: from a state of thinking that they know, that they can judge these events from above, that they are in a position to educate the survivors, to a state where they find themselves struggling with their own desire for power and privilege, with their own desire to forget the essential fragility that links us together. It's a process, Levi implies, that can help them remember that the "torturers" of those days were "made of the same cloth as we, they were average human beings, averagely intelligent, averagely wicked" (*Drowned* 202). How to generate and sustain this kind of humility—in the face of an uncertain future, in the face of our desire to collude with power, and in the face of our own vulnerability—becomes the basis of Levi's pedagogy in gray and the difficult lesson he wants his young readers and students never to forget.[22]

IV

In the previous section, I tried to explain how and why Levi turns to the gray zone and the figure of Rumkowski in an effort to educate his young readers. We saw the kind of problems he encountered in the classroom and the ways of seeing that underwrote those problems. And we saw how an aging survivor, desperate to communicate with the young, encouraged his readers to reckon with forms of ambiguity and complicity that challenge their ways of seeing—how, in short, Levi uses the gray zone as a pedagogical device to help his students understand the Holocaust, at least in part, as an ongoing threat that emanates from within their own souls, from their capacity for self-delusion, and from their own often unacknowledged desire for power and prestige. In what follows, I want to briefly consider how a similar set of issues and terms have become part of the national conversation in recent years.

Almost forty years have passed since Levi's death in 1987. In the intervening years, the sense that civilizations are vulnerable has only increased. Terrorist attacks, violent social upheavals, and natural catastrophes, as well as concerns over the rise of artificial intelligence, global warming, and nuclear war have only intensified. Levi was powerfully attuned to the ways that the "obscure unease" generated by such threats could fuel "widespread intolerance"—an intolerance of difference that expresses itself today on all points of the American political spectrum. Our continued willingness to be "dazzled by power and prestige," or to lose ourselves in technology, makes it possible for us "to forget our essential fragility" (*Drowned* 69). It's not hard to see how this heightened sense that our civilization is mortal—that it can collapse—has led to a public discourse that encourages people to speak with certainty and a lack of nuance, a form of confidence completely out of synch with reality. It prevents us from associating with people who do not share our political and social values, and the refusal corrodes our social bonds and democratic discourse. It's tempting to diagnose the rising anxieties about white extinction, white displacement, and white minority status—anxieties that have resulted in violence on the contemporary political scene in the United States—as symptoms of our unwillingness to reckon with our essential fragility, with the shared sense of vulnerability that we still struggle to name.

Whether or not we will acknowledge this shared vulnerability going forward remains to be seen, but recent events—including the #MeToo movement and Black Lives Matter—have helped to reshape the national conversation on power and privilege, among other things. The rise of these movements has caused us to become increasingly aware of our unconscious assumptions and the workings of power and privilege within our individual lives and the larger society. In many ways, Levi anticipated the conversations that are playing out on the national stage today. And we've seen how Levi, in his role as teacher, wanted his readers, and especially his young readers, to recognize the extent to which they might go to elide their own vulnerability. The struggle to reckon with that vulnerability is the hallmark of Levi's pedagogy in gray: a pedagogy that asks his readers to recognize the connection between our desire to collude with power and the act of forgetting the vulnerability—the essential fragility—that unites us. Levi hoped this kind of an education would encourage his readers to accept responsibility for the future—a future, as Levi reminded us, that is in our hands to shape. That terms like *vulnerability, privilege,* and *power* are now at the center of national conversations about how we live, and the kind of future we might create, is a testament to the ongoing importance of Levi's voice.

ANTHONY C. WEXLER is a senior lecturer in the University Writing Program at Johns Hopkins University. His research focuses on Jewish American literature and the Holocaust in American life. His current book project examines how a group of late-life novels challenge the ways the Holocaust has been received and represented in American life.

Notes

1   Paul Saint-Amour refers to this kind of future-oriented anxiety as the "traumatic power of anticipation": "the damaging intrusion of the future in a present already given over to 'worry'" (287). Levi, for a number of reasons, lived in such a state, especially in the final years of his life. There was the ongoing threat of nuclear war and the terrible discovery that many of the Germans he hoped to affect with his testimony remained willfully ignorant. The Bitburg affair in 1985 left him reeling at the general insensitivity toward victims. And to make matters worse, Levi watched as a culture of commodified remembrance was being consolidated in the United States. Alongside these trends, Holocaust deniers in Europe and the Middle East were finding new platforms from which to vent their claims. And Levi watched in horror as subsequent genocides took place across the globe. These factors, and others, contributed to his heightened sense that civilization was at risk of collapse.

2   Levi discusses this "obscure unease" in "The Eclipse of the Prophets," an essay originally published in the Italian newspaper, *La Stampa*, and later collected in *Other People's Trades*.

3   Levi takes aim at this deterministic view of history in his last work, *The Drowned and the Saved*: "No historian or epistemologist has yet proven that human history is a deterministic process"; who can say "that the history of human events obeys rigorous logic, patterns?" (150).

4   A similar line of thought is developed by Jonathan Lear in *Radical Hope: Ethics in the Face of Cultural Devastation*. Lear's book focuses on Plenty Coups, the last chief of the Crow—the Native American tribe living primarily in Southern Montana—and on his response to the cultural catastrophe that befell his people. Through Plenty Coups, and his specific historical situation, Lear explores the shared sense of vulnerability we feel as members of cultures that can collapse. Like Levi, Lear felt that he, too, was living with a "heightened sense that civilizations are themselves vulnerable" (7). And his book sets out to name the shared vulnerability in the hope that it will help us to "find better ways to live with it."

5   In this essay, I use the terms *students* and *young readers* interchangeably. Both groups were part of a younger generation with whom Levi was so desperate to communicate.

6   See Homer for a more comprehensive account of Levi's ideas about education. Homer is one of the few writers that I have discovered who reflects extensively on Levi's educational approach. He shows how Levi championed a form of education "that emphasizes the utility of recognizing pain and avoiding it," and that, for Levi, education was "the only counter" to "our ill-constituted selves" (202–3).

7   For a more comprehensive reading of Levi's last work and its connection to his last act, see my "Primo Levi's Last Lesson: A Reading of *The Drowned and the Saved*."

8 Levi, at the end of *The Drowned and the Saved,* argues against the need for war. "Satan is not necessary: there is no need for wars or violence, under any circumstances" (200). He also challenges the idea of preventative violence: "[F]rom violence only violence is born, following a pendular action that, as time goes by, rather than dying down, becomes more frenzied."

9 Toni Morrison's introduction to *The Complete Works of Primo Levi* is short and insubstantial. However, the length of the introduction matters far less than her willingness, as one of America's greatest African American writers, to endorse the work of a Sephardic Jew and Holocaust survivor from Italy.

10 A number of essay collections in English focus on these aspects of Levi's identity. See Gordon, ed.; Kremer; and Sodi and Marcus. Other topics in these collections include Levi's Jewish identity, his use of language, his science fiction short stories, his poetry, and his enduring legacy. A few recent essay collections in English focus on the most effective ways to teach Levi's work to students at different age levels. See, for example, Patruno and Ricci.

11 Victor Brombert, in a wonderful reading of this scene, reminds us that Levi, through his deployment of Dante, establishes a link between two scenes of teaching: one taking place between Levi and Pikkolo, and the other involving the effort of Dante's Ulysses to teach his men, a link, Brombert says, that is "not merely thematic, but historic and transcultural: from Homer to Virgil, to Dante, to Primo Levi, to the future reader" (*In Praise* 117).

12 For more information about Levi's epistolary exchange with Lévi-Strauss, see Belpoliti, *Primo.*

13 Levi was continually caught off guard by the surprise students expressed when they discovered that the author of the book they had been reading was still alive. In an interview from 1983, Levi describes feeling a flash of amazement when the students discover seeing the "author of the book they've been reading, that I'm still alive and that I speak Italian, not Latin or Greek" (*Voice* 110).

14 In these years, Holocaust remembrance had not been transformed into a civil religion in the West, and the survivor culture that would flourish in America in the late 1970s and 1980s had not yet emerged in Italy. It's also important to note that the "memorial turn" in Western culture had not yet taken place when Levi started visiting classrooms in the late 1960s, and the memories of survivors were not yet an integral feature of our knowledge of the Holocaust. In fact, Levi's last book, *The Drowned and the Saved,* was one of the important works that contributed to the memorial turn in the mid-1980s (Traverso). In these years, memory, as opposed to history, would become a central topic of academic scholarship, public debates, and the culture industry. Most of Levi's work, however, should be located before this memorial turn.

15 Following the encounter, Levi's Hungarian friend, Edith Bruck, suggested that "a part of Primo came to believe that humanity did not deserve to know about Auschwitz. If a sixteen-year-old boy could deny the existence of the atrocity," she went on to say, "the survivor has to remain silent, even if it's the worst thing he can do" (qtd. in Thomson 488). I mention

this scene, and Bruck's interpretation of it, in order to draw attention back to the problem at the heart of this essay: the challenges that Levi faced while trying to communicate with members of the young generation. We might also locate in Bruck's comments another factor that contributed to Levi's suicide.

16   In the chapter "The Intellectual in Auschwitz" from *The Drowned and the Saved*, Levi offers a fascinating comparison between himself and Jean Améry.

17   Levi's account of the connection between survival and complicity has, not surprisingly, led to criticism. How could Levi, a Holocaust survivor, temporarily blur the lines? How could an innocent survivor focus so much attention on these grey specimens? He knew the criticism would come, but these were risks he was willing to take in order to challenge his young readers' "understanding" of the events.

18   In a fascinating article, "Levi, Bellow and the King of the Jews," Marco Belpoliti considers how Saul Bellow's account of Rumkowski in his 1970 novel *Mr. Sammler's Planet* might have influenced Levi's writings about him.

19   This kind of misalignment had long interested Levi. In "Lorenzo's Return," an essay collected in *Moments of Reprieve*, Levi describes the sense of disconnection as follows: "Each of us, knowing or not, creates an image of himself, but inevitably it is different from that, or, rather, from those (which again are different from one another) that are created by whoever comes into contact with us" (149). Levi was also deeply aware of the disconnection between his own inner life and the kind of self he projected on the page. Cynthia Ozick, in an

essay called "The Suicide Note," links a form of self-deception that had been an important feature of Levi's earlier works to the manner of his death. Levi, she argues, spent his career acting the way a "civilized man ought to conduct himself," and as a result, the world came to see "a man somehow set apart from retaliatory passion. A man who would not trade punches" (36). In Levi's last work, she argues, he finally removed his earlier "civilized" mask and allowed his long-repressed rage to surface. This is why she reads his last work as a suicide note *avant la lettre*—a work that prefigures the transformation of Levi's rage into ultimate self-destruction. In this way, Ozick imagines a form of misalignment—a distinction between Levi's inner world and his public persona—as the key to understanding his last act. It's a compelling reading, but one that might say more about Ozick, and her vision of how a survivor is supposed to act, than it does about Levi or the specific emotions that traverse his last work.

20   The story "Retirement Fund" was initially published as part of a collection of fifteen science fiction stories called *Natural Histories* (or, in Italian, *Storie Naturali*). Published under the pseudonym Damiano Malabaila, these stories, which draw widely on chemistry, astrophysics, and molecular biology, focus on the destructive power of technology. The stories from this collection were published in 1990 in an English collection called *The Sixth Day and Other Tales*.

21   For a fascinating comparison between this hollowed-out version of Simpson and the central figures from Levi's first book, the *Muselmänner*, or absolute victims, see Gordon, *Ordinary* 171.

22   Adorno also suggests that education after Auschwitz should involve a process of "critical self-reflection" (193). Adorno explains: "One must come to know the mechanisms that render people capable of such deeds, must reveal these mechanisms to them, and strive by awakening a general awareness of those mechanisms, to prevent people from becoming so again" (193). Levi would have certainly agreed with Adorno here. However, unlike Levi, Adorno encourages his readers to reckon with their capacity to occupy the position of the persecutors, and not, specifically, with the figures who occupy positions along the gray band.

Works Cited

Adorno, Theodor W. "Education after Auschwitz." *Critical Models: Interventions and Catchwords.* Trans. Henry W. Pickford. New York: Columbia UP, 2005. 191–204.

Agamben, Giorgio. *Remnants of Auschwitz: The Witness and the Archive.* Trans. Daniel Heller-Roazen. New York: Zone, 2002.

Améry, Jean. *At the Mind's Limits: Contemplations by a Survivor on Auschwitz and Its Realities.* Trans. Sidney Rosenfeld and Stella P. Rosenfeld. Bloomington: Indiana UP, 1980.

Belpoliti, Marco. "Levi, Bellow and the King of the Jews." Trans. Hugo André MacManus. *Centro Internazionale di Studi Primo Levi* 10 Feb. 2020. https://www.primolevi.it/en/levi-bellow-and-king-jews-marco-belpoliti.

————. *Primo Levi: An Identikit.* Trans. Clarissa Botsford. New York: Seagull, 2022.

Brombert, Victor. *In Praise of Antiheroes: Figures and Themes in Modern European Literature 1830–1980.* Chicago: U of Chicago P, 1999.

Gordon, Robert, ed. *The Cambridge Companion to Primo Levi.* Cambridge: Cambridge UP, 2007.

————. *Primo Levi's Ordinary Virtues: From Testimony to Ethics.* Oxford: Oxford UP, 2001.

Homer, Frederic D. *Primo Levi and the Politics of Survival.* Columbia: U of Missouri P, 2001.

Kremer, Roberta S., ed. *Memory and Mastery: Primo Levi as Writer and Witness.* New York: SUNY P, 2001.

Lara, Maria Pia. *Narrative Evil: A Postmetaphysical Theory of Reflective Judgment.* New York: Columbia UP, 2007.

Lear, Jonathan. *Radical Hope: Ethics in the Face of Cultural Devastation.* Cambridge, MA: Harvard UP, 2006.

Levi, Primo. *The Drowned and the Saved.* Trans. Raymond Rosenthal. New York: Vintage, 1989.

————. *Moments of Reprieve.* Trans. Ruth Feldman. New York: Penguin, 1986.

————. *Other People's Trades. The Complete Works of Primo Levi.* Vol. 3. Trans. Antony Shugaar. Ed. Ann Goldstein. New York: Liveright, 2015. 2009–253.

————. *The Reawakening.* Trans. Stuart Woolf. New York: Simon and Schuster, 1995.

————. *The Sixth Day and Other Tales.* Trans. Raymond Rosenthal. New York: Summit, 1990.

──────────. *Survival in Auschwitz: The Nazi Assault on Humanity*. Trans. Stuart Woolf. New York: Simon and Schuster, 1996.

──────────. *The Voice of Memory: Interviews 1961–1987*. Ed. Marco Belpoliti and Robert Gordon. Trans. Robert Gordon. New York: New Press, 2001.

Lévi-Strauss, Claude. *The View from Afar*. Trans. Joachim Neugroschel and Phoebe Hoss. Chicago: U of Chicago P, 1985.

Ozick, Cynthia. "The Suicide Note." *New Republic* 21 Mar. 1998: 32–36.

Patruno, Nicholas, and Roberta Ricci, eds. *Approaches to Teaching the Works of Primo Levi*. New York: MLA of America, 2014.

Rosenfeld, Alvin H. *A Double Dying: Reflections on Holocaust Literature*. Bloomington: Indiana UP, 1980.

──────────. *The End of the Holocaust*. Bloomington: Indiana UP, 2011.

Saint-Amour, Paul K. *Tense Future: Modernism, Total War, Encyclopedic Form*. Oxford: Oxford UP, 2015.

Sanyal, Debarti. "A Soccer Match in Auschwitz: Passing Culpability in Holocaust Criticism." *Representations* 79 (2002): 1–27.

Sodi, Risa, and Millicent Marcus, eds. *New Reflections on Primo Levi: Before and After Auschwitz*. New York: Palgrave, 2011.

Thomson, Ian. *Primo Levi: A Life*. New York: Henry Holt, 2002.

Traverso, Enzo. "Revisiting the Life and Intellectual Legacy of Primo Levi." *Jacobin* 11 Apr. 2021. https://jacobin.com/2021/04/primo-levi-enlightenment-holocaust-auschwitz-memory-italian-jewish-legacy.

Wexler, Anthony C. "Primo Levi's Last Lesson: A Reading of *The Drowned and the Saved*." *The Palgrave Handbook of Holocaust Literature and Culture*. Ed. Victoria Aarons and Phyllis Lassner. Cham: Palgrave Macmillan, 2020. 27–43.

Mexican Antigones: In Search of a Stolen Mourning

Since Calderón militarized the country upon declaring a so-called war against narcotrafficking, extreme violence within Mexico has increased drastically.[1] In fact, the military deployment under the guise of pacification has had the opposite effect: we have been witnesses to the complicity between cartels and military forces and an increase in cases of forced disappearances, human trafficking, and femicides. Faced with the state's inability and negligence to respond by searching for those who have disappeared, many Mexican women have organized into groups to search throughout the national territory. They have learned to recognize the smell of death among all of the aromas of the land, as well as the difference between intact and disturbed ground; they have learned to find and handle human remains with the necessary caution to enable later analysis. Some of them, such as Yadira González, have even become certified forensic anthropologists. In sum, they have become Antigones against their will. As Antigone Gómez or Diana Gómez said: "I didn't want to be an Antigone, but it's what life made me become" (Uribe 15). The Mexican *Buscadoras* are Antigones in search of a stolen mourning.

Volume 34, Number 3   DOI 10.1215/10407391-10898255

© 2023 by Brown University and d i f f e r e n c e s : A Journal of Feminist Cultural Studies

A significant number of adaptations of the Greek tragedy *Antigone* by Sophocles (441 BC) have been produced in Latin America in response to the multiple forensic crises that have devastated the region. From the dictatorships in the Southern Cone in the seventies to the different armed conflicts in Colombia, Peru, Guatemala, and El Salvador, among others, and now, particularly in Mexico since the militarization of the country, Latin America has been the region of a systematic history of forced disappearances, including the phenomenon of the systemic killings of women in Ciudad Juárez, many of whom have also been registered as cases of missing people. The number of adaptations of *Antigone* that have been produced in this region stands out above all because there is a huge difference between the story of the Theban Antigone and that of the Latin American Antigones: the Greek Antigone has the body of her brother and knows exactly how Polyneices died, whereas the majority of Latin American Antigones are family members of the disappeared that search for the body, alive or dead, of their loved one and the truth about their fate. Antigone of Thebes demanded a dignified ritual for her brother; "Antígona furiosa" (Gambaro, 1986), "La Antígona peruana" (Grupo, 2000), *Antígona González* (Uribe, 2012), and "Antígona en Juárez" (de la Rosa, 2005) demand the materialization of the absence of their loved ones and a human sepulcher.

In his text *Mourning and Melancholia,* Freud argues that the crucial difference between these two psychic phenomena is that mourning takes place when the subject who suffers knows what they have lost. Contrarily, not knowing what has been lost or, in the case of the Latin American Antigones, not even knowing if they had lost something or not, sentences the subject to the melancholic condition. As Freud points out: "This would suggest that melancholia is in some way related to an object-loss which is withdrawn from consciousness, in contradistinction to mourning, in which there is nothing about the loss that is unconscious" (245). This does not mean that Latin American Antigones are not aware of their loss, but that, for Freud, unconscious melancholia is not necessarily the lack of the object per se, but that which was lost along with it: the patient knows whom they lost but not what they have lost in the lost object (245). The uncertainty imposes a suspended temporality and the suffering of a pain that is infinitely prolonged. Following Freud, it is clear that the mourning of the Latin American Antigones has been rendered impossible, since they don't know if they have lost someone or not; but, according to this same theory, the difficulty of mourning becomes enigmatic for the Greek heroine. If Antigone of Thebes has the corpse of her brother and knows the truth about his fatal end, why does she continue to lament? Freud is mistaken on a key point: mourning is collective or it is not. The truth is essential for social, political, and restorative justice, since its concealment obstructs the opening of a future to come, but it is not enough. One can only mourn if loss is recognized socially and collectively as such; the pain of mourning the bereaved must be registered as the sorrow of a subject member of the polis. What the Theban Antigone and the Latin American Antigones have in common is that their laments and their loved ones are not recognized as part of what is shared. It is true that all the Latin American women are citizens, but some are so only on paper. All of the Antigones in the world have been women whose citizenship has been denied de jure or de facto. For them, there is neither a legal nor a customary right to mourn.

So narrates Sophocles in the tragedy of Antigone, confirmed by the collectives of *Buscadoras* in México, the Madres y Abuelas de Plaza de Mayo (Mothers and Grandmothers of Plaza de Mayo), the Women in Black, the Madres de la Candelaria (Mothers of the Calendaria), the Mujeres Buscadoras de Calama (Seeking Women of Calama), the Agrupación de Familiares de Detenidos Desaparecidos (Association of Relatives of Detained Disappeared): knowledge of the truth is not enough for the process of mourning; sociopolitical recognition of the loss is needed as well, that is, recognition of the loss on the basis of the mourner being a member of the community and of the polis. In other words, what is missing is a collectivization of loss.

I would like to begin by bringing up a point from Bonnie Honig's interpretation in *Antigone, Interrupted*, where she develops a critique of what she calls a mortalist humanism. According to Honig, this humanism "asserts that what is common to humans is not rationality but the ontological fact of mortality, not the capacity to reason but vulnerability to suffering. This mortalist humanism is connected to what has been dubbed recently 'the turn to ethics' or 'the ethical turn'" (17). But what she implies in this quotation is that the ethical turn has abandoned the political battle. In her book, Honig proposes opting for a natalist humanism with the argument that this is agonistic, and so "draw[s] not only nor even primarily on mortality and suffering, but also on natality and pleasure, power [. . .], desire [. . .], and *thumos* [. . .]" (20). I share Honig's concern about neglecting the political battle. Nevertheless, I agree with the reading that Athena Athanasiou develops in *Agonistic Mourning: Political Dissidence and the Women in Black*, where she insists on a false opposition between natality and mortality or between the necessity to advocate for a humanism with one adjective or the other. According to Athanasiou, mourning is never truly *phoné* (77).

That is, mourning for a deceased or disappeared being is, at the same time, a critical denunciation of the trivialization of the disposability of certain humans who have been valued as expendable:

> [O]nce we challenge such configurations [the binary between affirmative militancy and regressive grief], we might be able to begin to make sense of the incalculably complicated and politically enabling ways in which these activists stage mourning as a site of agonistic resignification in order to interrogate the hierarchies, injustices, and foreclosures upon which the dominant regime of grievability is sustained. In embodying the spectral potentiality of displaced memory, they performatively bring forth an alternative public, however suffused with friction and precariousness, which redefines the ways in which people come together and go to pieces in public. (76–77)

In this sense, the battle for mourning to be recognized as worthy of attention is, following Judith Butler, the fight against a differential and unjust allocation of lamentability ("To Preserve" 74). It is a political act that denounces and intends to subvert a bio/necropolitics that perceives some humans as essential members of society and others as cynically replaceable.

The Mexican Antigones as "Bad Victims": In Search of a Stolen Mourning

Freud failed to see the sociopolitical expanse of mourning. Had he paid more attention to Antigone and a little less to Oedipus, perhaps he would have realized that his theory of mourning did not consider the decisive spaces of collective recognition of the community and of the public sphere in regard to loss. Antigone of Thebes calls into question this precise point in psychoanalytic theory, since the heroine knows the fate of her brother, Polyneices, and, additionally, is in possession of his cadaver. In her laments, we hear that she knows what she lost—according to Antigone, an irreplaceable member of the family—and still so, she continues to lament: "One husband gone, I might have found another, or a child from a new man in the first child's place; but with my parents covered up in death, no brother for me, ever, could be born. Such was the law by which I honored you. But Creon thought the doing was a crime, a dreadful daring, brother of my heart" (Sophocles 72). In her lamentations, there are two fundamental demands:

1.   A dignified sepulcher for Polyneices. This would be a human grave, says Antigone, which, in addition to preventing the corpse from being devoured by predatory animals, is defined as a rendition of honors in Thebes, her hometown, a place that she considers her *polis*: "O town of my fathers in Thebes' land, o gods of our house! I am led away and must not wait. Look, leaders of Thebes, I am last of your royal line. Look what I suffer, at whose command, because I respected the right" (73).

2.   The discrediting of Creon as a mediocre and cruel king. Addressing Creon himself, Antigone replies: "[A]nd yet what greater glory could I find than giving my own brother a funeral? All these would say that they approved my act did fear not mute them. A king is fortunate in many ways, and most, that he can act and speak at will" (52).

Since 2012, different "Antigone" collectives have organized throughout Mexico. Many declare that they are not looking for those who are guilty, but are "only" looking for their children.[2] I would like to pause to analyze this demand to "just look for the disappeared" and the clarification that some of the collectives are not looking for the guilty. What does "to just look for" mean? Is it possible to only look for the body and the fate of a disappeared when this function should be taken care of by the state? What I am interested in arguing here is that, beyond the extrapolitical intentions of the *Buscadoras*, their concrete intervention (material, literal) in national territory is a political action since their searches have transformed the history and destiny of Mexico: even beyond their possibly extrapolitical intentions or this statement just being a safety strategy,[3] their searches have discovered the culprits (organized crime, the so-called war on drugs, the inefficiency and collusion of the state, the patriarchal culture of Mexico). In short, beyond their chants, the *Buscadoras* are political agents: their lament and their action have exposed a forensic and security crisis in our country and the corruption of the Mexican narcostate.

I would like to bring up, on one hand, that the Mexican Antigones have been forced to assume the functions of the state, meaning their search should not be interpreted as merely a maternal and/or loving act, as if it were an extrapolitical action. Additionally, I am interested in denouncing the perversion of the tendency by certain media and, in large part, public opinion that calls for empathy with the lamentations of these women, as if their actions were beyond all agonistic space. The systematic phenomena of forced disappearances are not a tragedy that is exclusive to certain families with certain vulnerabilities. In our context, the appeal to empathy is a sentimental denial of this forensic crisis[4] as a national emergency.

The main point here is that the fight for a collective mourning is also a denunciation of the differential allocation of human value. A careful analysis of those who deserve public mourning and those that do not would reveal that those disappeared bodies were disposable before being materially so, that is, their lives were deemed expendable. The scandalous number of disappearance reports that the authorities have not responded to contain a discriminatory bias, as do the fabricated tale of the disappeared as enemies of the state and alleged criminal cartel members. Within such a framework, the enemy is not deserving of mourning. One must also think about the numerous disappeared women of Juárez and/or femicide victims whom the authorities did not consider worthy of searching for because "who knows what they were up to":

> *In 2017, I(dh)EAS, along with the collectives of family members of disappeared persons, prepared a protocol [A Practical Guide for the Implementation of Authorized Protocol in the Search of Disappeared Persons] to serve those who were in that search. The document begins with a blunt warning: "A practice by some authorities (according to what we have documented) is to try and 'link' the disappeared person to organized crime, using phrases such as 'they were on the wrong track' or in the case of women, suggesting that surely 'they were with their boyfriend' or 'were asking for it.' What they are trying to do is play down the seriousness of the disappearance and to a certain extent, justify it." (Rosete)[5]*

In this context of the authorities' propensity to revictimize the victims and of the importance of public opinion, the demand for an undifferentiated mourning undoubtedly brings with it new horizons of justice—among other issues, a fight to transform a discriminatory, unjust world with unequal allocations of ontological value. As Athanasiou precisely states, it is rather necessary "[t]o displace the certainty of the structural opposition between an alleged positivity of natality and negativity of mourning, and, instead, explore their mutual and undecidable imbrications" (75).

Since their activism and the search for their own collective mourning as political agency does not negate their victimhood within a framework of systemic violence, product of an alleged war against narcotrafficking and the negligence of the state, I have decided to call the Mexican *Buscadoras* "bad victims." They are rebel victims: the subversion of their passive position in no way takes away the pain of the absence of their loved ones.

Honig invokes Butler as one of the central figures of mortalist humanism, but I would point out that Butler bases her radical equity project on a grievability that denounces an unjust, differential allocation (racist, sexist, homophobic, nationalist, and so on) of the value of a human being's life. This differential allotment does not exclusively refer to an afterlife but refers also to the care of life as it is biologically and ontologically vulnerable, that is, life that politically requires equity in which all life is worthy of being safeguarded, protected, and cared for: "Precarity has to be based on the demand that lives should be treated equally and that they should be equally livable" (Butler, "Bodies" 67). In this sense, vulnerability is not a characteristic of life that must be overcome, but is, rather, protected in an equitable way. What a public lament denounces are the frameworks that produce social norms that value some humans over others. The political project of nonviolence proposed by Butler has, on one hand, a commitment to radical, social equality in *life* and, on the other, departs from an ontology of interdependency in which the well-being of each *life* is essential and even dependent on the well-being of others.

I would say, then, that what Honig calls Butler's mortalist humanism and that she places as truly ethical and extrapolitical, is an agonistic lamentalism in which mourning is a political figure of catachresis, since it critically articulates itself as a denunciation of the unequal allocations of lamentability. Following Butler in *Antigone's Claim: Kinship between Life and Death*, Antigone is a critical agent of political catachresis: "Antigone is the occasion for a new field of the human, achieved through political catachresis, the one that happens when the less than human speaks as human" (82). But why catachresis and why political? When Antigone of Thebes disobeys Creon's edict, she acts and speaks as if she were a man—in ancient Greece, only men were political agents—thereby subverting her place as victim and woman: "I am no man and she the man instead if she can have this conquest without pain" (Sophocles 52). This movement is catachrestic because although Antigone, by lamenting, does not change from being a woman and is still punished for behaving as if she were sovereign (in the end, they sentence her to death when they lock her alive in a cave), she does achieve, on one hand, to make it clear that Creon is a tyrant and, on the other, that he will be punished by fate and the gods. His own son, Haemon, Antigone's betrothed, advises Creon against his authoritarianism:

Creon: Is the town to tell me how I ought to rule?
Haemon: Now there you speak just like a boy yourself.
Creon: Am I to rule by other mind than mine?
Haemon: No city is property of a single man.
Creon: But custom gives possession to the ruler.
Haemon: You'd rule a desert beautifully alone. (64)

And finally, when Creon accuses him of being a swindler, Tiresias, the ancient soothsayer, openly calls him a tyrant: "And the whole tribe of tyrants grab at gain" (78). He also warns him of his macabre fate: "[T]he Furies sent by Hades and by all gods will even you with your victims" (79).

By taking the floor and justice in her own hands, Antigone recovers the political agency that she had been denied. She thus undermines, displaces, and seizes the tyrannic devices that assign value, in this case, a differential value between the lamentability of her brothers, Eteocles and Polyneices. As is the case for Antigone of Thebes, so, too, the task of the Mexican *Buscadoras* is catachrestic: they search in place of the authorities and when they unearth bodies, they return to themselves the political agency that they had been denied. The society and state have not only stripped them of the possibility of mourning. In addition, their torment carries with it the de facto denial of their citizenship, which they recover for and by themselves as they dig bodies out in collectivity. Nallely Gómez shares that in the groups of *Buscadoras*, she learned to speak out against despotism:

> *To fight, to break through that fear, to break the silence, to not stay silent, to go out and look and to take each other by the hand, as in the collectives, since we are many and join forces—it is the only way that they will listen to you because here, at times, the government wants to impose its wish of what is to be done, and I believe that, better yet, the government should do what is asked of it, shouldn't it? We are, in a way, learning to change the whole environment, because before it wasn't so, nobody said anything, and now yes, I have learned a lot more from my companions. (qtd. in Lorusso 522)*

De facto, the disappearance of people is a crime whose name is a concentrated form of meaning: the person disappears both as a human being and as a citizen. When the state refuses to search for a person, they deny them their belonging to the *polis*; that unsought person is treated as something less than human and something less than a citizen. They are Polyneices, native foreigners. That being said, I don't want to imply that the state is not responsible for searching for missing foreigners within its territory, since all humans are citizens of the world and as such deserve humanitarian treatment. Rather, what I want to say is that they who are not looked for are denied precisely that universal citizenship. In reality, the "citizen" refers only to the being who is recognized as part of a political community with obligations and rights and not necessarily of a national territory. If our right to a dignified burial is denied us, we remain unrecognized as citizens. The *Buscadoras* are the political catachresis of this denial. By grabbing hold of the pick and shovel, the Mexican Antigones take the place of the state and thus, from a displaced *topos*, give and take back their snatched citizenship. Cecilia Flores, the leader of the Madres Buscadoras de Sonora (Mother Seekers of Sonora) tells us: "What we do upsets them. We have found the bodies that they could not find, that they do not find because they don't want to. We are around 900 mothers in the state. We have found almost 300 bodies and have found 50 people alive" (qtd. in Rosete). Political agency is recovered by interrupting repeated violence by the sovereign: in the case of Antigone, Creon's edict, and for the Mexican *Buscadoras*, the negligence of the Mexican state. As Athanasiou explains regarding Butler, "Butler has rethought agency as 'the hiatus in iterability' [. . .]. What is called agency, then, consists in '[. . .] a repetition that fails to repeat loyally, a reciting of the signifier that must commit a disloyalty against identity—a catachresis—in order to secure its future, a disloyalty that works the iterability of the signifier for what remains non-self-identical in any invocation of identity, namely, the iterable or temporal conditions of its own possibility'" (76).

In their disobedience, the Mexican Antigones are bad victims: at the very moment of their search, they overthrow oppression and exercise their rights. Like Antigone of Thebes, the *Buscadoras* have been accused of committing the crimes of exhumation and of manipulation and alteration of the crime scene. This takes place in a paradoxical sequence in which it was the search itself that transformed the land into a scene and evidence of a crime, since, before their intervention, that land was no more than a few square meters of Mexican territory. Also, after many field searches, in an action that demonstrates the absence or weakness of its capacities in the face of the overwhelming consequences of the supposed war against drugs, the Mexican state was finally forced to grant individuals the right to search for their disappeared relatives, as can be read in section X of article five of the General Law on Forced Disappearance of Persons, Disappearance Committed by Individuals and the National System for the Search for Persons (Ley

General en Materia de Desaparición Forzada de Personas, Desaparición Cometida por Particulares y del Sistema Nacional de Búsqueda de Personas): "Joint participation: the authorities from different levels of government, in their respective areas of competence, will allow the direct participation of Family members, under the terms provided in this Law and other applicable provisions, in the search tasks, including the design, implementation, and evaluation of actions in individual cases, such as public policies and institutional practices" (Estados; my translation). Beyond the Article's consonance with the international human rights framework, it seems to me that recognition of this right has had a double consequence: on the one hand, a hypostatization of the guarantees against disappearance; on the other, the formation of people's search agencies. Both are the product of a rebellion away from the place of submissive victim to that of a bad victim.

I want to reemphasize that the activities of the *Buscadoras* collectives in Mexico are not extrapolitical. In addition to bringing to light the deterioration of certain functions of the state, the act of literally searching national lands has the performative effect of "interrogat[ing] the hierarchies, injustices, and foreclosures upon which the dominant regime of grievability is sustained. In embodying the spectral potentiality of displaced memory, they performatively bring forth an alternative public, however suffused with friction and precariousness, which redefines the ways in which people come together and go to pieces in public" (Athanasiou 76–77). In 2017, Mirna Medina, a member of *Las Rastreadoras* (The Trackers), a group of mothers who, with machetes and shovels in hand, go in search of their disappeared relatives, found the body of her son, Roberto, in a clandestine grave after three years of searching. Medina, however, continues to collaborate with *Las Rastreadoras*, as each disappeared loved one of the members of the organization also becomes a child of the entire collective. In the words of Medina, "*Las Rastreadoras* are part of me and I am part of them; it would be very unfair to leave them, abandon them. There are many who are looking for their disappeared and many who helped me in the search for my son. We keep working, we live working" (qtd. in "Encontré"; my translation). To the question of when they will finally be able to rest, Medina replied, "When we can no longer work due to age, due to health [. . .]. But this does not end until the disappearances end. We will work until we find them all." In *compañera* Medina's speech, there are at least two political scenes: the first, that they are the subject of the searches for their disappeared; and second, that they do not discriminate, either filially or in any other way, between those who are absent, since its imperative slogan is that everyone must be found.

The extrapolitical meaning of the interjection "We are not look-ing for those guilty" may continue to be worrying; however, here the respon-sibility of listening to and politically questioning the exclamation belongs to, let's say, to continue thinking with Antigone of Thebes, the Chorus. By this I mean that not only the victims must respond politically to this forensic crisis but also the others, we who are witnesses, members of this same *polis* that is Mexico. Undoubtedly, we are also affected, although in a very different way. As the collective Buscadoras Guanajuato (Seekers Guanajuato) wrote on May 10, 2022 (Mother's Day in Mexico) in a Facebook message,

> *"Nothing to celebrate, much to demand." And it is strategically accompanied by #10demayo2022 throughout the networks. Today, the* Buscadoras *mothers have nothing to celebrate. We will con-tinue to raise our voices to demand that the state do its job and our disappeared persons return home. We will continue to cling to that stubborn love to continue looking for them until we find them. Because disappeared persons belong to every-one. Because we are missing almost 100,000 we will continue in this fight. #TeSeguimosBuscando [#WeKeepLookingForYou]. (my translation)*

As the witnesses that we are, not in danger of death (as we are not Antigone *Buscadoras*), it is imperative that our political demand be to find those who are guilty—and not only to demand the integration of institutional-ized commissions whose mission is exclusively the construction of truth, reconciliation, and forgiveness, as has become a common political practice of transitional justice in Latin America from the late twentieth century to the present. In this sense, it is our duty to resist the popular imaginary of a feminized mourning, that is, a submissive mourning whose end is not a political responsibility but rather a resignation to loss through sentimental-ist narratives.

The Mexican *Buscadoras* are political subjects who enter the public scene in an agonistic and nonsentimental manner, but this does not mean that their testimonies and circumstances are not emotionally mov-ing. An agonistic mourning is carried out via strategies that demand, and in the specific case of the *Buscadoras*, search with their own hands for, the mourning and memory of their loved ones, thereby questioning the biopolitics of this alleged war against narcotrafficking in which their own have been valued as disposable and expendable. In short, these Antigones respond to trauma politically, not as *lloronas* ("crying women")[6] who wander

the streets or suffer in their corners without public demands to deal with
the loss. Rather, in their field searches, they subvert the pernicious social
imaginary of mourning as an intimate and familial elaboration.

We must not lose sight of the fact that all these politically active
groups call into question the possibility of intimate, domestic, and family
mourning. Socorro Gil is a seeker mother from Guerrero who looks not only
for her son: "We have the idea that we know where they pick up [kidnap]
our children, but we don't know where they are going to leave them. So,
if we can travel across the entire Mexican Republic, we are going to do it.
And if I don't find my son, maybe I will find another mother's son" (qtd. in
Rosete). These women challenge, as I explained earlier, the Freudian theory
of mourning, which completely loses sight of the fundamental need for the
recognition—that is always relational and therefore political—of loss as such
and of the social accompaniment to this mechanism. Even if we think of a
nonviolent loss, for example, of a loved one who dies of old age, in order to
carry out any traditional ritual and the burial itself, we are required to show
an official death certificate, that is, verification of the loss via a representative
of the *polis*. The demand of both Antigone of Thebes and the Latin American Antigones is simple: sociopolitical recognition of their loss and, with
it, the possibility of giving their loved ones a dignified burial in a terrain or
space socially, politically, and legally destined for burial, which dignifies it
as human. In this sense, I agree with Athanasiou that the collectivity and
sorority of mourning is a fundamental part of and not an accessory to their
subversion. As can be read in the testimony of Juana B. (below), a woman
who participates in the searches for missing relatives in Mexico, it is in being
with others that self-involved victimization becomes agency and political
demand. It is in the collectives that these women give language and political clarity to the unfair frameworks of commemoration. The seeker Nallely
Gómez also expresses it in this way: "And I do realize what a collective is,
well, where there is a lot of communication, right? Eh, with all of them,
with the searches, with the workshops, with the training, that we have our
companions, from the Platform and, well, my whole environment changed,
right?" (qtd. in Lorusso 521).

Juana B. explicitly mentions that it was in solidarity that she
developed her understanding of civic consciousness, knowledge about legislative procedures, and the importance of human rights:

> *The other lesson is how to show solidarity with the rest of the*
> *families that are going through the same process [. . .] how this*

learning has also led to having a much more active role as citizens in society in the legislative processes [. . .]. Another, obviously, [is] how to enter into this whole world of human rights, so important, so relevant and, well, before I was not completely indifferent, [but] now let's say that it's part of each of the activities that we do as a main point and above all being involved as a citizen. I think that has been the greatest lesson and, obviously, meeting people of all types who accompany the families, who in some way do it with the interest, precisely, of making this situation visible [. . .], problematic, and also learning from each other. (qtd. in Lorusso 521)

Juana B. is also a bad victim. According to the Freudian theory of trauma, the subject repeats the violent scene in order to return to it and anticipate it—not from a passive place, but precisely as the subject (agency) of the event (as action). In her testimony, we read Juana precisely as the subject of her activism, as an agent with strong political projects—not as a melancholic mother, but as a woman on the battlefield: literally there, even with her weapons (pick and shovel). Like Antigone, Juana acts as a citizen even though she does not count as one. True, Juana is, like all Mexicans, a citizen, but that is only true on paper. Each group of the *Buscadoras* was formed after many women went to the authorities to report the disappearance of their relatives, demanded their search, and provided clues to the police as to where their loved ones may be. They were all left hanging. In this sense, *Buscadoras* are women whose citizenship has been de facto denied. After reporting threats from a member of organized crime, authorities told Mirna Medina: "Well, woman, don't go looking" (qtd. in "Encontré").

The People in the Hidden Graves Are Not Trash

The collectives and solidarity groups give the individual *Buscadoras* the recognition that the Mexican state and the negligence of public opinion have denied them. Silvia García, a member of a *Buscadoras* collective, affirms:

In the collectives I believe that we are a family, we understand each other, we know the pain and what we feel, because many times we do not feel it with the family. It's looking into each other's eyes, without knowing how sad we are but knowing that I understand them and that they understand me. Yeah? I think

that sometimes you cry more with them than even with your fam-
ily. And when you're not with them, perhaps the authorities pay
less attention to you. And so, as a family, as a group, many of us
have to raise our voices—yes, to shout—so that everyone listens to
us, understands us, and knows that something very serious and
very sad is happening. (qtd. in Lorusso 523)

The sociopolitical conflict faced by the *Buscadoras* is a lack of recognition. As Charles Taylor states, social recognition is essential for the identity and well-being of individuals, while lack of recognition can seriously damage both (26). Mutual recognition is essential for nonviolent cohabitation, since nonrecognition or misrecognition is damaging. In this way, recognition is a duty that is not only political but also moral. According to Axel Honneth, when an "I" addresses another person as a "you," it implies addressing the other as part of the moral community of which one is also a member. This means that the "you" is not just an individual but, at the same time, a person who shares membership in the community as an "I" ("'You'" 5). For Honneth, what essentially constitutes a society are shared projects and values (5). This means that when a person's political or legal demand is not recognized as such, that person remains an individual (collective or group) that does not belong to society. All Antigones in the world are de facto not recognized as citizens, and neither are their dead or missing loved ones. Beyond recognition among family or peers, recognition as a moral person is institutionalized in the ascription to rights and obligations. In this context, the negligence in not searching for the disappeared builds a poor self-perception on the part of the victims. Tranquilina Hernández, a *Buscadora*, says: "The people who are in the hidden graves are not trash, they are not animals" (qtd. in Brito 34), evoking Antigone of Thebes, who refers to the unburied corpse of Polyneices as "a rich sweet sight for the hungry birds beholding and devouring" (Sophocles 32). It is thanks to the recognition gained in solidarity, generated in the collectives, that the *Buscadoras* regain respect and esteem for themselves and for their cause. Honneth and Taylor understand recognition as fundamental to personal integrity. For its part, Honneth's theory of recognition is not limited to face-to-face recognition between peers but also involves institutions and social structures (practices, discourses, and so on). Social integration in general terms is measured by the social recognition that individuals or groups meet with; and absence of recognition is experienced as moral harm as it undermines moral agency, by which I mean that the subject is prevented from acting politically in the public sphere as a member of the community.

The *Buscadoras'* lament reveals an unequal distribution of recognition in Mexico, and when the rules of the community that govern it are unfair, conflict erupts. In other words, the regulatory rules that govern us in Mexico express that not all members of our society have the same obligations or the same rights. Being part of a community is experienced as having common values and projects. Therefore, if the *Buscadoras'* lament is not recognized as worthy, or if the search for their missing loved ones is not seen as a social project for the entire community, then the question is precisely one of their belonging in this supposed society. The feeling of not sharing the moral horizon of the "us" to which we are supposed to belong or of being directly excluded from the commons leads to the need to problematize established norms. Recognition must be publicly (beyond family and peers) accessible and perceptible; it cannot be intimate and secret. Through shared understanding of their pain and political demand, collective members recognize each other and recognize the dignity of their lament and the social injustice of not being heard as moral agents. In this sense, solidarity is not only the care of the members of a group among themselves but also in terms of the symmetrical esteem that they have for one another, since it is collectively that they are able to achieve valuable objectives. The seeker Nallely Gómez comments:

> *Well, I think it's the best thing that could have happened to me, that is, after my brother's disappearance, you find yourself a new family because you talk to your colleagues or* listen to them and they understand you. *I really liked meeting them, even if it was by video call. Working with them and being told . . . learning about their cases, learning about their stories, I really like listening to them, and I ask them: Hey, what was your son wearing? What was your son like? Well, how was your son? What was your life like before he disappeared?* (qtd. in Lorusso *523; my emphasis).*

Only by seeing myself as an object from the perspective of the peers with whom I interact can I perceive myself as a self: "In so adopting a 'second-order' perspective on myself, I can come to cognitively understand myself as an agent whose actions elicit responses in others (which I generate in myself as I adopt the perspective of others) and whose actions thus have social meaning" (Wilhelm 59). Self-recognition as a moral agent is a reflective turn that depends on the recognition that others give us. This means that autonomy and freedom are relational and that recognition is a moral obligation. Therefore, the principles of social struggles are the moral feelings of indignation provoked by the nonrecognition that limits self-realization, and with it autonomy: "[E]ach of the negative emotional reactions that accompany the experience of having one's claims to recognition disregarded holds out the possibility that the injustice done to one will cognitively disclose itself and become a motive for political resistance" (Honneth, "Personal" 138).

In terms of mourning, recognition of absence is not enough for its working-through; social recognition is essential. Antigone of Thebes cannot abide by Creon's edict, because she wants to give Polyneices a funeral that honors him as part of humanity and not leave his corpse as if it were meat at the mercy of scavengers. The funeral that Antigone wants for Polyneices and that she describes as fair is the one that her other brother Eteocles received, one at which the entire community mourned him in traditional rituals that lamented his death. *Buscadoras* need social mourning rituals, as these are a sign of recognition of their loved ones' belonging to the human community.

If we carefully listen to Antigone of Thebes and the demands of the *Buscadoras,* we understand that the demand for recognition of their loss in the public sphere is at the center of their lament. What bothers Antigone the most is that Creon had prohibited rituals and homage to Polyneices. While weeping, Antigone tells Ismene: "Creon will give the one of our two brothers honor in the tomb; the other none. Eteocles, with just observance treated, as law provides he has hidden under earth to have full honor with the death below. But Polyneices' corpse who died in pain, they say he has proclaimed to the whole town that none may bury him and none bewail, but leave him unwept, untombed, a rich sweet sight for the hungry birds' beholding and devouring" (Sophocles 32). That there is no public lament is what Antigone finds to be condemnable. Tranquilina Hernández similarly demands that the searches be sped up: "We have to continue. The people who are in the graves are not trash, they are not animals; we have to hurry up and get them all out of there" (qtd. in Brito 34; my translation). According to Athanasiou, "[T]his agonistic politics involves deploying the actuality of counter-memory as a history in and of the present: that is, not as a mere affirmation of the present as it is, but rather as a critical performative engagement with the established matrix of memorability that produces and sustains presentness and the present" (72).

Working through the loss of a loved one does not mean replacing one with another or turning the page of our own history with them to leave them behind and in oblivion, but rather, making the history of the now absent subject and our bonds into an exercise of remembrance, transforming the loved one into someone memorable, worthy of remembering and *commemorating*. In this sense, claiming mourning as political deconstructs and subverts the allocation of memorability. Building history in and through mourning implies that the loss is named and recognized as such, that is, as a socially lamentable loss. In a Derridean sense, this would also be a history to come, to the extent that by fighting for those losses that the state and/ or the community want to deny as subjects worthy of lamentation, we also resist the repetition of that violence of differential allocation of memorability. Unlike the melancholy that causes a temporary suspension, mourning reinaugurates future time, for at the same time that it facilitates the elaboration of history, or precisely because of this, it opens up the future as a horizon of possibilities—instead of as melancholic confinement in a predetermined fate of infinite suffering. In the same way, mourning implies the construction of history because only in the processing of the loss can it be registered, named, and respected as memorable. In this way, melancholy is precisely resistance to the reality of loss and, therefore, to its registration as memory.

In the political sphere, mourning means preserving the memory of what was lost with that absence because, as Derrida writes, that which disappears with each loss is the possibility of a world: "[E]ach time [death is] another end of the world, the same end, another, and each time it is nothing less than an origin of the world, each time the sole world, the unique world" (95). Through agonistic mourning, a mortalist humanism in which all deaths are mourned can be synthesized with a natalist one, because in order for all losses to be lamentable, an ontology of vulnerability and equitable memorability must be inaugurated, in which all lives are worthy of protection and sociopolitical care for their growth. The unfortunate end of a world that every single death causes does not prevent the birth of a new one. However, how we deconstruct (which means both disarm and rebuild) the world that remains after a loss persists as a political task. The work of mourning is political, since both what is left behind and what is opened up show our ontological dependence on others, on each other.

When we lament the absence of someone, we really cry for the canceled possibility of a future with that loved one. We mourn a stolen future. The *Buscadoras* collectives facilitate the possibility of turning anger and melancholy into an active demand for justice. In solidarity among sorority, these women have managed to transform melancholy and the desire "to break it all" into *National Search Days*,[7] when they search for the bodies of their disappeared in the field, teach basic forensic identification techniques, search for living disappeared loved ones in hospitals and prisons, organize workshops in schools and in ecclesial and faith communities on prevention of forced disappearances, and refer awareness of the forensic crisis to local authorities, security forces, and the general public. These groups have managed to use their rage to demand justice and a better political future, and at the same time resist being consumed by sadness.

Collective responsibility thus consists of being "duelists" in its two meanings in Spanish: on one hand, to recognize each life lost as a collective loss and, on the other, and at the same time, to occupy public space in order to fight for justice. This is not a fight to the death, since the task is to maintain the political arena as a space of *polemos*, that is, a space for tension and opposition. To preserve the political space, we must, even though it may be beyond our rabid anger and our sense of right and wrong, keep the enemy alive. Annihilating the enemy may well be a political act, but it is not a project for world transformation, since here, it is equally important to calculate natality as an insurmountable phenomenon: the enemy is always reborn. Expending energy to eliminate the enemy is an endless project that eliminates the possibility of revolutionary transformation. As I suggest in *Eros: Beyond the Death Drive*, the battle for justice is an eternal confrontation that needs two different forces to protect the public space as a common ground. I think of battalions of duelists because dueling is, in both senses, erotic. Suffering a loss implies that, in the end, life is affirmed. Mourning is a period in which those of us who remain alive withdraw from the world to commemorate, in a series of rituals, our lost loved ones. It is an evocation and a time in which the whole world seems to have lost if not all meaning (as in melancholy), then at least a very special one. Duel as battle, as long as it is not to the death and respects the rules of confrontation, implies that the tension between the forces is maintained, that although there is a winner, triumph does not compromise the life of the other. Thus, if the battle remains in the discursive terrain, it will produce a democratic public sphere. The *Duelista* is, then, the figure that reveals itself to be the democratic citizen, whose political practice is nothing but erotic.

Finally, the narration of history is the only practice against repetition, since, just as mourning does, it opens the future to unprecedented possibilities. The work of mourning is the construction of history through its registry, the naming and acknowledgment of not only the loss but also what was lost with it. In this sense, by not telling the truth about the fate of the disappeared, the Mexican state has deprived their families and friends of the right to reinvent their lives (that is, the right to a future). And although the prospect of constructing the future may seem daunting, it is better than being the prey of a cruel and permanently paralyzed present.

In political terms, collective mourning has two powerful effects: the first is the reopening of a future of possibilities for life after loss. The second is an intervention that interrupts the effects of a sedimented ontology, according to which some lives lost do not matter. In other words, collective mourning has the power to change an unfair and violent biopolitics that dictates that some lives are more worthy to be mourned than others. Realistically, it will be impossible for the *Buscadoras* to unearth all the bodies that the nation has abused with their disappearance. However, the very action of searching has been a political intervention that has transformed the public sphere and has interrupted the perverse idea that this forensic crisis is the sole responsibility of organized crime. The *Buscadoras* may fail in their goal of digging them all up, but their civil disobedience has already succeeded, for their action has enacted the equality they deserve and are owed by the state in their right to mourn. As Butler writes, "[I]n the asking, in the petition, [they] have already become something new" ("Violence" 44)—I would say, to begin with, by being bad victims.

ROSAURA MARTÍNEZ RUIZ is a professor of philosophy at the Universidad Nacional Autónoma de México. She is the author of *Freud y Derrida: escritura y psique* (Siglo XXI, 2013) and *Eros: Beyond the Death Drive* (Fordham University Press, 2021, originally published in Spanish in 2017). Her current research project, "Violence, Subjectivity, and Collective Trauma," focuses on forced disappearance, collective trauma, and mourning politics.

Notes

1   This article is a result of the research project "Violencia, subjetividad y trauma colectivo," sponsored by the National Autonomous University of Mexico–Universidad Nacional Autónoma de México through DGAPA PAPIIT IN402721.

2   Likewise, the mothers of the *Plaza de Mayo* in 1978 "only" asked to be told if their children were alive or dead. "Why don't they tell us if they are alive or dead? We want that and nothing more: that they respond to us, and then we will leave," one of them said in a documentary fragment from "Entrevista a Madres y Abuelas en Plaza de Mayo 1 de junio de 1978" ("Interviews of the Mothers and Grandmothers in the Plaza de Mayo 1st of June of 1978") (Parque; my translation). Nevertheless, her complaint did not die out; it became the creation in Argentina of the National Bank of Genetic Data, and her white handkerchiefs turned green in the "green wave" feminists who fought for legal and safe abortion and finally triumphed in 2021 with its decriminalization.

3   Since the prime suspect in these crimes is organized crime in collusion with the authorities, many *Buscadoras* have chosen to state that they are not looking for the culprits as a safety strategy.

4   Poorly carried out exhumations, insufficient staff and forensic facilities, funeral homes turned into forensic medical services, bodies lost in the labyrinth of bureaucracy or delivered to the wrong families reflect the forensic collapse in Mexico.

5   i(dh)EAS is a Mexican NGO of stra-
    tegic human rights litigation. Pas-
    sages from Rosete's and Lorusso's
    texts are my own translations from
    the Spanish.

6   *La Llorona* is a Mexican legend
    that tells the story of a woman
    who, after losing her children,
    grieves her loss and calls for their
    return throughout Mexico.

7   Many feminist collectives in
    Latin America use this phrase as
    a political slogan to refer to the
    need or desire to break every-
    thing, as the patriarchal ideology

has permeated everything. As
of 2016, the Network of National
Links (Red de Enlaces Nacionales)
organizes National Search Days
(Jornada Nacional de Búsqueda)
every year. In this context, several *Buscadoras* associations and
NGOs gather in a troubled region
in Mexico to carry out searches
in open fields and forensic identification, as well as to look for
victims and to warn schools and
ecclesiastic communities against
enforced disappearance. These
groups also look to make federal
and local authorities sensitive to
this problem.

Works Cited

Athanasiou, Athena. *Agonistic Mourning: Political Dissidence and the Women in Black*. Edinburgh: Edinburgh UP, 2017.

Brito, Jaime Luis. "Tetelcingo: Bajo la visión implacable de las buscadoras." *Proceso* 29 May 2016. 32–34.

Buscadoras Gto. #10demayo2022. *Facebook* 10 May 2022. https://www.facebook.com/permalink.php?story_fbid=pfbid02o7kkbMwKGBQE2CPTAhYCW6EudCcSmaZpBtTkxXE1yoF5ooSn6pgfYY8b56goHHwal&id=104500384801717.

Butler, Judith. *Antigone's Claim: Kinship between Life and Death*. New York: Columbia UP, 2000.

——————. "Bodies in Alliance and the Politics of the Street." *Notes Toward a Performative Theory of Assembly*. Cambridge, MA: Harvard UP, 2015. 66–98.

——————. "To Preserve the Life of the Other." *The Force of Nonviolence*. New York: Verso, 2020. 67–102.

——————. "Violence, Mourning, Politics." *Precarious Life: The Powers of Mourning and Violence*. New York: Verso, 2004. 19–49.

de la Rosa, Perla. "Antígona: Las voces que incendian el desierto." *Cinco dramaturgos chihuahuenses*. Ed. G. de la Mora. Ciudad Juárez: Fondo Municipal, 2005. 187–228.

Derrida, Jacques "Letter to Francine Moreau." *The Work of Mourning*. Ed. Anne Brault and Michael Naas. Chicago: U of Chicago P, 2001. 94–103.

"'Encontré a mi hijo pero faltan miles más': Mirna Medina." *Pacifista* TV 12 Sept. 2017. https://web.archive.org/web/20220520111333/https://pacifista.tv/notas/encontre-a-mi-hijo-pero-faltan-miles-mas-mirna-medina.

Estados Unidos Mexicanos, Cámara de Diputados del H. Congreso de la Unión. "Ley General en Materia de Desaparición Forzada de Personas, Desaparición Cometida por Particulares y del Sistema Nacional de Búsqueda de Personas." 17 Nov. 2017. https://www.diputados.gob.mx/LeyesBiblio/pdf/LGMDFP.pdf.

Freud, Sigmund. "Mourning and Melancholia." 1917. *The Standard Edition of the Complete Psychological Works of Sigmund Freud.* Trans. and ed. James Strachey. Vol. 14. London: Hogarth, 1957. 243–58. 24 vols. 1953–1974.

Gambaro, Griselda. "Antígona furiosa." *Griselda Gambaro: Teatro 3.* Buenos Aires: Ediciones la Flor, 2011. 313–28.

Grupo Cultural Yuyachkani. *Antígona.* Lima: Yuyachkani, 2000.

Honig, Bonnie. *Antigone, Interrupted.* New York: Cambridge UP, 2013.

Honneth, Axel. "Personal Identity and Disrespect: The Violation of the Body, the Denial of Rights, and the Denigration of Ways of Life." *The Struggle for Recognition: The Moral Grammar of Social Conflicts.* London: Polity, 1995. 131–39.

——————. "'You' or 'We': The Limits of the Second-person Perspective." *European Journal of Philosophy* 29.3 (2021): 1–11.

Juárez, Santiago Mario, Juan Carlos Gutiérrez Contreras, and Zúe Valenzuela Contreras. *Guía práctica sobre la aplicación del protocolo homologado para la búsqueda de personas desaparecidas.* Mexico City: I(dh)EAS, 2017.

Lorusso, Fabrizio. "Desaparecer y buscar en Guanajuato: Respuestas colectivas frente a las violencias." *Korpus* 21 (2022): 507–30.

Martínez Ruiz, Rosaura. *Eros: Beyond the Death Drive.* Trans. Ramsey McGlazer. New York: Fordham UP, 2021.

Parque de la memoria. "Entrevista a Madres y Abuelas en Plaza de Mayo 1 de junio de 1978." *YouTube* 1 Aug. 2018. https://www.youtube.com/watch?v=OBlVz3VO09k.

Rosete, Erika. "Las madres buscadoras de América Latina: Sin miedo y con memoria." *El País* 29 May 2022. https://elpais.com/mexico/2022-05-29/las-madres-buscadoras-de-america-latina-sin-miedo-y-con-memoria.htmlrodani.

Sophocles. "Antigone." *Sophocles 1: Antigone, Oedipus the King, Oedipus at Colonus.* Trans. David Greene and Richard Lattimore. Chicago: U of Chicago P, 2013.

Taylor, Charles. "The Politics of Recognition." *Multiculturalism: Examining the Politics of Recognition.* Princeton: Princeton UP, 1994. 25–73.

Uribe, Sara. *Antígona González.* Oaxaca: Sur+ ediciones, 2012.

Wilhelm, Dagmar. *Axel Honneth: Reconceiving Social Philosophy.* New York: Rowman and Littlefield, 2019.

Damnations of Memory:
Monument Attacks in the United States, 2015–2021

Damnations of Memory

Since the mid-2010s, political protest in the United States has shifted to monuments like never before. Other countries have also seen a rise in monument attacks, but nowhere have there been more documented cases than in the United States. In the following, I explore these attacks as an acting-out of value conflicts. I ask what kinds of monuments were attacked, how the attacks were carried out, and about the attackers' explicit and implicit motivations. I look at three types of monument attacks: 1) monuments associated with racism and white supremacy; 2) monuments linked to genocides of Native Americans; and 3) the attack on the U.S. Capitol on January 6, 2021. I argue that attacks on monuments memorializing violence against African Americans and Native Americans were successful resolutions of value conflicts, whereas the assault on the Capitol was produced by, and deepened, a value paradox. As such, only the Capitol attack is an "acting out" in the sense of a misdirected act of aggression motivated by a misrecognition of the past.

Monument attacks are a peculiar type of collective and cultural memorial practice. Cultural memory has been defined as "a system of values,

Volume 34, Number 3   DOI 10.1215/10407391-10898269

artifacts, institutions, and practices that retain the past for the present and the future. It transfers knowledge and supports the emergence and elaboration of distinct identities" (Assmann 26). The study of cultural memory was inaugurated by the French sociologist Maurice Halbwachs. For Halbwachs, history does not exist as an objective set of facts, but is the product of a selective and interpretive process of mediation. What is remembered and how it is remembered are subject to power struggles. Even though monuments are commissioned by political and economic elites, the elites cannot fully control what they mean. Halbwachs's communicative approach informs the social study of collective memory and monuments: "Research into the politics of memory [. . .] focus[es] on the communicative pathways that mediate interactions between the informal public sphere of opinion-formation (such as public opinion and broader social movements) and the formal institutions of legal will-formation. Although this approach highlights the importance of the state as the primary nexus for memory disputes, it takes developments within civil society and international factors into account as well" (Verovšek 3). Attacks on monuments are acts of violence against artifacts that represent a past that has become intolerable in the present.

The political act of destroying monuments is as old as the building of them. Monument destruction was so routinized in ancient Rome that the act had its own name: *damnatio memoirae*, "damnation of memory." In the Roman Empire, images of political rulers were placed in all public, ritual, and domestic spaces. When a ruler was deposed, "his images were systematically mutilated or physically altered [. . .]. The Romans themselves realized that it was possible to alter posterity's perception of the past especially as embodied in the visual and epigraphic record" (Varner 1). Historicist ideas that monuments must always be protected or that history should never be rewritten only date back to the Enlightenment period of the eighteenth century. Before that, the memorialization of the past was explicitly political.

Cultural memory practices are vital in the making of political collectives. Political theory identifies two modes of collective memory practices. One celebrates the past as a heroic achievement. This is typical for the nation-states that emerged in the eighteenth and nineteenth centuries. The other mode, typical of postcolonial and postcommunist states that emerged in the twentieth century, focuses on struggle, trauma, and victimhood. Memorial practices in these nations are anchored in "historical wounds" (Chakrabarty 77). The current war over how to remember u.s. history is a struggle between these two modes of memorialization. Traditionally, the United States remembered its history in an unabashedly heroic mode.

But over the past decade, memorialization has partially shifted toward a wounded mode. The recognition of past trauma makes it necessary to reject heroic memorialization. Violent conflicts over historic monuments are a confrontation between these two modes of memorialization. The heroic mode defends heroic monuments; the wounded mode attacks heroic monuments. The wounded mode is evident in attacks on monuments associated with slavery and those linked to violence against Native Americans. The attackers on the u.s. Capitol framed their actions as both heroic and wounded. This produced an unresolvable value paradox.

If cultural memory is a "system of values, artifacts, institutions, and practices," then contests over monuments can also be interpreted as political valuing practices (Ecks 16). Monuments are attacked when the values they embody become unacceptable. Monument attacks are attacks on both the medium and the memory, the signifier and the signified. Monuments are erected when the remembrance of what they represent is considered good. Monuments are destroyed when the remembrance of what they represent is considered bad. Valuations are negotiations between different social actants. What is valuable and what is not depends on the criteria of value, thus various groups can differ as to what they recognize as good. Valuations depend on transparency about what is being valued and who is doing the valuing. Valuations differ by the degree to which they are institutionalized and routinized. How something is valued also depends on the expertise required to do a competent valuation. Monuments are evaluated both for what they signify and as signifiers. The will to destroy a monument springs from an intense value conflict. When a group sees what is signified as deeply at odds with its own values, and when the value of keeping the signifier does not make up for the offense it causes, the monument falls. But a resolution of value conflicts can only occur when heroic monuments are destroyed from an unambiguously wounded position. When a heroic monument is attacked from an ambiguous mixture of heroic and wounded modes, value conflicts are not resolved, but deepened.

In the United States, *damnatio memoirae* are as old as the republic. The first time a large monument was destroyed was days after the signing of the Declaration of Independence in 1776. In celebration of independence, a citizens' society called the Sons of Liberty pulled down the statue of King George III at New York's Bowling Green (Marks 61). This was the first large monument in North America to be destroyed as a political act. The destruction of George III's statue in July 1776 damned the memory both of the monarch and of what he signified: colonial dependence and political tyranny. The

Sons of Liberty had a different valuation of George III than the British. There was perfect transparency about who George III was and how to evaluate him: the Revolutionary War had just begun. British rule was not yet history; in fact, British troops would recapture New York a few months later. There was no need for historians to evaluate George III's biography or the history of the British colonies in North America. No expert committees had to be convened to evaluate the statue. The new Americans despised the presence of the British and the monarchy. Some may have argued that there was value in keeping the statue so that later generations would be reminded of past tyranny. Someone may have argued that the statue must remain because history should never be rewritten. But in 1776, the will to exact *damnatio memoirae* upon the British monarch was unequivocal. The destruction of a monument honoring George III enacted the opening paragraph of the Declaration: toppling the statue expressed that it was "necessary for one people to dissolve the political bands which have connected them with another." The George III monument was built by the British in a heroic mode and it was destroyed in a heroic mode.

Psychoanalysis adds another layer of insight: monument attacks can be seen as a form of acting out. Freud defined acting out (*agieren* or *abagieren*) as a form of nonverbal working through of past conflicts. Instead of a conscious remembering, the patient acts out a suppressed affect by repeating it (*Wiederholung*). The patient does not recognize the action as a repetition. *Ausagieren* can be a form of transference where the patient projects suppressed conflicts onto the therapist. For example, instead of remembering an authority conflict with their parents, a patient acts defiantly against the therapist. Freud detected a deep correlation between a patient's resistance against conscious remembering and acting out: "The greater the resistance, the more extensively will acting out (repetition) replace remembering" (151). Lacan later distinguished verbal acting out from the *passage à l'acte* as a nonverbal rupture in the therapeutic relationship (42). Lacan's *passage à l'acte* could take violent forms, either against the self or against others. Acting out can be broadened beyond dyadic therapeutic relations, as a form of collective action that reactualizes past hurt without conscious remembering.

The monument attacks that I analyze are both similar to and different from acting out. Monument attacks are different from acting out because they are not unconscious acts; instead, they are conscious ways of working through past hurt. Instead of a resistance to remembering, the attacks make remembrance explicit. Attacks are inversely related to the strength of remembering: the less the resistance is to remembering, the stronger is the attack. There are also remarkable similarities between attacks and acting out: both are ways of working through past hurt. Both are violent acts: always violent against an object, often violent against people. Monument attacks are often repetitions of past acts, both in form and in affect. For the pro-Trump attackers, their assault on the Capitol in 2021 was a repetition of the American Revolution of 1776. Acting out only occurs when the hurtful past is *misrecognized* and aggression is directed at a substitute target. Acting out is a *failed* attempt at a value resolution. In this sense, I argue that only the Capitol attack would qualify as acting out.

America's first damnation of memory happened in 1776. America's largest wave of monument attacks has happened since the mid-2010s. America's largest monument attack happened on January 6, 2021. For the attackers, the storm on the Capitol was both a heroic repetition of the patriotic uprising of 1776 and a wounded retaliation for previous attacks on heroic national monuments. By its odd mixture of heroic and wounded modes, the Capitol attack deepened value conflicts rather than resolving them. In the following sections, I will look in detail at the three most significant clusters of monument attacks in the United States in the past decade to elucidate their forms and motivations and to discern if they were carried out in a heroic or a wounded mode.

Defacing Racists

By far the largest cluster of wounded monument attacks addresses racism toward African Americans. The years since 2015 have seen a steep increase in the renaming, removal, and destruction of monuments to people associated with slavery, segregation, and white supremacy. The process began with a wave of unnamings. In 2014 and 2015, Duke and East Carolina universities removed Charles Aycock's name from campus buildings. Aycock was the governor of North Carolina from 1901 until 1905 and an advocate of white supremacy (Krueger). In 2015, the University of Maryland removed the name of H. C. Byrd from its sports stadium. As university president from 1936 to 1954, Byrd upheld segregationist policies, barring African Americans from gaining admission (Svrluga). Princeton University took Woodrow Wilson's name off of its public policy school and the Wilson College in June 2020. Princeton's president explained that Wilson's racist attitudes were "significant and consequential even by the standards of his own time," especially his resegregation of the civil service long after it had already been integrated (Carew). The University of Illinois at Chicago unnamed its law school in 2021.

John Marshall, for whom it was named, was the U.S. Supreme Court chief justice from 1801 to 1835. He was also a slave trader and supported slavery in his legal work ("Board").

Harvard Law School used to carry the seal of Isaac Royall Jr. (1719–1781) in recognition of his large donations. Royall was Massachusetts's richest enslaver and known for his excessive brutality. In 2015, a campaign group called #RoyallMustFall lobbied the university to distance itself from this tainted past. The Harvard movement was a socially mediated response to #RhodesMustFall, which started in 2015 in Cape Town and spread to other places with Rhodes statues. (In 2016, Harvard Law responded to #RoyallMustFall's campaign by adopting a new seal to sever its association with Royall (Duehren and Parker).

Monuments to the Confederate States of America are among the most contentious. The majority of Confederate monuments were built during the first two decades of the twentieth century at the peak of segregationist policies. Right-wing commentators argue that Confederate monuments are symbols of national unity that expressed the reintegration of Confederate history into United States history. These sites commemorated brave soldiers who sacrificed their lives during the Civil War (Ryback, Ellis, and Glahn 65). Attacks on Confederate monuments are considered by many on the Right to be attacks on Southern honor and tradition, with some even claiming that African Americans have cherished these monuments as much as whites have and that the monuments were never meant to symbolize white supremacy. Most academic historians contradict this right-wing reading, noting that Confederate monuments, especially the thousands of statues erected around the turn of the century, were designed "to intimidate African Americans politically and isolate them from the mainstream of public life" ("AHA"). Taking down these monuments, they argue, is not about rewriting history; it is about who should be honored in a public space. Slavers should not be honored. Confederate monuments were meant to glorify slavery and segregation, and this message was clearly understood by African Americans ("Stone").

In 2015, a white supremacist killed nine African Americans in a church in Charleston, South Carolina. These murders triggered the removal of dozens of Confederate statues across the South. In response, right-wing activists organized a defense of the monuments. Trying to stop the removal of Confederate general Lee's statue at Charlottesville, Virginia, a far-right coalition of the Proud Boys, the Ku Klux Klan, and the Twitter group @UniteTheRightVA organized a protest rally in August 2017. At a torch-lit march, the right-wing protesters shouted, "You will not replace us," "Jews will not displace us," and "White Lives Matter," articulating an existential connection between Confederate statues and the white race: destroying these statues was the same as destroying white people (Wildman). The next day, when the white supremacists congregated around Lee's monument, large crowds of counterprotesters gathered around them. As more right-wingers arrived in the city and marched toward the Lee statue, they clashed with the counterprotesters. A member of the Proud Boys rammed his car into a group of counterprotesters, killing one and injuring thirty-five.

In a press conference after Charlottesville, President Trump defended the white supremacists: "You also had people that were very fine people, on both sides" ("Full"). In his view, there may have been a few radicals among the protesters, but the majority were good citizens who simply wanted to defend a cherished monument: "Many of those people were there to protest the taking down of the statue of Robert E. Lee." In this account, historic monuments should never be removed; American history should never be rewritten.

In May 2020, George Floyd, a forty-six-year-old African American, was killed by police officers in Minneapolis during an arrest. One of the police officers put his knee on Floyd's neck for nearly ten minutes. Floyd's extreme distress was clearly visible from the mobile phone footage recorded by bystanders. He said "I can't breathe" at least sixteen times, but the officer kept the stranglehold. Social media footage of George Floyd's murder triggered what may have been the largest protest wave in U.S. history (Buchanan, Bui, and Patel). When videos of Floyd's murder went viral, protests erupted across the United States and in sixty countries worldwide. Protesters aligned themselves with #BlackLivesMatter (BLM), a movement started in 2013 in the wake of the police killing of Trayvon Martin, a young African American in Florida (Francis and Wright-Rigueur; Lebron). Most of the protests were peaceful, but when police officers were attacked, shops looted, and property damaged, hundreds of U.S. cities imposed curfews and more than thirty states called in the National Guard. At least 14,000 people were arrested. More than one billion dollars in insurance claims were filed (Kingson). During the protests, hundreds of monuments were defaced, destroyed, or removed. Monuments to Confederate history were the top targets. Almost one hundred Confederate monuments were demolished in 2020 (Treisman).

Monuments of former U.S. presidents also became targets of attack. Theodore Roosevelt's statue at New York's American Museum of

Natural History was taken down because it depicted white supremacy. Roosevelt's great-grandson approved: "The world does not need statues, relics of another age, that reflect neither the values of the person they intend to honor nor the values of equality and justice" (qtd. in Pogrebin). Statues of Thomas Jefferson and George Washington were attacked for their histories of slave ownership, and on June 22, 2020, protesters tried to tear down Andrew Jackson's statue near the White House.

To quell these protests, Trump signed the Executive Order on Protecting American Monuments, Memorials, and Statues and Combating Recent Criminal Violence on June 26, 2020. The order increased the maximum punishment for attacks on historic monuments to ten years jail time. As Trump says in the order, "[T]he first duty of government is to ensure domestic tranquility." The previous weeks had, according to the order, seen "a sustained assault on the life and property of civilians, law enforcement officers, government property, and revered American monuments such as the Lincoln Memorial." The attackers were said to be driven by extremist ideologies of "Marxism" and "anarchy." Radicals were allegedly targeting monuments because of a "desire to indiscriminately destroy anything that honors our past and to erase from the public mind any suggestion that our past may be worth honoring, cherishing, remembering, or understanding." The order details specific attacks, pointing out how they reveal a "deep ignorance of our history." "My administration will not allow violent mobs incited by a radical fringe to become the arbiters of the aspects of our history that can be celebrated in public spaces," Trump's order declared. To defend monuments was to "defend the fundamental truth that America is good, her people are virtuous, and that justice prevails."

Trump's speech at Mount Rushmore on July 4, 2020 similarly focused on monument attacks. CNN reporter Leyla Santiago introduced the speech in view of the ongoing George Floyd protests: "Kicking off the Independence Day Weekend, President Trump will be at Mount Rushmore, where he'll be standing in front of a monument of two slave owners and on land wrestled away from Native Americans" (qtd. in Krishnamurthy). The slaveholders referred to are George Washington and Thomas Jefferson, the Native Americans the Lakota Sioux.

At Mount Rushmore, Trump described the 2020 protests as "a merciless campaign to wipe out our history, defame our heroes, erase our values, and indoctrinate our children" ("Remarks"). Attacks on historic monuments were declared to be attacks on "our country, and all of its values, history, and culture." Destroying monuments was, according to

Trump, tantamount to a treasonous attack on American democracy: "Make no mistake: this left-wing cultural revolution is designed to overthrow the American Revolution." Trump would defend the monuments with all his might: "This attack on our liberty, our magnificent liberty, must be stopped, and it will be stopped very quickly." People who attack national monuments in the name of racial justice are, according to Trump and his supporters, attacking the foundations of racial justice: "They would tear down the principles that propelled the abolition of slavery in America." Referring to George Washington, Trump swore "he will never be removed, abolished, and most of all, he will never be forgotten."

The George Floyd protests added further urgency to the question of how to deal with the historical wounds of racism, segregation, and slavery. One of the most prominent initiatives came from Washington, DC, where Muriel Bowser, the Democratic mayor, was overall supportive of the George Floyd protests. She sponsored renaming a Washington street near the White House "Black Lives Matter Plaza" and had "Black Lives Matter" painted in huge yellow letters onto it. She also convened the District of Columbia Facilities and Commemorative Expressions (DCFACES) Working Group. The acronym is a double Freudian slip: it looks like "defaces" and evokes "dick faces." BLM Plaza, with the White House and the Washington Monument in the background, also features on the cover page of the DCFACES report, which makes explicit reference to how George Floyd's murder "fueled winds of change and unprecedented levels of activism in the battle for inclusion, equality, and justice. The movement following Floyd's death led cities, states, and the federal government to reflect and reconsider commemorations in the modern context" (DCFACES 3).

The working group was tasked with evaluating "named DC government-owned facilities and mak[ing] recommendations as to what, if any, actions need to be taken if the person the facility is named for is inconsistent with DC values and in some way encouraged the oppression of African Americans and other communities of color or contributed to our long history of systemic racism" (DCFACES 3). All "assets," such as schools, campuses, parks, public buildings, streets, and statues, must be aligned with DC values of accessibility, diversity, equity, liveability, opportunity, prosperity, resilience, and safety (DCFACES 4). Assets were scrutinized for violating DC values along five criteria: participation in slavery, involvement in systemic racism, support for oppression, involvement in supremacist agendas, and violation of DC human rights laws.

There were more than 3,000 assets in DC, of which 1,330 were named after a person and 153 were "persons of concern." When problems were identified in these persons' biographies, the group could recommend renaming, removal, or contextualization. Assets could be freed from further scrutiny or recommended for further research. Some of the historical figures found to violate DC values were Thomas Jefferson, Benjamin Franklin, Alexander Graham Bell, Zachary Taylor, Woodrow Wilson, and Andrew Jackson (DCFACES 17).

The first release of the DCFACES report recommended that the District "remove, relocate, or contextualize" eight national monuments because of who they honored: the Columbus Fountain, Benjamin Franklin's statue, Andrew Jackson's statue, the Jefferson Memorial, the George Mason Memorial, the Newlands Memorial Fountain, the Albert Pike statue, the George Washington statue, and the Washington Monument. Most monuments were to be "contextualized," for example, by adding George Washington's slave ownership to the narrative for his monuments (DCFACES 7).

DCFACES' proposals met with a furious response from conservatives. James Comer and Jim Jordan, senior Republicans in Congress, wrote a letter to Bowser that strongly objected to the recommendations and questioned the legitimacy of DCFACES: "We are shocked and appalled that Washington, DC—the seat of government for our great nation and named for our first President—would seek to erase the legacy of our nation's founders and trivialize their contributions to the American experiment" (Comer and Jordan). Bowser was asked to hand over all documentation relating to DCFACES to a judicial oversight committee, and to "refrain from wasting taxpayer dollars on misadventures in historical revisionism meant to placate radical left-wing activists."

After the conservative backlash, the report was quietly withdrawn (Weil and Brice-Saddler). An amended version was published soon after that does not mention any national monuments. But founding figures like Washington, Franklin, and Jefferson remain "persons of concern." For DCFACES, violations of DC's declared core values overrode any other positive valuation. Thomas Jefferson might have been the principal author of the Declaration of Independence, but his slave ownership overrode any value attached to his other achievements. DCFACES is a stark example of how a heroic mode of memorialization can be undone and remade by a wounded mode. Erstwhile "heroes" of the past were called out for the violence and trauma they caused. DCFACES presents a dramatic revaluation of historical figures. The wounds they were said to have inflicted outweighed any of their heroic actions.

Native Americans

The second cluster of American *damnatio memoirae* since the 2010s concerns violence against Native Americans. Two figures were especially targeted, Christopher Columbus (1451–1506) and Junípero Serra (1713–1784), both seen as representatives of racism and genocidal violence against Native Americans. This cluster of attacks, also motivated by a wounded revaluation of history, is largely located in the Atlantic Northeast (Columbus) and in California (Serra).

In the immediate aftermath of Charlottesville, a series of attacks targeted monuments to Christopher Columbus. Columbus now symbolized the genocidal expansion of European imperialism. In 2017, attackers destroyed Columbus statues in different cities. In New York, protesters sprayed "hate will not be tolerated" and "#somethingscoming" on the Columbus statue pedestal at Central Park (Nir and Mays). In 2020, the University of Notre Dame covered its Columbus murals, which were painted in the nineteenth century, because they display Native Americans prostrating in submission before white European colonizers ("Teaching").

During the George Floyd protests, protesters attacked several statues of Juan de Oñate (1550–1626), a Spanish conquistador responsible for genocidal attacks on Pueblo Indians in New Mexico. Other targets were statues of Kit Carson (1809–1868), a western frontiersman who came to symbolize the mistreatment of Native Americans by white settler colonialism.

Since 2015, several attacks have been carried out against statues of Junípero Serra (1713–1784), the "Apostle of California." During the late eighteenth century, Serra founded the first nine of twenty-one Catholic missions in California, including San Diego and San Francisco's Mission Dolores. Pope Francis canonized Serra on his first visit to the United States in 2015. Efforts to canonize Serra started in 1934 at the request of the bishop of Monterey-Fresno ("Padre"). Seven thousand five hundred pages of interviews and documents were compiled to prove that Serra deserved sainthood, but he was only beatified in 1985 when the spontaneous healing of a nun was attributed to him. In 2015, Pope Francis "bypassed the usual requirement of two verified miracles for declaring sainthood" to fast-track the process. Francis sees the current era as an age of renewed evangelization, which is why a great missionary like Serra took priority for sainthood.

Serra's canonization in 2015 was perceived by many as an indefensible glorification of colonial violence against Native Americans. After the canonization, Serra's statue at Carmel Mission was defaced with paint. Surrounding graves were also targeted by protesters, specifically the graves of people with European names, leading the police to investigate the attack as a racial hate crime (Rocha). In October 2015, Serra's statue in Monterey was decapitated. In 2017, a Serra statue at Santa Barbara was decapitated and painted red. Serra's statue at San Gabriel was attacked in 2017. After George Floyd's murder in June 2020, Serra's statue at San Francisco was toppled. Protesters sprayed "Stolen Land," "Olone [sic] Land," "Decolonize," and the encircled A icon for anarchy on the pedestal. The attack was part of a wider campaign against historical memorials in San Francisco's Golden Gate Park (Severn). The same year, activists destroyed the Serra statues at Sacramento and at Mission San Rafael Arcángel. In the summer of 2020, activists threatened to bring down Serra's statue at Ventura. Fearing violence and unrest, Ventura city council stripped the statue of its legal landmark status and dismantled it in the middle of the night to avoid direct conflict ("Ventura").

Native American protest groups toppled Serra's statue in downtown Los Angeles in June 2020. "We have reached a time and space when the oppressed are taking a firm stance, saying 'enough is enough,' a time when we have to dismantle a system that does not work, and never has worked, for our people of color [. . .]. It is time to teach the truth and remove the lies and the oppression. It is time to remove the commemoration of hate, bigotry, and colonization," said Jessa Calderon, a representative of the Chumash and Tongva people ("Junipero"). The protesters tied a rope around Serra's neck and pulled until the statue crashed to the ground.

Violence against monuments to Serra responds to a long history of violence against Native Americans. The Catholic missions in California were pioneer outposts of the Spanish empire (Tutino). In the late eighteenth century, Spain was expanding northwards, competing with Russian, French, and British empires. Serra's missions expanded by converting Native Americans through deception and coercion. The missions were agricultural estates run on the back of forced labor (Madley). Living conditions were bad: "The Franciscans interned neophytes [. . .] in sex-segregated, filthy barracks-type quarters" (Field et al. 293). Many died of infectious diseases. Sexual abuse was rampant, perpetrated by priests, traders, and soldiers stationed in the missions. Native Americans were kept like prisoners: "The missions resembled penal institutions [. . .] with the practice of locking up some neophytes at night and restricting movements outside the mission grounds, the use of corporal punishment, and the relatively tight control of behavior" (Lightfoot 62). Once Native Americans were baptized, they became the property of the mission, and leaving was no longer allowed. Like slaves, runaways from the mission were hunted down, brought back, and punished. Violent confrontations between Native Americans and the missions were frequent, and in the decades following the establishment of the missions, Native Americans lost more than half of their people (Bean). Due to disease and abuse, the number of neophytes in the California missions dwindled, from more than 18,000 in 1800 to less than 1,000 in 1839 (Field et al.). In the wake of the Spanish missions, "natives faced an era of death" (Tutino 477). Serra's missions "caused a demographic collapse throughout the region" (Field, "Complicities" 196).

The defenders of Serra paint a different picture. They argue that Serra's missions were not an outpost of the Spanish empire but a protective buffer against colonial oppression (*Man*). When Serra saw how Spanish soldiers brutalized the natives, these defenders claim, he walked three thousand kilometers to Mexico City to implore the viceroy for better protection. The frequent use of floggings and physical punishments may be undeniable, but they were normal practice at the time; punishments were meant to purify the soul; and in any case, Serra did not participate in them (*Man*). Several activist groups, such as the Coalition for Historical Integrity (CHI) and Defend Serra, came to the defense of Serra's memory against the attacks. Attacks on Serra statues "felt like attacks on a family member, on someone you love," said Monica Garcia, a member of CHI. "When we see him torn down, and all these false accusations, it really becomes an attack on *my* face, and *my* values," argued Anna Tretko of Defend Serra. "I just really could not believe the degree of desecration, and the hate that brought it down. There has never been an event in my life as a Catholic like walking around a destroyed, vandalized, desecrated memorial to a saint," said Audrey Ortega, a Catholic citizen of Sacramento (*Man*).

There are further instances of historical figures associated with violence against Native Americans. For example, Alfred Kroeber, a first-generation U.S. anthropologist, became a target of protest, accused of racist attitudes in his work on Native Americans. In his encyclopedic *Handbook of the Indians of California* of 1925, Kroeber writes in detail about Californian groups. Several of his accounts reveal a racist attitude, as when he describes the Ohlone group as "dark, dirty, squalid, and apathetic" (466). He reports that they never smiled and never looked one in the eye, although he concedes that their "obvious paucity and rudeness" was partly to blame on Serra's Catholic missions (466). In 2021, Kroeber Hall, the home to the University of California, Berkeley's Department of Anthropology, was officially unnamed. Students petitioning for the change explained that renaming Kroeber Hall should be part of a deeper revaluation of California's Native American history: "Un-naming should not be mistaken as an erasure of history, nor as an attack on the anthropology department as a whole. Instead, it should be seen as an actionable step toward the commitment this institution has made to its Native American students, the Tribal communities it serves and the Ohlone communities whose land we currently occupy and continue to benefit from" (Cesspooch et al.). The cluster of attacks on monuments symbolic of violence against Native Americans shared the same wounded logic of *damnatio memoriae* as the attacks on racist monuments. The form of the attacks was the same. Only the painful history embodied in the monuments varied.

"If you don't fight like hell, you're not going to have a country anymore"

January 6, 2021 was the largest monument attack in u.s. history. It is also the most polysemic of all the monument attacks. What exactly happened was at first fiercely contested, both across entrenched political lines and within the Trump camp. What the event should be called was immediately controversial. Democrats called it an "attack," a "riot," an "insurrection," and an "attempted coup." Many Trump supporters denied that there was violence, calling it a "patriotic" demonstration or a "tour" of the Capitol. Some agreed that there was a riot but claimed that it was carried out under a false flag: the true attackers were left-wing agitators and FBI operatives.

The purpose and meaning of the attack has been highly contested. Was it an assault on democracy, the u.s. Constitution, and the peaceful transfer of power? Was it a defense of democracy, the Constitution, and the lawful transfer of power? Was this an assault on Congress as an institution? Was it a smear campaign against Trump and his supporters? An assault on the Capitol as the symbolic seat of government? An attack on the Capitol as a historic landmark? An attack on the electoral vote counting process? An attack on any member of Congress who rejected Trump's narrative of a stolen election?

Six people died during or as a result of the attack. One hundred and forty police officers were violently assaulted. The Department of Justice started the largest investigation in its history. By early 2023, more than 1,000 people had been identified and charged with crimes, and dozens have been convicted and sentenced to prison. Most of the attackers were charged with unlawful entry into, or violence aimed at, a restricted government building; others have been charged with sedition and obstruction of an official proceeding ("Garland").

Interpretations of January 6 still vary greatly. Even by 2023, 20 percent of U.S. adults support the Trump supporters who took over the Capitol. Among Republican voters, 32 percent support the takeover. Approval of the Capitol attack has been constantly *rising* since 2021 (Orth).

For Trump's opponents, January 6 was a negative "impact event," a singular moment of right-wing extremism and an unprecedented attack on American democracy. As has been said of other impact events, the Capitol assault was "perceived to spectacularly shatter the material and symbolic worlds that we inhabit [. . .]. The emphasis is here on the violent overturning of the social, cultural, and—in the case of extreme trauma—symbolic frames and the destruction of the material world in which we constitute meaning as social beings that inhabit shared social worlds" (Fuchs 12).

In turn, the Trump side argued that January 6 was not a singular event. Instead, it was an episode in the long struggle against the "radical left." To their minds, January 6 was a patriotic repetition of 1776 and the struggle for independence. The storm on the Capitol was a heroic defense of the nation's heroic values. What the "radical left" had done to heroic monuments and American values had been far worse than what happened at the Capitol.

Trump's opponents had to work hard against the heroic memorialization of January 6. Speaking from the Capitol on January 6, 2022, to mark the first anniversary of the attack, President Biden rejected all claims that the "deadly assault" on "this sacred place" was in the historical tradition of 1776 and Independence. It was a blatant lie, he said, "that the mob who sought to impose their will through violence are the nation's true patriots. Is that what you thought when you looked at the mob ransacking the Capitol, destroying property, literally defecating in the hallways, rifling through desks of senators and representatives, hunting down members of Congress? Patriots? Not in my view" (Biden). That the attack on a heroic monument could itself have been a heroic act had to be fiercely denied.

The National Commission to Investigate the January 6 Attack on the United States Capitol Complex was established to refute any heroic memorialization of the events. At the first hearing of the Commission in

July 2022, Senator Liz Cheney referenced a continuous history of peaceful transfers of power, with Trump as the sole exception:

> *There, in a sacred space in our constitutional republic, a place where our presidents lie in state, watched over by statues of Washington and Jefferson, Lincoln and Grant, Eisenhower, Ford, and Reagan, against every wall that night encircling the room, there were* SWAT *teams [. . .]. [T]hese brave men and women rested beneath paintings depicting the earliest scenes of our Republic, including one painted in 1824, depicting George Washington resigning his commission, voluntarily relinquishing power, handing control of the Continental Army back to Congress. [. . .] The sacred obligation to defend this peaceful transfer of power has been honored by every American president . . . except one.*

The Capitol is one of the nation's sacred spaces; the attackers wanted to desecrate it; Trump is the only president in U.S. history who had ever tried to pervert the peaceful transfer of power. There was absolutely nothing heroic about this attack on a heroic symbol of U.S. democracy.

Opponents of Trump had to work so hard to destroy heroic memorializations because the Trump side had many convinced that the Capitol protesters were the true patriots. The "Save America March" of January 6 was organized by a pro-Trump group called Women for America First (WFAF), which had also set up the Facebook page "Stop the Steal" after the elections. The executive director of WFAF, Kylie Jane Kremer, began tweeting about the march in December 2020: "The calvary [sic] is coming, Mr. President!" The poster contained in the tweets described the goal of the march: "to demand transparency & protect election integrity."

The first time that Trump spoke about a monument attack was in 2017 after the Charlottesville events. Any other president would have condemned the far-right extremists who shouted "White Lives Matter" and brutally attacked counterprotesters, but Trump sided with the "very fine people" allegedly among them. Trump's narrative was that attacking monuments meant attacking American values and that defending monuments meant defending American values. Monuments were heroic, and defending monuments was heroic, too.

Trump's speeches following the George Floyd protests also argued that defending monuments meant defending heroic values: "This attack on our liberty, our magnificent liberty, must be stopped, and it will be stopped very quickly," as he said at Mount Rushmore ("Remarks"). Trump telling his supporters on January 6 that "we love you, you are very special" confirmed the framing of the attack as a patriotic uprising in defense of American values and freedom ("Video"). The attackers' references to the American Revolution confirm that many thought they were repeating the 1776 uprising against political tyranny. Cries of "Freedom," "1776," and "Defend the Constitution," along with the many flags associated with the American Revolution, staged the storming of the Capitol as a repetition of the War of Independence.

In an address to the Faith and Freedom conference in 2022, Trump repeated the interpretation of January 6 as a patriotic event in the tradition of 1776. His "movement" was committed to the "core values" of 1776: "We believe that the Declaration of Independence and the American Constitution represent the principle of human civilization. Our founding documents are not a source of shame. They are a source of great pride. [. . .] We believe in law and order [. . .]. We reject censorship, blacklisting. and cancel culture" (Faith). He again blamed the "radical left" for attacking both these core values and the monuments that represent these values: "[T]oday, each of these principles is under tremendous threat, under a threat like never before. Everything we hold dear [. . .] is under merciless assault from the radical left. These people are taking a sledgehammer to the very foundations of our society [. . .] trying to shred our Constitution, trying to demolish the rule of law [. . .]. The greatest danger to America is not our enemies from the outside." Trump believed the attackers are "driven by envy and intolerance, bigotry, malice, and even rage against nature itself."

With this heroic framing, the Trump side could not help but be conflicted about January 6. Right after the attack on the Capitol, WFAF distanced themselves from any violence perpetrated "by a handful of bad actors." They also used a wounded argument by claiming that the radical left had routinized violence as an acceptable form of politics: "Unfortunately, for months the left and the mainstream media told the American people that violence was an acceptable political tool. They were wrong. It is not" (Steakin, Santucci, and Faulders). The "violence" referenced here was the unrest after George Floyd's murder in 2020, accepted among left-leaning politicians. The violence at the Capitol came from a wounded position.

In the aftermath of January 6, Trump also emphasized a wounded framing. In a January 6 tweet, Trump said that "[t]hese are the things and events that [happen] when a sacred landslide election victory is so unceremoniously & viciously stripped away from great patriots who have been badly & unfairly treated for so long." Trump struggled to frame the Capitol assault in a purely heroic mode. Instead, he assumed a wounded position in order to reclaim the events as heroic. In a statement against the January 6 Commission hearings in June 2022, Trump followed the same strategy: "They are desperate to change the narrative of a failing nation, without even making mention of the havoc and death caused by the radical left just months earlier" (Statement). However, Trump's claims to being a wounded victim deepened the value confusion about what January 6 meant.

There is overwhelming evidence that the people who marched on the Capitol understood their own actions as heroic. The flags waived on January 6 abounded with historical references to different periods in u.s. history (Quito and Shendruk). Confederate flags remembered the Civil War of 1861 to 1865, with proslavery connotations. Most of the flags referenced the Revolutionary War period, 1775 to 1783. Trump supporters carried "We the People" banners that quoted the first line of the u.s. Constitution. Many carried the Betsy Ross flag, an early version of the star-spangled banner, with thirteen stars representing the colonies that fought for Independence in 1776. The Come and Take It flag carried by others originated in a revolutionary battle at Fort Morris in 1778. The motto "Don't tread on me" with a rattlesnake featured on several flags associated with American Independence: the Culpeper Minutemen, the Gadsden, and the South Carolina Navy. The Three Percenters flag represented a progun extremist group that makes the bogus claim that it only took 3 percent of the American population to kick out the British in 1776, meaning that a handful of armed patriots are capable of overthrowing an entire government (Quito and Shendruk).

The Capitol attackers' shouts give further evidence of how they made sense of their actions. Attackers screamed "stop the steal." The mob singled out "weak" Congress members as targets of attack: "You took an oath!" or "Fuck the traitors!" A Trump supporter explained the gallows in front of the Capitol: "The people in this house, who stole this election from us, hanging from a gallows out here in this lawn for the whole world to see, so it never happens again" (qtd. in Hodges).

One of the protesters explains why the crowd shouted "1776" and carried flags associated with Independence: "1776 was the year that we gained our Independence from England. So we chant '1776' because it reminds us of revolting against our government" (Four). Americans ostensibly needed to defend their country and their democratic ideals just like the founders of the Republic had done in 1776. The attack on the Capitol became the reenactment of the War of American Independence. The protesters shouted "1776!"; "Defend the Constitution!"; and "We are the People! Fuck the political class!" The rioters chanted "Whose house? Our house!" as if this was the rightful repossession of a building belonging to "the people." They shouted "Take the Capitol!" and "Freedom!" (*Four*).

After January 6, the Trump side struggled to arrive at an unambiguous evaluation. Trump's emphasis on a wounded past only deepened the conflicts. While some justified the violence as patriotism, many disavowed it. Some initially denied that there was any violence, or claimed that the event was faked by the Left. Attacking the Capitol in order to defend American democracy could not reestablish value congruence. Trump's narrative up to January 6 was that heroic monuments are attacked by a cowardly Left and successfully defended by heroic patriots. That a heroic nation could be defended by assaulting Capitol police officers, destroying property, and defecating in the halls of a national monument could never be made value congruent with the heroic framing of the "Save America" rally. The Capitol attack pushed Trump and his supporters into the position of political extremists they had previously assigned to the Left. A "cultural revolution [. . .] designed to overthrow the American Revolution" was instigated by Trump, not by the Left.

"He will never be removed, abolished, and most of all, he will never be forgotten"

Over the past decade, a steep rise in attacks by activists added to increasing numbers of sanctioned removals. Many sanctioned removals happened in anticipation of unauthorized attacks, or to avoid further attacks. For example, after the Unite the Right rally, Charlottesville's authorities first shrouded General Lee's statue in black and later removed it to avoid future violence. Activism against monuments has intensified, and authorities have become more responsive to activists' pressure. This has blurred the lines between sanctioned and unsanctioned monument removals.

Monument defenses have been both authorized and unauthorized, staged both by authorities and by citizens. An example of an authorized defense is Trump's Executive Order on Protecting American Monuments, Memorials, and Statues and Combating Recent Criminal Violence of June 2020. The right-wing rally at Charlottesville is an example of an unauthorized citizens' defense of a monument.

The power to decide if a monument should be maintained or removed has also become more egalitarian. Until 2020, most monument removals were authorized actions taken in consultation with experts.

DCFACES exemplifies how valuations of monuments rely on expert evidence. In turn, many of the most recent attacks on monuments did not refer to experts. Black Lives Matter protests did not commission historians to write reports on Confederate policies or on race relations in the nineteenth century.

Damnatio memoirae happens when a value conflict between what a monument represents and what political collectives consider good rises to the level of physical destruction. Memorials to representatives of racism and colonialism are felt to be more at odds with current values than ever before, and the will to assess monuments by current values rather than by past values is far greater than at any time in the past. DCFACES makes explicit that monument removals are driven by value conflicts. Participation in slavery, involvement in systemic racism, support for oppression, involvement in any supremacist agenda, and violation of human rights were named criteria for removing, renaming, and recontextualizing monuments. Key figures of American Independence, such as George Washington, Thomas Jefferson, and Benjamin Franklin, were not exempted from a harsh revaluation. For DCFACES, George Washington violates the values of Washington, DC. DCFACES exemplifies a fundamental shift from a heroic to a wounded mode of memorialization. A patriotic, self-celebratory way of remembering U.S. history is being displaced by a postsupremacy focus on past wounds. The rise of wounded memorial practices is emblematic of the United States becoming a postcolonial nation.

While the attack on the Capitol was motivated by a value conflict, carrying out the attack could never resolve it. Instead, it deepened existing value conflicts. That many Trump supporters later disavowed the attack, saying that true Republicans would never resort to violence, affirms that the Capitol storming could not resolve the conflict. Democracy could not be defended by attacking a key symbol of democracy. When Trump's framing shifted from a heroic defense of national monuments to a wounded attack on them, he only made the symbolizations messier.

The march on the Capitol was both an attack on and a defense of heroic U.S. values. It was a twisted attempt to restore value congruence. Attacking the Capitol to defend American democracy was bound to deepen the value paradox. By calling upon his supporters to march to the Capitol and to "fight like hell," Trump incited a violation of all the values he claims to defend (Trump, Rally).

"Acting out" can happen when a hurtful past is *misrecognized* and aggression is directed at a substitute target. Acting out is a *failed* attempt at a value resolution. In this sense, the attacks on monuments associated with violence against Native Americans and African Americans were not instances of acting out; they came from a clearly wounded position. These acts were motivated by a heightened recognition of a hurtful past and were directed at the right targets. They dramatized an intense value conflict that was successfully resolved by the demolition of offensive monuments.

The Capitol assault presents a different case. It was also motivated by a value conflict and sought its resolution, but the framing of the attack as heroic came from a fundamental misrecognition and ignorance of history, both the longer history of the United States since 1776 and the most recent history of protest. If a defense of u.s. democracy had indeed been the goal, the u.s. Capitol would not have been the right target. Later attempts to justify the Capitol assault as a wounded response only deepened the paradox. On January 6, Trump supporters acted out their misrecognition of the past, present, and future with deadly consequences.

STEFAN ECKS cofounded Edinburgh University's Medical Anthropology Programme. He teaches social anthropology in the School of Social and Political Sciences and has conducted ethnographic fieldwork in India, Nepal, Myanmar, and the United Kingdom. Recent work explores value in global pharmaceutical markets, changing ideas of mental health in South Asia, multimorbidity, poverty, and access to healthcare. Publications include *Living Worth: Value and Values in Global Pharmaceutical Markets* (Duke University Press, 2022) and *Eating Drugs: Psychopharmaceutical Pluralism in India* (New York University Press, 2013), as well as many journal articles on the intersections between health and economics.

Works Cited

"AHA Statement on Confederate Monuments." *American Historical Association* 28 Aug. 2017. https://www.historians.org/news-and-advocacy/aha-advocacy/aha-statement-on-confederate-monuments.

Assmann, Aleida. "Cultural Memory." *Social Trauma—An Interdisciplinary Textbook.* Ed. Andreas Hamburger, Camellia Hancheva, and Vamık D. Volkan. Cham: Springer, 2021. 25–36.

Bean, Lowell John, ed. *The Ohlone Past and Present: Native Americans of the San Francisco Bay Region.* Menlo Park: Ballena, 1994.

Biden, Joe. "Remarks by President Biden to Mark One Year since the January 6th Deadly Assault on the u.s. Capitol." *White House* 6 Jan. 2022. https://www.whitehouse.gov/briefing-room/speeches-remarks/2022/01/06/remarks-by-president-biden-to-mark-one-year-since-the-january-6th-deadly-assault-on-the-u-s-capitol/.

"Board Approves New Name for UIC Law." *UIC Today* 20 May 2021. https://today.uic.edu/board-approves-new-name-for-uic-law/.

Buchanan, Larry, Quoctrung Bui, and Jugal K. Patel. "Black Lives Matter May Be the Largest Movement in u.s. History." *New York Times* 3 July 2020. https://www.nytimes.com/interactive/2020/07/03/us/george-floyd-protests-crowd-size.html.

Carew, Sinéad. "Princeton to Drop Woodrow Wilson's Name from School." *Reuters* 27 June 2020. https://www.reuters.com/article/us-usa-protests-princeton-idUSKBN23Y0TU.

Cesspooch, Ataya, et al. "Native Student Organizations Want to Un-name Kroeber Hall, Are Frustrated with Faculty Pushback." *Daily Californian* 25 Aug. 2020. https://www.dailycal .org/2020/08/25/native-student-organizations-want-to-un-name-kroeber-hall-are-frustrated -with-faculty-pushback.

Chakrabarty, Dipesh. "History and the Politics of Recognition." *Manifestos for History.* Ed. Keith Jenkins, Sue Morgan, and Alun Munslow. New York: Routledge, 2007. 89–99.

Cheney, Liz. "Read: Liz Cheney's Opening Statement at Jan. 6 Select Committee Hearing." *Politico* 9 June 2022. https://www.politico.com/news/2022/06/09/liz-cheney-jan-6-committee -full-statement-00038730.

Comer, James, and Jim Jordan. Letter to Muriel Bowser. 4 Sept. 2020. https://oversight.house .gov/wp-content/uploads/2020/09/Letter-to-Mayor-Bowser-9-04-20.pdf.

DCFACES Working Group. "DCFACES Working Group Report." 1 Sept. 2020. https://mayor.dc.gov /sites/default/files/dc/sites/mayormb/page_content/attachments/DC%20FACES%20Executive %20Summary_r10sm.pdf.

Declaration of Independence. 4 July 1776. Transcript. *National Archives.* https://www.archives .gov/milestone-documents/declaration-of-independence#:~:text=The%20Continental %20Congress%20adopted%20the,1776%2C%20delegates%20began%20signing%20it (accessed 15 Jun. 2023).

Duehren, Andrew M., and Claire E. Parker. "Corporation Accepts Proposal to Change Law School Seal." *Harvard Crimson* 15 Mar. 2023. https://www.thecrimson.com/article/2016/3/15 /corporation-hls-seal-change/.

Ecks, Stefan. *Living Worth: Value and Values in Global Pharmaceutical Markets.* Durham: Duke UP, 2022.

Field, Les W. "Complicities and Collaborations: Anthropologists and the 'Unacknowledged Tribes' of California." *Current Anthropology* 40.2 (1999): 193–210.

——————, with Alan Leventhal and Rosemary Cambra. "Mapping Erasure: The Power of Nominative Cartography in the Past and Present of the Muwekma Ohlones of the San Francisco Bay Area." *Recognition, Sovereignty Struggles, and Indigenous Rights in the United States: A Sourcebook.* Ed. Jean O'Brien. Chapel Hill: U of North Carolina P, 2013. 287–309.

Four Hours at the Capitol. Dir. Jamie Roberts. HBO Documentary Films, 2021.

Francis, Megan Ming, and Leah Wright-Rigueur. "Black Lives Matter in Historical Perspective." *Annual Review of Law and Social Science* 17 (2021): 441–58.

Freud, Sigmund. "Remembering, Repeating, and Working-Through." 1914. *The Standard Edition of the Complete Psychological Works of Sigmund Freud.* Trans. and ed. James Strachey. Vol. 12. London: Hogarth, 1958. 145–56. 24 vols. 1953–1974.

Fuchs, Anne. *After the Dresden Bombing: Pathways of Memory, 1945 to the Present.* New York: Palgrave Macmillan, 2012.

"Garland Vows to Hold All January 6th Perpetrators Accountable under the Law." CNN. *YouTube* 5 Jan. 2022. https://youtu.be/3dqO8_hnDsM.

Halbwachs, Maurice. *Les Cadres sociaux de la mémoire*. Paris: F. Alcan, 1925.

Hodges, Lauren. "Trump Still Says His Supporters Weren't behind the Jan. 6 Attack—But I Was There." *NPR* 2 Jan. 2022. https://www.npr.org/2022/01/02/1068891351/january-6-insurrection -capitol-attack-trump-anniversary.

"Junipero Serra Statue in LA Comes Down." *L.A. Taco* 22 June 2020. https://www.youtube .com/watch?v=JZHFjoof2ag.

Kingson, Jennifer A. "Exclusive: $1 billion-plus Riot Damage Is Most Expensive in Insurance History." *Axios* 16 Sept. 2020. https://www.axios.com/2020/09/16/riots-cost-property-damage.

Kremer, Kylie Jane (@KylieJaneKremer). "The calvary is coming, Mr. President!" 19 Dec. 2020, 1:50 p.m. Tweet.

Kreuger, Sara. "UNC-CH Removes Names Aycock, Carr and Daniels from Campus Buildings." *WRAL News* 29 July 2020. https://www.wral.com/story/unc-ch-removes-names-aycock-carr -and-daniels-from-campus-buildings/19210169/.

Krishnamurthy, Chaitra. "CNN Calls Mount Rushmore 'Monument of Two Slave Owners,' Angry Internet Says 'Media Hates America.'" *MEA WorldWide* 3 July 2020. https://meaww .com/cnn-reporter-mount-rushmore-monument-two-slave-owners-internet-media-hates -america-reactions.

Kroeber, Alfred. *Handbook of the Indians of California. Bureau of American Ethnology Bulletin* 78.1 (1925): 1–995.

Lacan, Jacques. "The Function and Field of Speech and Language in Psychoanalysis." *Écrits: A Selection*. Trans. Alan Sheridan. London: Routledge, 1989. 33–125.

Lebron, Christopher J. *The Making of Black Lives Matter: A Brief History of an Idea*. New York: Oxford UP, 2017.

Lightfoot, Kent G. *Indians, Missionaries, and Merchants: The Legacy of Colonial Encounters on the California Frontiers*. Berkeley: U of California P, 2004.

Madley, Benjamin. *An American Genocide: The United States and the California Indian Catastrophe, 1846–1873*. New Haven: Yale UP, 2016.

Man of God, A Mission of Love: St. Junípero Serra Documentary. Spirit Juice Prod., 2021. *Knights of Columbus*. https://www.kofc.org/en/news-room/st-junipero-serra-documentary /index.html (accessed 3 July 2023).

Marks, Arthur S. "The Statue of King George III in New York and the Iconology of Regicide." *American Art Journal* 13.3 (1981): 61–82.

Nir, Sarah Maslin, and Jeffrey C. Mays. "Christopher Columbus Statue in Central Park Is Vandalized." *New York Times* 12 Sept. 2017. https://www.nytimes.com/2017/09/12/nyregion /christopher-columbus-statue-central-park-vandalized.html.

Orth, Taylor. "Most Americans—But Fewer Than in 2021—Disapprove of the January 6 Capitol Takeover." *YouGov* 4 Jan. 2023. https://today.yougov.com/topics/politics/articles-reports/2023 /01/04/most-americans-disapprove-january-6-capitol-attack.

"Padre Junípero Serra—The Path to Canonization." *California Catholic Conference*. https:// cacatholic.org/article/padre-junipero-serra-path-canonization (accessed 3 July 2023).

Pogrebin, Robin. "Roosevelt Statue to Be Removed from Museum of Natural History." *New York Times* 21 June 2020. https://www.nytimes.com/2020/06/21/arts/design/roosevelt-statue -to-be-removed-from-museum-of-natural-history.html.

Quito, Anne, and Amanda Shendruk. "Decoding the Flags and Banners Seen at the Capitol Hill Insurrection." *Quartz* 7 Jan. 2021. https://qz.com/1953366/decoding-the-pro-trump -insurrectionist-flags-and-banners.

Ray, Lexis-Olivier. "'This Is the Beginning of Healing': Descendents of Tongva, Chumash, and Tataviam Tribes Organized the Toppling of Junípero Serra Statue in the Birthplace of L.A." *L.A. Taco* 22 June 2020. https://lataco.com/serra-statue-chumash-tongva.

Rocha, Veronica. "Decapitated and Doused with Red Paint: Vandals Target St. Junípero Serra Statue at Santa Barbara Mission." *Los Angeles Times* 14 Sept. 2017. https://www.latimes.com /local/lanow/la-me-ln-junipero-serra-statue-vandalized-santa-barbara-20170914-htmlstory .html.

Ryback, Timothy, Mark Ellis, and Benjamin Glahn. *Contested Histories in Public Spaces: Principles, Processes, Best Practices.* London: International Bar Association, 2021.

Samuels, Brett. "Trump Releases 12–page Response to Jan. 6 Hearing." *The Hill* 13 June 2022. https://thehill.com/homenews/administration/3522080-trump-releases-12-page-response -to-jan-6-hearing/.

Severn, Carly. "'How Do We Heal?' Toppling the Myth of Junípero Serra." KQED 7 July 2020. https://www.kqed.org/news/11826151/how-do-we-heal-toppling-the-myth-of-junipero-serra.

Steakin, Will, John Santucci, and Katherine Faulders. "Trump Allies Helped Plan, Promote Rally That Led to Capitol Attack." ABC *News* 8 Jan. 2021. https://abcnews.go.com/US/trump -allies-helped-plan-promote-rally-led-capitol/story?id=75119209.

"Stone Ghosts in the South: Confederate Monuments and America's Battle with Itself." NBC News. *YouTube* 4 June 2020. https://www.youtube.com/watch?v=msIDM8MyGqg.

Svrluga, Susan. "U-Md. Student Government Endorses Demand That Byrd Stadium Be Renamed, Citing Racist Legacy." *Washington Post* 8 Apr. 2015. https://www.washingtonpost .com/news/grade-point/wp/2015/04/08/u-md-students-demand-byrd-stadium-be-renamed -citing-racist-legacy/.

"Teaching with the Columbus Murals." *Notre Dame University.* https://www.nd.edu/about /history/columbus-murals/ (accessed 3 July 2023).

Treisman, Rachel. "Nearly 100 Confederate Monuments Removed in 2020, Report Says; More Than 700 Remain." NPR 23 Feb. 2021. https://www.npr.org/2021/02/23/970610428/nearly-100 -confederate-monuments-removed-in-2020-report-says-more-than-700-remain.

Trump, Donald J. Executive Order #13933. Executive Order on Protecting American Monuments, Memorials, and Statues and Combating Recent Criminal Violence. 26 June 2020. Federal Registrar Doc. 2020–14509. Filed 1 July 2020, 11:15 a.m. https://www.federalregister .gov/documents/2020/07/02/2020-14509/protecting-american-monuments-memorials-and -statues-and-combating-recent-criminal-violence.

——————. Faith and Freedom Conference Speech. 17 June 2022. Nashville, TN. https://www .c-span.org/video/?521049-1/pres-trump-speaks-investigation-faith-freedom-conference.

—————————. "Full Text: Trump's Comments on White Supremacists, 'Alt-left' in Charlottesville." *Politico* 15 Aug. 2017. https://www.politico.com/story/2017/08/15/full-text-trump-comments-white-supremacists-alt-left-transcript-241662.

—————————. Rally before U.S. Capitol Riot Speech. 6 Jan. 2021. Transcript. *AP News* 13 Jan. 2021. https://apnews.com/article/election-2020-joe-biden-donald-trump-capitol-siege-media-e79eb5164613d6718e9f4502eb471f27.

—————————. "Remarks by President Trump at South Dakota's 2020 Mount Rushmore Fireworks Celebration." *Trump White House Archive* 4 July 2020. https://trumpwhitehouse.archives.gov/briefings-statements/remarks-president-trump-south-dakotas-2020-mount-rushmore-fireworks-celebration-keystone-south-dakota/.

—————————. Statement by President Donald J. Trump. *The Hill* 13 June 2022. https://thehill.com/wp-content/uploads/sites/2/2022/06/Statement-by-Trump-1.pdf.

—————————. "Video Statement on Capitol Protesters." *C-Span* 6 Jan. 2021. https://www.c-span.org/video/?507774-1/president-trump-video-statement-capitol-protesters.

—————————(@realDonaldTrump). "These are the things and events that happen when a sacred landslide election victory is so unceremoniously & viciously stripped away from great patriots who have been badly & unfairly treated for so long." 6 Jan. 2021, 11:01 p.m. Tweet.

Tutino, John. *Making a New World: Founding Capitalism in the Bajío and Spanish North America*. Durham: Duke UP, 2011.

Twitter. "Permanent Suspension of @realDonaldTrump." *Twitter Blog* 8 Jan. 2021. https://blog.twitter.com/en_us/topics/company/2020/suspension.

Varner, Eric. *Mutilation and Transformation:* Damnatio Memoriae *and Roman Imperial Portraiture*. Leiden: Brill, 2004.

"Ventura City Council Votes to Remove Junipero Serra Statue." *CBS Los Angeles* 16 July 2020. https://www.cbsnews.com/losangeles/news/ventura-city-council-removal-junipero-serra-statue/.

Verovšek, Peter J. "Collective Memory, Politics, and the Influence of the Past: The Politics of Memory as a Research Paradigm." *Politics, Groups, and Identities* 4.3 (2016): 529–43.

Weil, Julie Zauzmer, and Michael Brice-Saddler. "DC Committee Recommends Stripping the Names of Thomas Jefferson, Benjamin Franklin, Francis Scott Key and Others from City Government Buildings." *Washington Post* 1 Sept. 2020. https://www.washingtonpost.com/dc-md-va/2020/09/01/dc-building-school-renaming/.

Wildman, Sarah. "'You Will Not Replace Us': A French Philosopher Explains the Charlottesville Chant." *Vox* 15 Aug. 2017. https://www.vox.com/world/2017/8/15/16141456/renaud-camus-the-great-replacement-you-will-not-replace-us-charlottesville-white.

On Our Last *Leges*

Uncommon Law

*M*illenarianism, nemesis complex, death drive, disaster, and catastrophization are tired historical themes that require careful definition if they are to retain any valence of meaning. The world has always been coming to an end, and it is without question only a matter of time, aeons perhaps, before the globe is a cold and lifeless planet spinning in infinite space. Such vague prescience needs to be discarded in favor of material specifics and a definition of *catastrophe* that understands it as the end of a particular process, or in Samuel Johnson's definition, "the conclusion or final event of a dramatic piece." The Latin root is helpful, and particularly so for a jurisprudential analysis, in referencing *casus* and *stropha*, the turning point, trip, or downward fall of a case. The lawyer Thomas Blount, in his *Glossographia*, has *catastrophe* defined as subversion, "or the last part of a Comedy [. . .] or the inclination unto the end, as *vitae humananae catastrophe*, the end of a [hu]man's life." In the *longue durée*, catastrophe is a fairly quotidian reference. The comedic sense of endings and beginnings is properly the apprehension of the cycle of existence, and so a certain caution and direction are necessary in my claim that in the United States, Europe

Volume 34, Number 3   DOI 10.1215/10407391-10898283

without brakes, the system of common law has reached a turning point, is on its last *leges* as traditionally understood, because partisan political infection, the unchecked winds of policy, *ludibrium imaginum* or the riot of streamed images, has shattered the sensibility of the common that historically and doctrinally lies at the root of a customary system, the commonality, of a case law tradition or *commune ley.*

Remediation

My focus is a particular overturning and new beginning, generated by the remediation of law, its visual turn, and so the inversion of the scriptural gravity of the legal, of the heavy signifiers of normativity, and the beginning of the tragicomedy of the imaginal in the juridical. All that was shared liquifies into antinomic nonrecognition: the scope and animus of viral relay allowing for endogenous spheres of rhetorical polemic and alternate facts, a plural commons. Begin with an image of the end, a meme of catastrophe, taken from a case brought by the Texas Department of Criminal Justice to protect the identity of a pharmacy that was the source of drugs used in lethal injections against an advocacy group that had posted an image of an exploding head immediately after naming the pharmacy that had supplied such drugs (see fig. 1). The legal issue was whether the image could be said to expose the pharmacy to "a substantial threat of physical harm." The Court of Appeals thought it could not, without deeming it necessary to reproduce the image, "a graphic depiction of an 'exploding head,' although without any explicit linkage to physical violence as the cause" (*Texas Dept. of Criminal Justice v. Levin* 225, at 240 [Texas Court of Appeals]). On reflection, that seems a very curious thing for Justice Bob Pemberton to opine. Outside of spontaneous combustion, it is hard to think of any nonviolent reason that a head would explode or a skull shatter in the fashion depicted. It might not be the result of lethal injection, but the fulmination that decapitates the graphic subject is an image of destruction and death. It represents a catastrophe for the jigsaw figure. More than that, the Appeals Court fails to advert to the fact that it is not a singular image but an animated depiction, in which animation, repetition, sound, or motion is neither referenced nor reproduced.

The logic of the Appeals Court decision is indicative of a juridical deflection, fear, and scotomization of the image. The textual and discursive is to be preferred, for historical reasons, for comfort, as a *dispositif* of control, and so if there was a threat to the pharmacy, it was to be found instead in a professorial hypothetical in an email that was sent to an Oklahoma

Figure 1
From *Texas Dept.
of Criminal Justice
v. Levin* (online law
report)

Figure 1
From *Texas Dept.
of Criminal Justice
v. Levin* (online law
report)

pharmacy that supplied lethal injection drugs by one "Prof. Humez." The professor had written somewhat earlier to a different pharmacy, in another state, and had argued that manufacturing drugs expressly to kill people "flies in the face of one of those commandments Moses got from Jehovah on Sinai." He proceeds to add that "[a]s the folks at the federal building can tell you, [it] only takes one fanatic with a truckload of fertilizer to make a real dent in business as usual" (240). This statement created a threat but not, according to the Appeals Court, a *substantial* threat (232), as required by the relevant precedent case (*Texas Department of Public Safety v. Cox*). It was "closer to the mark," while the image, which did not even reach this level of discursive manifestation, was deemed free, by implication, of "the apprehension of physical harm" and was at most a "vague assertion of risk" (237).

The Texas Supreme Court heard the appeal and doubled down on the textualist bias of the Court of Appeals. It does, however, reproduce a still image extracted from the animated fulmination of the cerebellum. The official report prints this in monochrome, as if this were not another radical alteration of the depiction, and then dismisses its signification. In the words of Justice Green, "[W]e have no reason to believe that the exploding clay head symbolizes anything other than the sentiment that 'my mind is blown,' as in 'I cannot understand how this is happening' or 'this makes no sense' [...]" (*Texas Department of Criminal Justice* (S.C. 2023), 685 [Supreme Court of Texas]). It is again the text, the professorial electronic epistle, that takes the weight of interpretation and the accent of viewing. For the Supreme Court, the email was sufficient to threaten substantial physical harm; it was a serious threat and fell within the "physical safety exception to the PIA [Public Information Act]" (685). The basis for this finding, a textualist interpretation, is largely figural: "in recent times" threats of harm have "certainly escalated in degree and type" and cannot be viewed as vague assertions of risk. In the spring of 2014, Texas was "a very unsettled and dangerous world" and

"security risks had escalated in general [. . .]" (684) What is surprising is that the one optical figure, reproduced somewhat unusually in the text, interrupting the linearity of the discourse and the unity of legal method, is not viewed, analyzed, dissected, or scrutinized in any detail whatsoever.

The one observation that is made by Justice Green of the exploding head is that it is clay, which shows a disturbing inaccuracy of viewing, as the figure is made of jigsaw puzzle pieces that are digitally disassembling. The pieces represent the cellular structure of the body, the DNA that is the architectonic of meaning, and constitute the subtle material constituents of the body and its sensory apparatuses. In the less threatening monochrome image that the court report reproduces (fig. 2), not only is the animation lost but the sanguine red interior lining of the pieces is also erased. That the meme is of a person of color, a sepia skin tone and blood-toned inside, is neither remarked nor seen. That the starfish symbol is also the color of danger but at the same time symbolic of divine healing, guidance, and rebirth goes unnoticed. The key is that the details are overlooked. It cannot be incidental that the one organ represented, now sundered from the skull, is an eye that floats and looks back at the viewer in a form that invokes a close link to the divine eye that was used historically to denote sovereign presence surveilling the polity.[1] *Video et rideo* was the old expression, I see and I laugh, because the aerial looks through the pretense and crimes of human folly (see Lenton). To see is to pierce, to intrude, and in Christian theology to wound: *videbunt in quem transfixerunt*, according to the crucifixion scene (John 9.37). The disembodied gaze is far from innocent, but rather overlooks, sees through, pierces in the sense of wounding and, to borrow from the frontispiece of *Leviathan*, represents a greater power than any here on earth (Hobbes).

The intellectual insouciance, the juridical adiaphorism that underlies the scotomizing of the image represents one level of resistance to the common. The depiction of the exploding head is manifest in the judgment, it appears, and in that emanation becomes sensible and real, a face of legality. That it should manifest so as to be dismissed, drained of color, deprived of movement, stilled, which is to say killed, is a manifestation of fear of the image and of the contemporary viral Internet commons, the realm of gifs, memes, streams, clips, shares from which this comes. The judicial gaze represses and in doing so inaugurates an enigmatic path, a circum-ambulation in which what is not seen takes on an unconscious aesthetic force, or in Aby Warburg's formula, it becomes a dynamogram, an image symptom and symbolic energy whose aesthetic force survives, animating and reanimating in different conjunctures and lawscapes as a phantom of time, outside law, yet paradoxically manifest in judicial decision.[2] In the argot of the Internet it is a byte, a visual virus, and in the negative sense in which she uses it, what Chiara Bottici terms an imaginal relay (135–37).[3] The express dismissal, the claim that the image does not cause an apprehension of threat, is most indicative of a second dimension of this occlusion of the ocular. The remediation of law is trivialized by the Court. The imaginal, the viral relay of images of a suspended reality, of equivocal ontological status, fake law, is operative in a mode of internal exclusion. The image is taken into law so as to be excluded. The exploding head is a meme that is treated as a trivial cartoon, a childish picture, a page from the book of the illiterate. Rather than being viewed, it is written over, spoken through, discursively deformed, and the image of explosion is itself ironically exploded into verbal divagations or the *discurrere*, the running away of discourse. Even though the meme is what is most noticeable about the case, and will likely long outlive the text in social circulation, and hence presumably its inclusion in the judgment, it is misrepresented, deanimated, killed not once but twice on the page. And judicial discourse doesn't see color.

One of the principal effects of remediation is to "make the medium as such visible" (Guillory 324). The exploding head is precisely such an instance of visibilization in which it becomes specifically evident that legal method and judicial community are ill equipped to apprehend the apprehensions of the image. We face a point of diffraction of discourse, an instance of fissure, an incompatible encounter of distinct media breaking the web of legal discourse through the rend or tear of the optical depiction. There are no juridical opificers of the image (Sterne 124), and in broader terms—those of overturning, catastrophe, endings—what is at issue is a con-frontation of disciplines, an impossible interdisciplinarity, a legal presence in the culture wars, here dismissing an animated clip while necessarily also stumbling into the viral commons and remediated forms of the quotidian cultural affray of contested gender and racial performances. Discipline has a peculiar double valence in law, both as punishment (flagellation) and as method, *dispositif* and *episteme*.[4] For present purposes there is both the *inter* and the disciplinary. The inter—being between, among, mixed amid—suggests the loss of discipline in the sense of going outside of the familiar boundaries of the juridical. From a catastrophist perspective, one can also note that to inter is to bury, to mourn and leave a subject and method either cremated or decomposing underground. An abandonment of the rod. It is a point well captured in medieval Latin, where *inter* comes to mean indistinct, as in "roughly" or "about," but neither "precisely" nor "certainly" nor really "amid and among."[5]

The question raised is not, because it is always the case with law, why the legal institution and its judicial gatekeepers lag behind the contemporary commons. That is intrinsic to the conservative juridical tradition, it is their role, the maintenance of the web by means of slow, tralatitious, incremental change. The point is rather the diffraction of the *dispositif*, the fissure occasioned by incompatible media made visible by the haphazard and incautiously random remediation of legal transmission in the form of animé, pictures, cartoons, and clips (Foucault 76).[6] Take one more brief example. The First Amendment guarantees access to court records and filings. Courthouse News Services sought access to e-filings in a case in Broward Circuit Court and brought the case on the basis that the responsible court officials had not made the filings available on the day they were filed and frequently took one to three or more days to make them available. This made them somewhat useless for news reporting purposes. In short, two officials were responsible for filtering and releasing filings and each, the inappositely named Rushing and the defendant Forman, blamed the other for the delays: "Defendants deflect these arguments by pointing fingers at each other" (*Courthouse* 8). There follows an image of two spidermen figures pointing at each other (fig. 3). Chief u.s. District Judge Mark E. Walker comments that "it comes as no surprise to this Court that the Defendants' litigation tactic is to point fingers, as illustrated below [. . .]" (10). The caption to the image is "Clerk Forman and Chair Rushing." Neither, of course, suggests speed, but the sudden appearance of the meme as an indicator of mirroring behavior is remarkable for the sudden shift in medium, for the differential temporality, for the color and the other unremarked indicators that the image relays.

Figure 3
"Double Identity."
Spider-Man Episode
19 (1967)

The nexus between picture and discourse is to be found in a reference to the defendants attempting to create "an administrative labyrinth"
or throw a metaphorical net over their constitutional violations. The meme
itself gets a brief footnote reference and quotation from an article in *Screen
Rant* (Raymond), but the questions of what it might mean, signify, or occlude
for law, its normative significance or insignificance, its precedential weight,
its cognitive value, its place in the discursive formation, are left without
comment or response. On a brief viewing, the figures are far from equal. The
spiderman closest to the NYPD van is in the classic police firing pose, feet
apart, arm forward, back defended by the law enforcement vehicle, with the
force of law visually authorizing action. The figure on the right, next to two
wooden crates, is in a more aggressive posture, moving forward with their
hand forming, almost by trompe l'oeil, a gun. Superheroes, cartoon figures,
outlaws posed in differentially normative positions open up a visual array of
implexities that the judge who inserted them neither addresses nor explains.[7]

Though it may seem trivial, childish even, as well as inadvertent
and at most incidental to the judgment, to the law laid down—an injunction
was granted—it is, to the contrary, I am suggesting, of extreme significance
as marking a revaluation, a sea change, in sensory priorities. The image,
available only in the online report, marks a perceptual change, a dramatic
shift in legal sensibility and the introduction of a distinct medium into the
relay of legal faith, presumably on the basis that this picture, the modality
of vision, is a more effective channel for transmitting legality than the dead
letters of the text. Here, and not without irony, in the United States the puri-
tan ban on images transmitted to common law in the sixteenth century in
the form of a faith without images, a law of texts, *sola scriptura* in Luther's
phrase, is shattered (Aston 890). The unhearing eye was theologically and
spiritually a danger, a lure and threat to the faith carried by scripture. That
siren, or in Knox's argot, that strumpet the image, returns in digital media

Figure 4
Map of Texas from
*Housecanary v.
Quicken Loans*

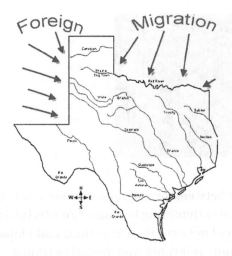

and with it, too, the challenge to creed and tradition (*traditio*) that exposure of institutions, visibilization of enforcement practices, and free circulation of video threatens. Remediation raises comparable questions for the jurisdiction of law, a break-up of the guild community, a sundering of the common sense of an exclusively and exclusorily legal commonality that now faces the fissures generated by remediations that introduce into the heart of law the diversity of communities and kaleidoscope of colors that make up the polity, the many. What used to be the *communis opinio* of the Bar, the oral histories and tacit conventions, the patterns of how things were properly done are unveiled by the incursion of minor symbols, stills, clips, images from across the spectrum of the web and its omnipresent lenses, CCTV, phones to dashcams. In a case concerning dirty lawyer tricks from 2018, District Judge Fred Biery bemoans the collapse of this very *sensus communis* and reprimands the attorneys with a number of images, including a small map of Texas threatened by migration from the North (fig. 4).[8]

In an ironically formulated dismissal, the judge complains: "A long time ago in a galaxy far, far away, the San Antonio litigation legal community consisted of about 300 lawyers who knew each other on a professional and social level, some of whom were quite capable of trying these kinds of cases and whose handshake agreements were kept, making court orders often unnecessary" (4). Here it is the regional San Antonio Bar that is threatened by and broken up through the incursion of "foreign," which is to say Northern, migrants, lawyers from out of state. The monochrome map, with its threatening all-capital-letters coda and its arrows flung at the borders, is a crude double sign of fragmentation of the seamless web or unbroken history of law's textual transmission as much as it is a lament for the breaking up of the tight-knit community, the commons of a particular Bar. The multimodal character of the text, albeit crudely done and lacking color, which appears only in an appendix image, is indicative. What arrives by night can take the subject by surprise. Here, indeed, the ostensible message is lack of decorum and frequent incivility in abstruse and underhanded litigation strategies. "Rambo tactics," "elementary-school behavior," "games," and significantly texting and email, in Biery's view, have precluded "earspace," meaning the in-person of face-to-face talk and listening (4).

The retrospection, *nostos* or nostalgia, for a smaller legal community, seriousness, proper dress sense, shared manners, adult behavior is of course somewhat undermined by the wifty and expansive use of a number of regressive elements in the order itself. The map is ludicrous and in the Latin would qualify as *sensus ridiculus*, a mere assertion, an illustration of lack of learning, of weak frivolity masking xenophobia. There is an element of the regressive not only in the simplex diagram but in the reference, expanded to the full text in the appendix, of the opening to the Star Wars movies. There is a posting of The Rule: For the Practice of Law, the *soi-disant* Texas Lawyer's Creed, requiring respect, peaceable behavior, efficient resolutions. To this is added a monochrome photograph of a severe-looking Abraham Lincoln pronouncing ex cathedra the priority of compromise and of peacemaking over litigation. The retrospective message, however, is undermined by the media of their relay in which juvenile movies, a statist map, and two other images rend the juridism of the text and most importantly introduce quite different communities and valences into the very form of the legal transmission. Imagery and especially crudely reproduced figures, as in Judge Biery's diagrammatic figure, repeat childhood patterns, the first books of the soon-to-be literate, and the communities, aesthetic, ideological, commercial, and technical, that travel in these viral, variable semi- and counterpublic spheres. What the judge introduces in the remediation, and this is only a very simple instance, is paradoxically precisely the variety of forms of manners, the foreign and the digital immigrants that his arrows were intended to signal should be kept out. The images allow in what the discourse seeks to exclude, and it is this ironic overturning, this overlooked transition, that should be the focus of any study of law's anarchic remediation and its collapsing sense of the commons of common law.

A dual process of overturning is at play in tracing the fate of the commons of law. Remediation is first an acceleration, an image-driven "*theatrocracy* [. . .] on speed," a viral law that increasingly inhabits the imaginal spaces and streamed relays of the quotidian videosphere (Peters 302).[9] In imaging immigration, Judge Biery ironically introduces into his decision precisely the medium of the imaginal that most actively and immediately crosses borders, transgresses boundaries, and unsettles the discipline and limits of law. It is a two-way street in which the judge's recourse to images projects the judgment into the videosphere and the no longer private quotidian virtual spaces of legal professional life. It is an attempt to govern visiocratically, by means of affect and image as extended modalities of jurisdiction, now transferred into jurisvision. The other facet of such acceleration, however, is the incursion of the visual, of memes and screengrabs, of the everyday of the Internet, its fragmentary and mobile, evanescent and unexamined streams, into the practice of law and the arbitrium of judgment. A novel immediacy displaces the long-term and slow-moving *traditio* of the juridical commons. At one level, Judge Biery is not wrong. Affect, phantasmata in the modalities of unreflective speed, instantaneous interest, ignorance of limits, lawless lawyers represent not simply a drift in practice but a change in the optics and temporality of the juridical. Technology brings the event, the imagined occasion and relationships, the visual phantasm of the instance into the judgment. An exploding head, spidermen pointing, arrows flying at the borders of Texas are all images of quotidian precarity and moments of threat, scenes of breakdown of what was formerly common to law. Where the judges in our examples err is in failing to treat the visual phantoms, the memes and other images inserted in their judgments, as remediations of juridical reason, as a novel gaze shifting the apparatuses of governance into distinctive videospheres and viral commons. The point is that it is a two-way street, a matter of implexity as well as complexity in which the law is promulgated as an image, as something more and other than discourse.

Juridical Theology

The other face of this increasing speed and videological form of juridical judgment is that of populism: divestment of the aura of professionalism and a crossing of the border between legal reason and political commentary, normative constraint and naked power grabs. It is here a question of the overturning of the *dispositif* of law, the changing apparatuses of juridical power that increasingly threaten to emerge as one more interest group and political force. If it is the temporality of law and the slowness of change that mark juridical reason as distinct from policy and politics, then the acceleration of images shatters that difference and pluralizes the ima-ginal community of lawyers. As in so many features of the United States, its common law is distinctive and far further accelerated than its counterparts elsewhere in the Anglophone or former commonwealth jurisdictions. There are institutional reasons for this that deserve brief mention, most notably that the u.s. common law is the youngest of the jurisdictions. Youth, as Aristotle was wont to observe, desires everything too much, is impatient, rushed. The neotenic jurisdiction is subject also to a peculiar and precarious inter-nal conflict. Founded upon English common law, an imperial and colonial regime of imposition, it was only in the latter half of the nineteenth century that the new republic sought to rid itself of the tinctures of Anglicanism and devise a system of precedent of its own (Goodrich, "Opinions"). The forging of a new jurisdiction, a *mos americanus iuris docendi*, in the old language of law, was marked by a denial of the provenance of the inherited structures and by the pragmatism that was in fashion among the "long-headed youths" of the Metaphysical Club, who began devising the intellectual strategies of the newly established legal academy and its distinctive local doctrines or *ius commune.* Where English common law was predicated upon custom and practice time out of mind, or since time immemorial, defined as 1189, u.s. common law sought independence, its own agency, at the same time that it depended upon linguistic structures and juridical forms that devolved from Law French, and beyond that the Latin of the *Corpus Iuris*, whose red letter phrase still forms the titular adornment of the codes of u.s. law.

The pickle jar of precedent and the history of the *mores* of a legal tradition may seem a distant topic in relation to contemporary decisional catastrophes—overturnings—but the stakes are always historical and mate-rial. The inherited Anglican tradition, albeit hidden and denied, was at root a monastic tradition, emergent from the monasteries in the twelfth century, and explicitly a dual system, religious and secular, canonic and monarchi-cal, ecclesiastical and civil.[10] While the reference may seem esoteric, its purpose is to draw attention to critical features of the paradoxically named common law that have escaped the attention of radical commentators, that there were significant ethico-religious roots to the tradition that manifested in a unitary guild and second-order norms of inculcated, tacit conventions of decisional behavior. For the Anglican common lawyers—first monks and then wearers of the coif—sergeants at law, benchers, utter barristers—it was a quotidian perception that "justice and law do lie down together," that antiquity was president because the age-old legal community was housed in a hierarchy that directly reflected the nine orders of angels in the very structure of the Inns of Court.[11] My point, and it is a precarious and preliminary one, is that the legal tradition, custom and use time out of mind, the *corpus mysticum* of state and the *arcana* or mysteries of governance, were both carried and kept in order by a unified theistic guild of elite lawyers in their emblematic community on the banks of the river Thames and itinerant therefrom. Predicated upon a scriptural tradition and customs in common, ludic learning practices, rites of eating, revels and rituals, the key to Anglican legal tradition was that the common opinion of jurists, the rules and institutions of an established juristic regime preceded and constrained the contemporary lawmaker.

The historical roots of the oldest social science have provided a method of slow reading and limited change that would ensure property rights and statuses ordained by royal decree, by Monsieur Capital, and latterly by neoliberal and welfare social policies. There is, however, something more at stake in law, which is the tralatitious, long-term avenues of transmission of a community of thought, a collective sensibility comprised in the discursive formation that legal institutions and modes of investiture inculcate across the ephemera of individual lives. It is here that u.s. common law is somewhat distinctive in its neophyte character, its youngling status, its feeble scholarly armature and methods. The *corpus iuris secundum* that adorns law libraries and offices across the States is an ambivalent and mixed set of borrowed rules and Indigenous practices. It explicitly recognizes that it is not *prima regula* or the first order of knowledge, but rather that it comes after and on the shoulders of Anglican common law, which tradition itself was a variant, and according to the Renaissance French historians, a confused form of local French law, in turn a derivative of the so-called universal law of Rome, the codes of papal and imperial legality that emerged from the eleventh-century receptions onward of a dual law or in more contemporary terms a juridical theology.[12]

Ahead in both progressive and regressive modes of libertarianism, the u.s. context is relatively free of a legal *dispositif* or apparatuses of jurisprudential knowledge that would constrain social and political action. In the common-law tradition, the preponderance of normative constraints are communal, tacit, and in technical terms unwritten in the strict sense of *ius non scriptum*.[13] This simply means that, as Lord Chief Justice Camden put it, "If it is law, it will be found in our books. If it is not to be found there, it is not law" (*Entick v. Carrington* 1066). If one can find it in the legal scriptures, the treatises, cases, reports, somewhere, one can use it as part of the *communis opinio iuris* or common opinion of the Bar. More than that, it is a habiliment, a habit, an office incorporated into the structures of a tradition and community of thought that exists far more between the lines than on the page, in performance and the theater of practice than in strict application of the dead letters of a text. What constrains the practice and historically has kept some form of faith in the rule of law has been a materiality of transmission within institutional and inculcative settings that transmit a culture, ethics, and methodology of restraint, of incremental change limited both by textual norms or hermeneutic method and by a communal sense of the authority of poets, doctors, and philosophers—*auctoritates philosophicorum, medicorum, poetarum* (Coke 264).[14] Those sources, the heavy signifiers of classical, medieval, and early modern institutional writings, commentaries, treatises—syntagms—reports provide, within the Anglican and more broadly European tradition, a long-term ethics of practice, a species of *caritas*, a moral order—good or bad—that constitutes a slow-burning falling, as in cases, rather than overturning or catastrophe: an incremental progression distinct from and to the side of the immediate winds of policy and the instantaneous opinations of politicians.

Where such an institutional and didactic juridical tradition of existential inculcation does not exist in any substantial form, as in the United States, then policy will dominate, politics will drive legal decision, and communal forms will be split by partisan preferences that suddenly appear and then disappear in hasty syncopations, weak thought, forensic rhetoric on speed. As juridical theology dissipates in the glare of new media and politicized appointment processes, the paper-thin, legally very recent *dispositif* of legal community and culture in the United States also shifts in corresponding or mirroring fashion from ethics to adiaphorism, from morality to insouciance, communal sensibility to advocacy of private interests. All of which is to hint that the key mistake made by critical legal studies, by leftist jurisprudence and cause lawyers was one of temporality, meaning an absence of an inculcated historical sensibility and accompanying institutional modes of common learning. Juridical theology, which is to say the juristic sense of community, the rites and ceremonies of a tradition of legal public performances, the scriptural methodologies and hermeneutic contributions, were political in a structural sense and according to a long-term temporality that was resistant to the quotidian noise of partisan debauch and policy fragmentations. The commons of common law were an architectonic, a series of structures, apparatuses of knowledge that moved slowly. Outing that guild and community, exposing the norm to the myriad lenses and endless streaming of new media equalizes statuses, divests dress codes and shatters both class barriers and epistemic boundaries in modes that are difficult to predict and often painful to observe. A flood of viral relays, Internet intrusions into all the alcoves and crevices of court, chambers, office, legal home and legal life, dissipates the fragile sense of community of thought that for good and ill was the marker of tradition and the ambulatory itinerancy of common lawyers.

The social bond, *vinculum iuris* in juridical argot, appears ever more diffracted and confused. The Left argues conservatively for respect for the rule of law, and the Right argues radically for the political character of all legal judgment. Charismatic political demagogues and draunt ideologues alike take up the Shakespearean theme of kill all the lawyers. Exposure shows the inventions of trial law to be all too human and in consequence *ad hominem* and *ad feminam* attacks on decisions as personal political opinions distract popular attention from the judgment *ad rem* or according to its substance. By the same token, remediation draws the judiciary into the factionalism and dysfunction of populist relays of imaginal political debate. The key criticism of such judicial interventions is lack of qualification, a dearth of aesthetic seriousness, a default of method and sensibility that should otherwise recognize the symptomatic force of the image and the radical prospects of remediation. In this overturning, and most specifically the viral visibilization of law that makes the medium of legal judgment apparent, the *in camera* process and introspective journey of deliberation depicted and streamed a presence that both validates the critique of legal politics and supports a critical apprehension that the collapse of the symbolic, the loss of faith in legal institutions, lies in a failure of methodology, an epistemic vacuity in the face of the acceleration of economic and technical change as it impacts legal process and the formulation of decision.

Juristic Monochromacy

It may seem a curious critical argument to point to lack of tradition and structure, but the issue is intellective and institutional. The relative weakness or permeable character and overmutable quality of u.s. legal reason lies in a relative autonomy, outlined above, from the history of common law and the inculcative institutions of ethical patterns and critical skills over the *longue durée* of legal reason. These include foundational writings, the *Institutes* and *Commentaries*, the common opinion and community of thought that inscribe invisibly over time and space, in the mode of *ius non scriptum*, as well as didactic rites such as dining rituals, chamber

judgments—a bencher would emerge from a cupboard to judge student arguments—revels, French law clerk *basoche* or satirical theatrics, moots, bolts,
courts of love, and circuits of performance.[15] Born in the folds of pragmatism
and then legal realism, the u.s. academy and training institutions have, by
contrast, had something of a chameleon character, an instantaneous and
reactive approach, and an extremism that vacillates wildly between nihilism
and optimism, satire and self-importance, fad, fashion, and status obsession
(Goodrich, "Satirical" 487–91). The u.s. *sensus communis iuris* is in sum an
ephemeral feature, and the community of thought has tended to the transi-
tory, individualistic, and ironically private, less shared ideation than cult of
personality in a bizarre species of star system (Goodrich, "Duncan" 975–77).
As the juridical sensibility, the fractured community of thought becomes
ever harder to delineate and define, the symptoms expressed, the slips that
are on view in the judicial uses of images provide a vital glimpse into how
the legal community of thought is changing, the influences that play out in
the moment of invention of decision, and the gaze that constitutes the lens
of judgment.

   The superficiality of vision, the lack of ocular focus, the blindfold
that supposedly replaces opinion with impartiality, in fact, operate here as
projection of prejudice. Not to look closely is simply to impose a prior view,
to presuppose the character, quality, and color of the subject, to overlook by
overlaying assumption upon fact. The process of abstraction whereby facts
become norms and the "is" transforms into the "ought," *sein* into *sollen*,
seems to entail a looking away, a blurring of detail and of focus that results
in displacing the viewed by legal precognition that is also miscognition.
One striking example can be taken from a case involving Andy Warhol's
series of colored silkscreen prints of a monochrome photograph of the singer
Prince.[16] The photo portrait of the artist, by Lynn Goldsmith, itself a significant aesthetic accomplishment, presents a frontal view, inclusive of head,
shoulders, and a quarter torso (fig. 5). The Warhol silkscreens, by contrast,
are truncated, of the face alone, and, of greatest significance, overlaid with
dramatic patterns of vivid color. The photo portrait is flattened, altered in
terms of depth of contrast and by the removal of certain minor details. In
most of the images, the contrast is replaced with brightly and contrastive
colors in varied patterns and background, and in some instances the image
is drained of almost all pigment and tone (fig. 6). The decision of the Second
Circuit makes virtually no reference to color and certainly offers no analysis
of the hue and cry, the stain of the polychrome works. At most, Warhol had
indulged in "imposing" his style on the "primary work" whose "essential

Figure 5
Prince, Lynn Gold-
smith (1981)

Figure 6
Silkscreens from
*Andy Warhol Foun-
dation v. Goldsmith*

elements" remained recognizable (*Andy* [2021] 42). The judge could presumably see through the screen of color and gaze upon the fiction of an original,
a monochrome figurative representation of *haec imago*, of this face. Such
looking through the screen and staring upon an imagined uncolored vis-
age requires a signal scotomization of the silkscreens, an erasure not only
of the color but of the very materiality of the image that is being judicially
looked through in favor of an imagined depiction. In the summative words
of Judge Lynch, "[T]he Prince Series retains the essential elements of its
source material, and Warhol's modifications serve chiefly to magnify some
elements of that material and minimize others. While the cumulative effect
of those alterations may change the Goldsmith Photograph in ways that give
a different impression of its subject, the Goldsmith Photograph remains
the recognizable foundation upon which the Prince Series is built" (43).
There is no question that Lynn Goldsmith should be paid for her work and
that a contract implied in fact for the use of the photograph could be the
legal ground of compensatory damages, but the question is not juristic, it
is jurisvisual: what is it that the judge sees when looking at these colored
compositions? The tinctures of overlay must impact at some point. How can

the dramatic changes, the alterations of field of vision, and the aesthetic of the image escape scrutiny, analysis, and review? It is almost as if the judge sees literally, in linear and monochromic style, a prior or other image, a legal fiction of a figure that in its very abstraction loses color and content, is exsanguinated of hemoglobin and life. It is not seen, but rather the artistic remediation is immediately remediated by the judicial gaze fixated upon a skiagraphic outline, a lineal diagram, a sketch that is resident either in the past or in the extimacy of judicial invention.[17]

The absence of color in the legal view of the countenance is a manner of refusing to countenance color as mattering. It may just be an example, a case, and one that will perhaps be overturned on other grounds, but the refusal to recognize the remediation of the photo portrait is symptomatic and occurs consistently across the range of legal disciplines. The Court in *Warhol* remarks at one point, with characteristic superciliousness, that in conducting their inquiry into copyright infringement, "the judge should not assume the role of art critic and seek to ascertain the intent behind or meaning of the works at issue. That is so both because judges are typically unsuited to make aesthetic judgments and because such perceptions are inherently subjective" (41). So what is in effect promulgated is "don't look now," which means suppression of the act, veiling of the judicial sensibility that is simply that of a different sort of art critic, a blindfolded viewer. It becomes a structural feature of juridical decision that color be unseen, deflected from consciousness and deliberation, deemed superfluous to fact and norm alike. The structure is one of overlooking color, an evisceration of the material surface and affect of viewing that can only then act out in the decision as the unseen and undesired substrate of judgment. It is an exercise in repression of materiality, a denial of appearances, of the reality of what is seen in favor of a white and Christian sense of a hidden reality and of greater things as yet unseen or, paradoxically, seen through a glass darkly, and here pretty much not at all.

To resist subjectivity, to act as if blind to the sensibility, materiality, and color of the artwork, is but to displace subjective judgment by subjective legal "judgment" and to look away, deflecting vision by means of presupposition and projection, filling the void with the phantoms that necessarily emerge in the candleless theater of the judicial cranium. To see a color-blind future is more accurately to reinforce the status quo, the hierarchy of inherited prejudices, the sumptuary law, the heraldry and emblemata that directly designated the status of specific colors.[18] It hardly needs saying that such refusal of the color of appearances, the hues of manifestation, the tinctures of the real is a dangerous approach to the visible world, to the living color of subjects and fictive subjects in a volatile political context and a highly polarized social and legal situation. The laborious exercise of legal analogy fails to take advantage of the gap, the *ana*, of *analogos*, the image that rends the discursive text precisely with color, the seismograph of a picture of a singer of color, repainted, revised, emended aesthetically and playfully by the artist of soup cans.

The contradiction of putative legal similarity is most evident in the judge's simultaneous denunciation of aesthetic vision—of critical apprehension and viewing of the images—and his own fundamentally subjective assertion that "[t]he Prince Series retains the essential elements of the Goldsmith Photograph without significantly adding to or altering those elements" (43). Such a color-blind view is symptomatic and in juristic terms is an explicitly affective gaze in which the question for resolution, as formulated in another case involving colors, is that of "the total concept and feel" of the works in question (*Warhol* [2021] 324). It is the impression of the likeness of the two works that determines if there has been infringement and the subjective erasure of color plays a significant role in the affect of objectivity that the Appeals Court both relays and denies. The failure to address the remediation of the image reflects a much more general akinesia and myopia in the face of imaginal law, the new modality of the commons, the viral world that lawyers, too, imbibe and inhabit. More than that, more dangerous than that, it is here a form of blindness to matter and surfaces, a strange prosopagnosia that manifests in the juridical viewing of the portrait as an image.

Conclusion: Overturning Regimes of Vision

Regime change, new appointments to the Supreme Court of the United States, the Capitol Hill riots, populism, and ideological polarization constitute immediate political shifts and an increasing pace of overturnings, both social and legal. The boundary between law and virulent though mutable policy directions is redefined in significant part by remediation and specifically an imaginal online and streamed environment that enters the lives, the chambers, the courts, and, increasingly, judicial decisions. The old legal maxim that the judge determine with downcast eyes, that there be a blindfold on *Justitia,* is ever more out of keeping with the technologies of relay and transmission of law. Courts overturn and overrule as a quotidian feature of their activity, but that process of evolution was textual, a linear progression—*nulla dies sine linea* as the lawyers were wont to intone to their apprentices, no day without its lines. The hermeneutics of the text was distinct from the rhetorical and theatrical performances of the courtroom, the scriptural relay being in large part protected by the black-and-white typography, the order of print, the diagrammatology and other regimentations of the page. Remediation in the form of digital relay and hyperlink incorporations have shifted the boundary between the legal and political, the normative and the social. To coin an ugly phrase, law becomes *viserbal*, its ontology increasingly a spectral hauntology making it impossible any longer to simply look away.

In acceleration there is opportunity, both practical and critical. The increasingly visual character of legal transmission, the augmented use of screenshots, cctv, cell phone, dashcam, and headcam images introduces sound, motion, and color into the thinking of law. I have focused on color, the stains, hues, tinctures that emerge in judicial decisions only to be overlooked, seemingly too dramatic and novel to be textually accounted for, or otherwise dismissed as exornations to be subjugated to the inkhorn divinity of print. The purpose of legal records, archives, and now galleries and albums of images is that of creating a pattern and discernible path of development. The subjects of law can now often see what the judicial subjects deciding say, the view from the bench. In cinematic terms the images and clips form the *plan subjectif*, the viewpoint of the lens of legal decisions. This is literally and allegorically an exposure of the postcritical legal mind, a royal road to the invention of judgment, and a pathway through the "layers of positivist shellac."[19] Such exposure allows a signal opportunity to move behind the heavy signifiers of legal argot. It provides a means for attending to detail, critical scrutiny, close viewing, and apprehension of color as structural features of viewing and as a fulcral facet of current political polarization.

Judicial monochromacy, the translation of the black and white of print, of so-called black letter law and gothic typeface, to the social scene is ironically both antinomic and antipathetic. To think and see in monochrome is to privilege a conflict, to focus on two opposed poles of the spectrum and so, quite literally, to polarize. Black and white is already a contradiction, an optical error, and a mode of exclusion of the luxuriance and diversity of colors. The opportunity is that of looking more closely, distinguishing, detailing, differentiating and divagating according to the strict *ambulatio* of the eye, the nonlinear gaze, the lateral wandering of optical apprehension according to the rhizomes of the visual. Consider, for example, that a corporation is a

Figure 7
Sexy Gazebo, Maya
Hayuk (2008–2009)

Figure 8
The Universe II,
Maya Hayuk (2009)

legal fiction, an "as if" or *non-entia imaginaria* in Vaihinger's terms, which he persuasively argues it is dangerous to hypostasize because the phantom, the as if of legal argument, is a living being, a manifestation of fiction that has singularly real effects over time (246). The corporation is not a person but rather a mystic body, an apparatus of power, with administrative norms governing its exercise. As such an entity, Starbucks wanted an advertising campaign for its Frappuccino drinks and through its agent advertising company approached an artist, Maya Hayuk, to devise such a scheme. After working together for some time toward multicolored visuals for the drink, Hayuk pulled out of the relationship and no contract was signed. A while later, Starbucks launched a campaign with kaleidoscopic colored images that were strikingly similar to original artworks of Hayuk's.

The case is one of copyright infringement, and the role of the court is to determine whether there is a substantial similarity between the original artwork and the advertising campaign images: a question of color and design. Despite the case being specifically concerned with visual details, ocular similarities and differences, not one image is reproduced in the judgment, although they are all incorporated by reference. It is from the plethora of pictures in the filings that the comparison has to be made. Hayuk's copyrighted images, *Sexy Gazebo* and *The Universe II* (figs. 7 and 8), inaugurate a series of striking, multicolored, kaleidoscopic designs with a distinctive vortex character marked by diamond shapes lanced to a tip. The question in the case is whether there is a substantial similarity between the artist's artworks and the Frappuccino advertising designs (figs. 9, 10, and 11). Such being the question, it is extraordinarily deflective that Judge Laura Swain does not compare the images visually and indeed precludes any reasoned precedent of viewing by excluding the multicolor designs from the published report. She offers no detailed analysis of colors, no extended view of design or form but only a scathing conclusory point of

Figure 9
Starbucks advertisements for Frappuccino from *Hayuk v. Starbucks*

Figure 10
Starbucks advertisements for Frappuccino from *Hayuk v Starbucks*

Figure 11
Starbucks advertisements for Frappuccino from *Hayuk v. Starbucks*

view that "the Court finds, as a matter of law, that none of the Frappuccino Works is substantially similar to 'the total concept and feel' of protectible elements of any of the Hayuk Works" (*Hayuk* 292). She goes on to say, with equal generality, that the aesthetic elements and choices are dissimilar and distinguish the *comparata*, leaving no "substantial similarity."

   In slightly more detail, the judge describes, or rather lists, the individual colors, both background and rays, shapes and drips, but views them in terms of division, as if each were a separate and distinct feature opposed to and divided from the other colors and antinomically juxtaposed with the "other," the noninfringing corporate advertisement. The zero sum of judicial decisions becomes a zero viewing, a lackluster zetetic that fails to open to the images, to stay with the colors, to apprehend the implexity of color, image, and representation. The judicial gaze divides and opposes, creating an antinomy between the colligated images and colors. As the art historian Georges Didi-Huberman has argued extensively, the stain of color, the tinctures and hues show what cannot be figured or said. They are intrinsic to the affective force of images, and crucially, their implexity and force reside in their combination, as conjunction and interrelation, which here means pattern and effect of affect ("Image"). Key to the judicial gaze is a symptomatic inability to see the relation between the colors, the colorist flushes, the dance and play of taints, dyes, tinges, paints, and pigments. The colors are juxtaposed in a relation of relationlessness. It is this irrelation, the inability to perceive the colors as a composition, as imbricated and inter-mingled with each other, as a play of interrelations, an implexified dance of differences, that precludes any adequate judgment *ad apparentiam* or according to appearance.

The separation of colors, the individualizing of specific hues without any context of multiplicity of colors and their visual imbrication effectuates, in a specific context of aesthetic similarities, a polarization of colors that reduces and opposes two works of art as if they were only antagonistically related. Judicial monochromacy at the level of compari-son of aesthetic compositions fails in its apperception of these ontographic expressions to apprehend the variety, vibrancy, multiplicity, and diversity of colors manifest together in dramatic and harmonious interrelation. Colors blend and fold into each other, bounce off similarities and differences, and express an ever-changing variety of moods intricately bound up with the shifting temporal and spatial context of viewing. The polarizing effects of monochromacy are precisely the consequences of the imposition of an irre-lation of colors, the failure of the juridical and by extension cultural gaze to appreciate the uniqueness of hues at the same time as seeing color as always already a combinatorial of multiple tinctures extant precisely and inexorably with and within each other. The antinomy of the monochrome sets colors against each other because it sees not the spectrum, but the apposition in which one color contradicts the other. To recognize and critically appreci-ate an aesthetic of law is to acknowledge that remediation brings not color but colors into judgment. It is the plurality and kaleidoscopic interrelations of such colors, the vibrancy and dance, the hues and changing tinctures in their mobile expressions that manifest both artwork and culture, or in the trinitarian classification of Roman law, persons, things, and actions.

Remediation requires that the juridical gaze, the legal lens, expand to apprehend and appreciate the implexity of colors and the colorist complexity of the commons of common law.

PETER GOODRICH is a professor of law at Cardozo School of Law, New York, and a visiting professor in the School of Social Science, NYU Abu Dhabi. Recent work includes *An Advanced Introduction to Law and Literature* (Edward Elgar, 2021) and *Judicial Uses of Images: Vision in Decision* (Oxford University Press, 2023).

Notes

1   For well-known examples, see the eye of a vigilant justice (*princeps iustitiiae advigilans*) in Aneau 81. For an English version, see the pectoral sovereign eye (*sapiens dominabitur astris*) in Wither 31. The source for the emblematic representations is the reception of the hieroglyphic tradition. The main source was the monumental and highly influential Piero Valeriano, *Hieroglyphica, sive de sacriiis Aegyptorum*. Orus Appolo de Aegypt in *De la signification des notes Hieroglyphiques des Aegyptiens* provides a useful list and definitions. Michael Stolleis's *The Eye of the Law* provides an erudite modern history.

2   The term comes from unpublished correspondence and is picked up and developed in Didi-Huberman, *The Surviving Image* 110–11.

3   Bottici discusses the relay of a social unconscious and phagocytosing—self-consuming—images, pictures that generate a false war within a culture.

4   On the root of discipline in the rod, and flagellation, see the remarkable Rev. William Cooper's *Flagellation and Flagellants: A History of the Rod in All Countries*. On discipline as *dispositif*, see Agamben's *Opus Dei* on the genealogy of office (ch. 3) and *The Highest Poverty* on habit and habitus (28). On legal disciplinary apparatuses, see Legrand.

5   See Baxter and Johnson, eds., s.v. *inter*: about, roughly, 1185; *inter canem et lupum*, at twilight, 1265, 1295; *inter totum*, in all, 1086.

6   Of the optical concept of diffraction, Foucault writes: "These points are characterized in the first instance as points of incompatibility: two objects, or two types of enunciation, or two concepts may appear, in the same discursive formation, without being able to enter—under pain of manifest contradiction or inconsequence—the same series of statements" (76).

7   The term *implexity* comes from Didi-Huberman's "Image, Language: The Other Dialectic" (22) and means internal complexity, the element of one color in the other, of one aspect implicated in and inseparable from others.

8   See *HouseCanary Inc. v. Quicken Loans*. The image here, identical to that used in *HouseCanary*, but with red arrows and blue coda, is taken from Judge Biery's opinion in another case, *Aquifer Guardians v. Federal Highway Admin.* 548.

9   This theme is developed in Peters, "Theatrocracy" 31.

10 On this aspect of the early history of the common law profession, see Baker.

11 As, for example, in Legh (fol. 135v).

12 The classic study is Pierre Legendre's *La Pénétration du droit*

romain dans le droit canonique classique de Gratien à Innocent IV, which is pursued in numerous more theoretical works, including Legendre, *Le Désir*. In English, see Legendre, *God in the Mirror*.

13 *Ius non scriptum* simply means unwritten law in the sense of uncodified law. Common law is written in the sense of being recorded in writs and plea rolls, commentaries and cases, but the scope and flexibility of content depends on tradition and memory as set down in the main by the authors of early modern common law.

14 In full: *"Auctoritates philosophorum, medicorum, et poetarum, sunt in causa aligandae et tenendae."* (The opinions of philosophers, physicians, and poets are to be alleged and received in causes.)

15 See Peters: "[L]aw's aesthetic power is essential to its force" (*Law* 5), and slightly further on, her argument that the history of legal performance is constitutive of Western jurisprudence. Her point in the present context is important for understanding a more anachronic sense or transhistorical force to the legal community of thought and patterns of practice.

16 See *Andy Warhol Foundation v. Lynn Goldsmith* (2021), reversing the earlier 2019 ruling. The Supreme Court, by a majority, just affirmed the appellate court's monochromatic decision. As Justice Kagan, dissenting, appositely remarks, "The majority does not see it. And I mean that literally. There is precious little evidence in today's opinion that the majority has actually looked at these images, much less that it has engaged with expert views of their aesthetics and meaning" (*Andy* [2023]). It bears note that Justice Kagan provides a visual analysis, using other exemplars of optical differentiation.

17 My erudite editor requests a footnote here to define *extimacy*, a Lacanian coinage that references a projection of the intimate into the exterior, something that Emanuele Coccia, in *Sensible Life: A Microontology of Images*, would likely term an "objective unconscious," the exteriorization of the interior image.

18 Patricia Williams notes "the aesthetic visual power" that hides race behind a veil of color-blindness (28).

19 I am borrowing here from the linguistically inventive Pierre Legrand 6.

Works Cited

Agamben, Giorgio. *The Highest Poverty: Monastic Rules and Form-of-Life.* Trans. Adam Kotsko. Stanford: Stanford UP, 2013.

——————. Opus Dei: *An Archaeology of Duty.* Stanford: Stanford UP, 2013.

Andy Warhol Foundation for the Visual Arts, Inc. v. Goldsmith. Federal Reporter, Fourth Series, vol. 11, 26 Mar. 2021, 26–55. United States, Court of Appeals for the Second Circuit.

Andy Warhol Foundation for the Visual Arts, Inc. v. Goldsmith. 143 S.Ct 1258 (2023).

Aneau, Barthélemy. *Picta poesis: Ut pictura poesis erit.* Lyon: Mathieu Bonhomme, 1552.

Aquifer Guardians v. Federal Highway Admin. Federal Supplement 3d, vol. 779, 22 Apr. 2011, pp. 542–77. United States, District Court of Western District of Texas, San Antonio.

Aston, Margaret. *Broken Idols of the English Reformation.* Cambridge: Cambridge UP, 2016.

Baker, J. H. *The Order of Serjeants at Law.* London: Selden Society, 1984.

Baxter, J. H. and Charles Johnson, eds. *Medieval Latin Word-List.* Oxford: Oxford UP, 1934.

Biblia Sacra Vulgata (Vulgate). *WordProject.* https://www.wordproject.org/bibles/vg/index.htm (accessed 26 June 2023).

Blount, Thomas. *Glossographia: Or a Dictionary, Interpreting All Such Hard Vvords, Whether Hebrew, Greek, Latin, Italian, Spanish, French, Teutonick, Belgick, British or Saxon; as Are Now Used in Our Refined English Tongue. Also the Terms of Divinity, Law, Physick, Mathematicks, Heraldry, Anatomy, War, Musick, Architecture; and of Several Other Arts and Sciences Explicated. with Etymologies, Definitions, and Historical Observations on the Same. Very Useful for All Such as Desire to Understand What They Read.* London: Newcomb, 1656.

Bottici, Chiara. *Imaginal Politics: Images beyond Imagination and the Imaginary.* New York: Columbia UP, 2014.

Coccia, Emanuele. *Sensible Life: A Micro-ontology of Images.* New York: Fordham UP, 2014.

Coke, Edward. *The First Part of the Institutes of the Lawes of England, or a Commentarie on Littleton, Not the Name of a Lawyer Onely but of the Law Itselfe.* London: Society of Stationers, 1628.

Cooper, William. *Flagellation and Flagellants. A History of the Rod in All Countries.* London: William Reeves, 1895.

Courthouse News Serv. v. Forman. 606 F.Supp.3d 1200 (2022). United States, District Court of Northern District of Florida.

Didi-Huberman, Georges. "Image, Language: The Other Dialectic." Trans. Elise Woodard et. al. *Angelaki* 23.4 (2018): 19–24.

———. *The Surviving Image: Phantoms of Time and Time of Phantoms: Aby Warburg's History of Art.* Trans. Harvey Mendelsohn. University Park: Pennsylvania State UP, 2016.

Entick v. Carrington (1765). 19 Howell's State Trials 1057.

Foucault, Michel. *The Archaeology of Knowledge and the Discourse on Language.* Trans. A. M. Sheridan Smith. Abingdon: Routledge, 2013.

Goodrich, Peter. "Duncan Kennedy as I Imagine Him: The Man, the Work, His Scholarship and the Polity." *Cardozo Law Rev* 22 (2001): 971–90.

———. "Opinions and Decisions: Legal Essays." *Cambridge History of the American Essay.* Ed. Jason Childs and Christy Wampole. Cambridge: Cambridge UP, 2023. 425–40.

———. "Satirical Legal Studies: From the Legist to the Lizard." *Michigan Law Review* 103.3 (2004): 397–517.

Guillory, John. "Genesis of the Media Concept." *Critical Inquiry* 36 (2010): 321–62.

Hayuk v. Starbucks Corp. United States, District Court of Southern District of New York.

Hobbes, Thomas. *Leviathan or the Matter, Forme and Power of a Commonwealth Ecclesiastical and Civil.* London: Crooke, 1651.

HouseCanary, Inc. v. Quicken Loans, Inc. Civil Action No. SA-18–CV-0519–FB, 2018, pp. 1–7. United States, District Court of Western District of Texas, San Antonio.

Johnson, Samuel. "Catastrophe." *A Dictionary of the English Language*. London: Dilly, 1799.

Legendre, Pierre. *God in the Mirror: A Study of the Institution of Images*. Abingdon: Routledge, 2019.

——————. *La Pénétration du droit romain dans le droit canonique classique de Gratien à Innocent IV*. Paris: Jouve, 1964.

——————. *Le Désir politique de Dieu*. Paris: Fayard, 1988.

Legh, Gerard. *The Accedens of Armory*. London: Totell, 1576.

Legrand, Pierre. *Negative Comparative Law: A Strong Programme for Weak Thought*. Cambridge: Cambridge UP, 2022.

Lenton, Francis. *Characterismi: or, Lentons Leasures Expressed in Essayes and Characters, Neuer before Written On*. London: Newcomb, 1631.

Levin v. Texas Department of Criminal Justice. 2014 WL 10298844 Tex. Dist. (Texas District Court).

Orus Appolo de Aegypt. *De la signification des notes Hieroglyphiques des Aegyptiens, cest a dire des figures par les quelles ilz escripuoient leurs mysters secretz, et les choses sainctes et divines*. Paris: Keruers, 1543.

Peters, Julie Stone. *Law as Performance: Theatricality, Spectatorship, and the Making of Law in Ancient, Medieval, and Early Modern Europe*. Oxford: Oxford UP, 2022.

——————. "Theatrocracy Unwired: Legal Performance in the Modern Mediasphere." *Law and Literature* 26 (2014): 31–64.

Raymond, Charles Nicholas. "The Origin of the Spider-man Pointing Meme." *Screen Rant* 4 Jan. 2020. https://screenrant.com/spider-man-pointing-meme-cartoon-origin/.

Sterne, Laurence. *The Life and Opinions of Tristam Shandy, Gentleman*. 1760–1767. New York: Penguin, 1997.

Stolleis, Michael. *The Eye of the Law: Two Essays on Legal History*. London: Birkbeck Law, 2009.

Texas Department of Criminal Justice v. Levin. 520 S.W.3d 321 (Texas Court of Appeals).

Texas Department of Criminal Justice v. Levin. 572 S.W.3d 671 (Supreme Court of Texas).

Texas Department of Public Safety v. Cox Tex. Newspapers, L.P. S.W.3d, 343, 1 July 2011, pp. 112–29. Texas State, Supreme Court.

Vaihinger, Hans. *The Philosophy of "As If."* 1924. New York: Routledge, 2021.

Valeriano, Giovanni Piero. *Hieroglyphica, sive de sacriiis Aegyptorum*. Lyon: Honoraty, 1579.

Williams, Patricia. *Seeing a Color-Blind Future: The Paradox of Race*. London: Virago, 1998.

Wither, George. *A Collection of Emblemes, Ancient and Moderne Quickened vvith Metricall Illustrations, Both Morall and Divine: And Disposed into Lotteries, That Instruction, and Good Counsell, May Bee Furthered by an Honest and Pleasant Recreation*. London: Allot, 1635.

FALL 2023, VOL. 42, NO. 2

TULSA STUDIES IN WOMEN'S LITERATURE

FEATURING ARTICLES ON:

CHINESE MOTHERS

HEBREW POETS

IRISH WOMEN ACTIVISTS

BLACK AMERICAN MEDICAL HISTORY

TRANS WRITING

AFRICAN AVIATION

@TSWLJOURNAL // UTULSA.EDU/TSWL // LIKE US ON FACEBOOK

Keep up to date on new scholarship

Issue alerts are a great way to stay current on all the cutting-edge scholarship from your favorite Duke University Press journals. This free service delivers tables of contents directly to your inbox, informing you of the latest groundbreaking work as soon as it is published.

To sign up for issue alerts:

1. Visit **dukeu.press/register** and register for an account. You do not need to provide a customer number.

2. After registering, visit **dukeu.press/alerts**.

3. Go to "Latest Issue Alerts" and click on "Add Alerts."

4. Select as many publications as you would like from the pop-up window and click "Add Alerts."

read.dukeupress.edu/journals

Printed and bound by CPI Group (UK) Ltd, Croydon, CR0 4YY

10/06/2024

14513267-0001